Innovation Management

Innovation is both the creative and the destructive force at the center of economic development. It is perhaps the best explanation of current human prosperity, yet core to some of our most pressing societal problems. But how does innovation come about? How does it get managed in organizations? Moving from the most foundational ideas to the most cutting-edge debates in the field, this book serves as an invaluable companion to the field of innovation management. Each chapter summarizes, discusses, and critiques key academic texts, relating them to specific themes and connecting them to broader discussions in the field. Through this unique format, readers will gain insights into the important ideas and debates about innovation, how to manage it, and what it means for business and society. This book also brings interdisciplinary perspectives from economics, sociology, psychology, history, and management into the conversation about how to think about innovation scientifically.

Rasmus Koss Hartmann is Associate Professor of Management in the Department of Management, Society and Communication at Copenhagen Business School. Professor Hartmann's research has been supported by the Danish Council for Independent Research's Elite Research grant and the Carlsberg Foundation, and has been shortlisted for awards from the Academy of Management and the European Group on Organization Studies. He has previously been employed at Massachusetts Institute of Technology and at the University of Southern Denmark where he also received the Special Prize for Research-based Education.

Innovation Management
Foundations and Futures

Rasmus Koss Hartmann
Copenhagen Business School

CAMBRIDGE
UNIVERSITY PRESS

Shaftesbury Road, Cambridge CB2 8EA, United Kingdom

One Liberty Plaza, 20th Floor, New York, NY 10006, USA

477 Williamstown Road, Port Melbourne, VIC 3207, Australia

314–321, 3rd Floor, Plot 3, Splendor Forum, Jasola District Centre, New Delhi – 110025, India

103 Penang Road, #05–06/07, Visioncrest Commercial, Singapore 238467

Cambridge University Press is part of Cambridge University Press & Assessment, a department of the University of Cambridge.

We share the University's mission to contribute to society through the pursuit of education, learning and research at the highest international levels of excellence.

www.cambridge.org
Information on this title: www.cambridge.org/9781009431521

DOI: 10.1017/9781009431576

© Rasmus Koss Hartmann 2025

This publication is in copyright. Subject to statutory exception and to the provisions of relevant collective licensing agreements, no reproduction of any part may take place without the written permission of Cambridge University Press & Assessment.

When citing this work, please include a reference to the DOI 10.1017/9781009431576

First published 2025

A catalogue record for this publication is available from the British Library

A Cataloging-in-Publication data record for this book is available from the Library of Congress

ISBN 978-1-009-43152-1 Hardback
ISBN 978-1-009-43156-9 Paperback

Cambridge University Press & Assessment has no responsibility for the persistence or accuracy of URLs for external or third-party internet websites referred to in this publication and does not guarantee that any content on such websites is, or will remain, accurate or appropriate.

To
Mia, Aya, and Magnus

Today, the luckier economies of the world have achieved levels of per capita prosperity at least twenty times those of 1870, and at least twenty-five times those of 1770 – and there is every reason to believe prosperity will continue to grow at an exponential rate in the centuries to come. Today, the typical citizens of those economies can wield powers – of mobility, of communication, of creation, of destruction – that approach those attributed to sorcerers and gods in ages past.

J. Bradford DeLong

The space of the technologically possible is much greater than that of the economically profitable and socially acceptable.

Carlota Perez

Contents

Preface *page* ix

1 **Why Study Innovation Management?** 1
   1.1 Schumpeter: Creative Destruction 1
   1.2 McCloskey: The Origins of Capitalism as We Know It, or Why Are We Rich Today? 5
   1.3 Chandler: The Rise of Managerial Capitalism and the Idea of Corporate R&D 9

2 **Why Is Innovation Difficult?** 14
   2.1 Abernathy: From Fluid to Specific 14
   2.2 March: The Trade-Off between Exploitation and Exploration 17
   2.3 Rosenberg: The Nature of Uncertainty 20

3 **How Do Technologies Improve?** 24
   3.1 Foster: The Technology S-Curve 24
   3.2 Tushman and Anderson: Technology Cycles 30
   3.3 Vincenti: Technological Interdependencies and Performance Shifts 34
   3.4 Adner and Kapoor: Eco-Systems and the Pace of Substitution 37

4 **What Makes Some Innovations More Challenging Still?** 40
   4.1 Christensen: Disruption and Unattractive Markets 40
   4.2 Henderson and Clark: Product Architectures and Organizational Architectures 45
   4.3 David: General Purpose Technologies and Their Reach 49

5 **How Does Knowledge Shape Ideas?** 54
   5.1 Galenson: The Life Cycles of Creatives and Two Types of Creativity 54
   5.2 Ward: Structured Imagination, or the Downsides to Knowledge 58
   5.3 Shane: Prior Experience, or the Upside to Narrowness 62
   5.4 Jones: Is (Great) Invention Getting Harder? 66

6 **Can Organizations Exploit *and* Explore?** 71
   6.1 Adler et al: Re-thinking the Trade-Off between Exploration and Exploitation 71
   6.2 Brown and Duguid: Organizational Learning and Inevitable Innovation 81
   6.3 Cohen and Levinthal: Absorptive Capacity and the (Other) Effects of R&D 84

7 Should Innovation Be Managed? 91
- 7.1 Cooper: Innovation through Stages — 92
- 7.2 Mouritsen et al: Management Accounting and Justifications for Innovation Projects — 96
- 7.3 Criscuolo et al: Bootlegging — 99
- 7.4 Foss: Letting Emergence Reign (or Not) — 103

8 How Are New Technologies Brought to Market? 110
- 8.1 Moore: The Chasm, and Finding Beachhead Markets — 110
- 8.2 Lieberman and Montgomery: First-Mover Advantages and Risks — 115
- 8.3 Navis and Glynn: Collaboration, Then Competition — 119

9 What Do Entrepreneurs Do? 125
- 9.1 Schumpeter: Enter the Entrepreneur, Resplendent — 126
- 9.2 Baumol: The Allocation of Entrepreneurs to Entrepreneurship — 129
- 9.3 Gans et al: Entrepreneurship without Creative Destruction — 134
- 9.4 Nightingale and Coad: Gazelles and Mostly Muppets — 141

10 How Does the State Shape Innovation? How Should It? 146
- 10.1 Acemoglu and Robinson: Institutions Matter (Again) — 146
- 10.2 Mazzucato: The Entrepreneurial State — 151
- 10.3 Adler: Dealing with Crisis — 155

11 What Is the Societal Impact of Innovation? 160
- 11.1 Perez: A Cyclical Model of Technological Revolution — 160
- 11.2 Zuboff: New Logics of Accumulation, or a Different Kind of Exploitation — 165
- 11.3 Autor: Will Robots Take Our Jobs? — 170
- 11.4 Bessen: Technology, Wages, and Engel's Pause — 174

12 How Does Innovation Shape Organizing? 178
- 12.1 Bodrozic and Adler: Organizations, Transformed — 179
- 12.2 Beane: Learning, Interrupted — 182
- 12.3 Dell'Acqua et al: Fast, Asleep — 187

13 Will Innovation Change Innovation? 192
- 13.1 Baldwin and von Hippel: Innovation without Organizations — 193
- 13.2 Altman et al: In an Age of Costless Communication — 198
- 13.3 Cockburn, Henderson, and Stern: Inventions in the Methods of Invention and the Shape of the Future — 204

14 Theories and Some Implications 210

References — 217
Index — 231

Preface

I always disliked textbooks, both as a student and as a teacher. In that sense, it is more than a little paradoxical to be writing one. What I always disliked was the sense they gave of being overly comprehensive and somehow final, like this was the "end of history" of a topic. Their main purpose, it seemed to me, was often to present a seemingly unending list of more or less stylized facts, reducing the complex arguments of a research paper to a single sentence in the process.

I would later be told that "research is a conversation," which made me think back to textbooks as particularly *bad* at capturing that sense of both disagreement and dynamism. Later, I would also read about how technology either substitutes or complements labor and, with some categorical slippage, again think back to textbooks as exemplary of (often poor) substitutes for reading of source ideas. And yet, for all these problems, students would often ask for textbooks because they understandably found it to be a bit of dive into the intellectual deep end to grapple directly with research papers, especially early in their studies. This is understandable. Research papers are written by academics for academics, and so they take things for granted about their reader that it is blatantly unfair to take for granted about students even at advanced levels, and even more unfair to take for granted about students just beginning to engage with a topic area. Of course, this does not imply that we should consider papers somehow beyond the reach of students. On the contrary, one of the major points of an academic education is to learn the craft of research and engaging directly with the writings that practitioners of that craft use to communicate to each other is part of learning the craft. You become a management scientist by working with and like management scientists, not by reading management science decaf.

And thus, the question that emerged was how to go about putting such a book together, how to build a textbook of sorts that complemented rather than substituted direct engagement with challenging material. What you have in front of you is the first answer to that question. More precisely, it is a beta version of an answer and one that will continually evolve as students help me think more and better about progressively better answers to the question.

The primary purpose of this book is to provide a systematic introduction to innovation management theory, but to do so in a way that brings readers *closer* to the source ideas. It is intended to support students in readings of original texts. It is a hybrid between the conventional textbook and a curated and annotated volume of selected readings. It is, in a sense, an elaborate version of what could be called a "reader" in innovation management theory. It is meant to be used alongside those original texts to make them more accessible and to sort the textual and ideational wheat from the chafe. Despite academic authors' best efforts, there is often a lot of chafe in academic writing (my own certainly included) owing to genre conventions, jargon, signposting, and many other things. Knowing that is part of understanding the craft, but facing it head-on makes it hard to understand what is, in fact, good research craft and what is, in Abbott's (1981) terms, professional regression.

The secondary purpose is to convey a particular image of innovation theory as a body of knowledge with many interconnections. Some of those are explicit, and when you read you will see references back and forth between the ideas in the various chapters. There was a time when the provisional title of this book was *Footnotes to Schumpeter* because everything did sort of connect back to and feel in some way like a footnote to something that Schumpeter had written about (the sage and business-minded advice of the publisher was to abandon that title). Other interconnections can be created through theoretical analysis. We can, so to speak, use texts to make each other better and more interesting. While interconnected, ideas are not all in agreement and I do not intend (as textbooks often do) to create a sense of finality. Hopefully, what will emerge will be a sense of where in the literature there are connections, continuities, disjuncture, agreements, and unfinished discussions. Rather than including the latest and greatest empirical results and their attendant weighing-in on discussions, I have chosen to emphasize theoretical ideas that prepare students to read and make sense of such empirical discussions in more advanced classes. Of course, there are some of those latest-and-greatest, but mostly toward the end of the book, where it also – by design – begins to become much more speculative and tentative. We start on solid ground. At the end, we jump between ice floes.

It is worth stating the somewhat obvious at the outset. As has to be the case, this book contains both a select set of ideas and a select reading of those ideas. They are my selections, and they reflect both my understanding of innovation research as a whole and my theoretical priors. In selecting between possible ideas to include, I have *largely* tried to choose ideas that represent a consensus view of what are canonical concepts, the foundational pillars of innovation management theory that most professional innovation scholars would consider "mainstream" and, we would like to believe, relatively enduring. I have, however, also tried to introduce some less mainstream and slightly more provocative ways to think about issues and have tried to paint a somewhat broader and less disciplinarily committed picture than you might find in most innovation management textbooks. To that end, we will be touching quite a lot of disciplinary ground. We will be moving from the economics of innovation through economic history over science and technology studies, organization, and management studies (of both the sociological and economic variety), strategy, and psychology. We will also be reading things that deliberately fall somewhat outside of the mainstream or that are not central to it. That does not make for a particularly straightforward story, and that is fine. If something is a straightforward story, chances are it is not true.

This balance between the mainstream and critical perspectives provides, I hope, a somewhat more interesting and more conversational access point to the ideas of the book, because it gets us away from the common problem in textbooks of presenting things as indisputable. While I will continually try to connect the foundational ideas to each other, I will also try to problematize them and dispute them, to use them as sounding boards for reflection or as a repertoire of potential interpretations that might or might not be relevant in understanding particular contexts – theories' implications for practice, I believe, depends on the practice and when dealing with innovation and technology, what we are dealing with is both uncertain and contingent. While some of the texts you will read are interested in the predictors of "performance," you will not really see me present them as "recipes" for that performance, but more as hypotheses that under certain conditions certain practices can contribute to driving certain outcomes that inevitably have certain more or less predictable side effects. That level of predictive power seems to me to be the best that management science can do, and I am not sure that will change, or that the point of progress in the science of management is to change that.

You are welcome to disagree with that point and many of the ones I present in this book. I do try to be as explicit as possible about when I am stating generally held views – views that reasonable people in the field of management science tend to find reasonable – and my own, less generally held views or speculations. The point is that disagreements with the ideas I express in this book are an excellent starting point for learning something.

1 Why Study Innovation Management?

> **Texts in This Chapter**
>
> Schumpeter, J. A. 1942/2008. *Capitalism, socialism and democracy* (Chapter 7). Harper Perennial Modern Thought Edition.
> McCloskey, D. N. 2010. *Bourgeois dignity: Why economics can't explain the modern world* (Chapter 1). University of Chicago Press.
> Chandler, A. D. 1977. *The visible hand: The managerial revolution in American business* (Introduction). Harvard University Press.

In this chapter, we lay out the basic frame for studying innovation management. To do so, we are going to try to understand why innovation is important, for society, for companies, and for individuals, and to do that we take our point of departure in the "urtext" of innovation research, namely, Schumpeter's work on *Capitalism, Socialism and Democracy* and especially the notion of Creative Destruction. To follow that up, we are going to untangle how innovation management fits within a broader context of capitalism as an economic system, within a particular ideology, and within the operations of the modern corporation.

1.1 Schumpeter: Creative Destruction

> If, as Alfred North Whitehead once asserted, the history of Western thought may be adequately described as a series of footnotes upon Plato, it may equally be said of the study of technological innovation that is still consists of a series of footnotes upon Schumpeter. Although the footnotes may be getting longer, more critical and, happily, richer, in the recognition of empirical complexities, we still occupy the conceptual edifice that Schumpeter built for the subject. Inevitably, therefore, Schumpeter's concepts constitute our point of departure.
>
> Rosenberg (1976), p. 524

The signs of Creative Destruction are all around us. As consumers, we are incessantly presented with new products, services, and solutions.

Things that were once staples of everyday life disappear. We regularly find out that we need things that were until recently nonexistent, even unimaginable. What we recognize as the largest companies, those that most dramatically shape our consuming lives by providing us with all this novelty, are mostly new ones. Just a generation ago, many of them either had not been founded or were in their absolute infancy. The technologies that these companies use similarly did not exist a generation ago. The same can be said of the technologies that shape our working lives. More and more of us work or will work in jobs that a generation ago made up a small share of the overall workforce or simply were not invented. We will also fulfill those jobs under organizational arrangements that are new. If you live in a Western city, you will see what were once factories being turned into fashionable housing and offices for a new kind of work and for a new kind of production. This churn, this constant change, is Creative Destruction unfolding.

Schumpeter's book *Capitalism, Socialism and Democracy* was written in 1942, amid the horrors of a World War and at a time when many were deeply disillusioned with capitalism as an economic system. While many today share the disillusionment with capitalism, the real difference between then and now is that in the 1930s and 1940s, socialism really was an alternative, with a substantial share of the world's population living in socialist economies. At the time, many looked to the Soviet Union and saw a well-functioning economic model, while in the West they would see something not quite undesirable. They would often *not* see the free markets and perfect competition on which capitalism is predicated, but monopolies, and think (with Adam Smith in mind) that this had to be economically inefficient and (with Karl Marx) that the tendency toward monopolies was inherent in capitalism, as was exploitation of the working class. If you looked, you might see the same today. They would also see vast inequality, with incredible wealth held by what we would call the 1 percent and the 99 percent have just suffered through a desperate depression.

Schumpeter's book was an effort to understand socialism and capitalism and their respective relationships with democracy. In what is perhaps the most concise characterization of capitalism ever written, this would be Schumpeter's argument: "Creative Destruction is the essential fact about capitalism. It is what capitalism consists in and what every capitalist [firm] has got to live in" (p. 83). To understand that we need to understand how Schumpeter thought about capitalism. "The essential point to grasp," he writes, "is that in dealing with capitalism we are dealing with an evolutionary process … Capitalism, then, is by nature a form or method of economic change and not only never is but never can

1.1 Schumpeter: Creative Destruction

be stationary" (p. 82). Capitalism is inherent, unstable, and dynamic. To live in a capitalist economy is to live in circumstances that, for better and worse, constantly change.

There is a poetic streak, I think, to Schumpeter's account of this constant change. Creative Destruction is a very evocative and quite intuitive way to capture something that is quite profound: that capitalism implies a constant "industrial mutation" that "incessantly revolutionize the economic structure *from within*, destroying the old one, incessantly creating a new one" (p. 83, italics in original). To him, there is a storm, a "perennial gale of Creative Destruction" blowing through capitalist society, like the Hindu god Shiva dancing through the world, tearing down what is and letting the new emerge from the ashes.

While we may not appreciate the causes of this process or the profundity of its implications, the *threat* of Creative Destruction is keenly felt by businesses. Schumpeter talks about Creative Destruction as an "ever-present threat" (p. 85), one that "disciplines before [new competition] attacks" (p. 85). It creates a paranoid anxiety for firms that they must compete not just in the short term on price and quality by constantly marginally improving. This is the kind of competition that firms are always in. In the slightly longer term, they also have to deal with "competition which commands a decisive cost or quality advantage, and which strikes not at the margins of the profits and the outputs of the existing firms but at their foundations and their very lives. This kind of competition is as much more effective than the other as a bombardment is in comparison with forcing a door" (pp. 84–85). The threat of such Creative Destruction constantly looms, even over monopolies, and makes them act *as if* they were in a state of cutthroat competition, because even if they are not currently competing they still compete against potential future entrants to their industry that will seek to overtake their position.

For Schumpeter, *innovation* is the fundamental impulse spurring Creative Destruction, the force that propels change in the economy. He employs a relatively broad definition of innovation, covering "new consumer' goods, new methods of production or transportation, the new markets, the new forms of industrial organization" (p. 83). Today, we tend to use that as the definitional starting point for distinguishing between different forms of innovation, rather than use the umbrella term, but do bear in mind that innovation can take other forms than those presented here. *Product innovation* is what people typically think about when they think of innovation, because it refers to either new physical products or (increasingly) services. These tend to be highly visible. *Process innovation* covers new techniques or tools for creating products or services.

These tend to be less visible and attention-grabbing because they often are sold in business-to-business markets but are indisputably important. *Market creation* refers to the opening up of new markets, whether by extending the geography in which a solution is marketed or in extending technologies into new fields. Innovations in transportation get relatively little attention in most modern innovation research but is nonetheless profound in its consequences. Consider, for instance, the implications that the humble forty-foot container has had on global trade and as a consequence on what you consume (Lewinson, 2008). New forms of organization refer (somewhat counterintuitively to many contemporary readers) not to new forms of organization *within* industry, but new forms of organization *of* industry. This might include new forms of networks or interfirm collaboration, but Schumpeter would have imagined things like cartels and other forms of what might today be called anticompetitive behavior.[1]

These subclassifications are worth noting in part for their own sake – as we will return to, they each have their own set of causes and a vastly different set of effects on organizations. Contrary to what many would have you believe, being good at one does not imply being good at the other, as we will return to in the essays that follow. It is also worth noting that we can make several very meaningful additions to the list. These might include innovations in business models (e.g., new ways to create and capture value) or innovations in techniques (e.g., new ways to *use* products or services). Similarly, new forms of organizations *within* industry are also worth considering. The ways that firms organize (legally through constructions like corporations or practically around ideas like the divisionalized form) are often taken for granted but are in fact innovations that were invented and brought into being (see Section 11.1 for an elaboration).

The other important thing to understand about these five forms of innovation is that they in interaction create what Schumpeter would surely see (and what you should see) as the miracle of capitalism. They allow for the long-run expansion of output and the driving down of prices, putting goods and services that were once only accessible to the hyper-rich into the hands of all of us. Innovation is what allows those of us who are fortunate enough to be born into the affluent societies of the Western world to enjoy standards of living that were frankly unimaginable just 200 years ago. To be clear, capitalism has incredible and far-reaching downsides. It creates gaping holes in our souls as both workers and consumers (as we will return to) and is a driving force in creating

---

[1] For a deeper exposition of this point, see the introductory chapter of Becker et al (2011).

1.2 McCloskey: The Origins of Capitalism

ecological damage on a potentially catastrophic, existentially threatening, scale. But be clear also that the kind of growth in material wealth that capitalism has created is a miracle that is unprecedented in world history, as Deirdre McCloskey's work will make eminently clear (in Section 1.2). Irrespective of what you think about the future, there is no way that innovation is not a part of it, either as an engine of progress or as the thing that gets us out of the mess that we, as a species, are in.

Going forward, we are going to see Creative Destruction come up repeatedly as a mainstay of innovation management theory. We will see it as the constant threat that Schumpeter describes. In this capacity, all the various ways that established firms and industries could be destroyed by innovation weigh heavily (and should weigh heavily) on the minds of incumbent firms. We will see the dilemma that it poses between competing at the margins *and* at the center of profits as constitutive of one of the key challenges of innovation management: of balancing exploration and exploitation both at the level of the firm allocating its resources between different activities and at the level of how a technology should be developed. We will also see it as an opportunity. Just as innovation can destroy, it can also elevate new entrants and new ideas to prominence. Attackers can have advantages over incumbents, and Creative Destruction is something that people can actively try to bring about. We will see the sense of turmoil that Schumpeter describes as a stable of industrial change but also as something that firms alternatively try to bring to an end or to leverage. We will see the tension between the immaculate wealth creation and the far-reaching and painful destruction as a key challenge facing society. And we will see how the constant flux, the constant search for new and better alternatives is currently reshaping the way both that innovation happens and that firms organize. We live, for better and for worse, in fantastically interesting times and understanding innovation and its implications is a central part of understanding them.

Inevitably, we take our point of departure in Schumpeter.

1.2 McCloskey: The Origins of Capitalism as We Know It, or Why Are We Rich Today?

Contrary to what many experience today, human history is – in material terms – mostly a story of *non-change*. Then, germinally around the end of the eighteenth century and forcefully through the Industrial Revolution and up to today, everything changed. McCloskey makes this evocatively clear:

> Economic history has looked like an ice-hockey stick lying on the ground. It had a long, long horizontal handle at $3 a day extending through the two-hundred-thousand-year history of *Homo Sapiens* to 1800, with little bumps upward on the

handle in ancient Rome and the early medieval Arab world and high medieval Europe, with regression to $3 afterward – then a wholly unexpected blade, leaping up in the last two of the two thousand centuries, to $30 a day and in many places well beyond. (p. 2)

We are fortunate to live on that blade. As McCloskey makes clear, for all the very real ailments of modern capitalism and all of its incredibly real, incredibly destructive effects, the world we live in is undisputedly *much better* for *a greater share* of *more people* than has been the case at any other point in human history. This is the case because of *economic growth*.

In his book *The Lever of Riches*, economic historian Joel Mokyr argues that economic growth in a society can come from several sources. We can grow richer through "Smithian growth" (named for Adam Smith, who needs no introduction), which comes from increased trade. Increased trade allows for larger markets and for increased specialization and with that comes increased productivity, which makes society richer. We can also have "Solovian growth" (named for Robert Solow, an American economist working in the second half of the twentieth century). This comes from increased investment in what economist call capital goods, that is, more sophisticated production equipment. Having more production equipment allows workers to be more productive and society to produce more goods with the same scarce inputs. To this one might add "Marxian growth" (after Karl Marx), which would come from increasingly brutal exploitation of workers or of natural resources. Just as having more production equipment can make workers more efficient, pushing them harder can increase productivity, but only up to a certain backbreaking point. Extracting more resources from the planet or society can do something similar (see Section 11.2).

These things surely matter in explaining why we are richer today than we were in the past, but they *cannot* as McCloskey argues explain the blade of the hockey stick. That change is too momentous to be explained by trade, capital accumulation, exploitation, or any other single concept in the economist's theoretical toolbox. Except, that is, for *one* kind of growth, the kind that Mokyr calls *Schumpeterian growth*: growth in human knowledge and ideas and innovation. Innovation *more than anything else* explains the material wealth of the modern world.[2] That is why

---

[2] The reason that innovation can explain growth in ways that more material factors cannot relates to the particular economics associated with *ideas*. The short story is that ideas allow for what Mokyr calls "free lunches" (Milton Friedman famously argued that there is no such thing as a free lunch), because they can, for instance, be infinitely replicated at little or no cost, at least in principle. The longer story about the unique economics of ideas, which in many ways resemble the economics of digital goods, is well told in Shapiro and Varian's book *Information Rules* (1998).

1.2 McCloskey: The Origins of Capitalism

we need to understand it. Not just because it is essential for firms to compete effectively, but because innovation is what makes *society* better off. Yes, innovation may be overhyped and glorified and lionized and romanticized, but it is also fundamentally the reason we no longer live in caves and hunt with spears (spears were an innovation, of course).

The question for McCloskey, then, is what brought about all this innovation? Why did the Industrial Revolution happen, and why does it continue to happen? Why did we get on the hockey stick's blade when we did not, say, 200 years before (in which case we would be unfathomably well-off today) or 200 years later (in which case you probably would not be reading this book, but toiling away in a field somewhere)?

Her answer is that things began to change because *ideology* had been changing.[3] Following the Reformation, new ideas began to emerge about the urban middle class of hiring, owning, professional, or educated persons (i.e., the "bourgeoisie"), first in the Low Countries and later in Britain and ultimately in the United States. To be clear, it was *not* the Reformation and the attendant emergence of what German sociologist Max Weber (1930) calls the "Protestant work ethic" that created the modern "the Spirit of Capitalism" (because, if that were the case, why do we see capitalism today in distinctly non-Protestant countries?). It was that with the reformation came a new way of thinking and talking about the bourgeois class. This thinking, in an evolved version, is still with us today and profoundly shapes how people think and talk about innovation in society and organizations.

Where before this group of merchants had been viewed with some contempt, they began to be viewed more favorably, as dignified and not repugnant. Up to this point, the best and brightest had gone to work in the courts, the church, or the military, because those were "honorable" professions. Alas, they are also mostly conservative ones. But with changing attitudes toward merchants, "[i]t became honorable ... to invent a machine for making screws or to venture in trade to Cathay" (p. 12). "Ordinary conversations about innovation and markets became more approving" (p. 7), "general opinion shifted *in favor* [italics added] of the bourgeoisie and especially in favor of its marketing and innovation" (p. 7). This process

---

[3] Do note that there are many other answers to this question, such as those advanced by, for example, Rosenberg and Birdzell (1986) or McCraw (1995), and clearly there is not one single explanation. On the contrary, many things changed and collectively created this change. One fun, but nonetheless serious, explanation emphasizes the diffusion of coffee into Europe in the period leading up to this transformation. In Pollan's words, "[c]offee showed up in Europe at exactly the right moment ... Coffee helped disperse Europe's alcoholic fog, fostering a heightened alertness and attention to detail, and ... dramatically improving productivity" (2021, p. 122).

had been going on for a while (that is the way it is with the ebb and flow of the tides of history) before the Industrial Revolution took off. What at the end of the eighteenth century emerged from that process was that ideology changed in such a way as to make Creative Destruction the socially desirable thing *that it had not been before*. The result of that change in ideology has been a "novel and immense and sustained, almost lunatic, regime of innovation" (p. 19). With this regime arose what Schumpeter in his day and we in ours recognize as capitalism, that dynamic economic system of which Creative Destruction is the essential fact.

To be clear, what was new was neither capitalism nor innovation. Capitalism existed long before the early nineteenth century, but this was capitalism in the sense of commercial activity, with trade, with prices emergently determined by supply and demand, with financial credit, with money and accumulation of wealth. None of those things, as McCloskey makes eminently clear in her subsequent chapters, were new. Innovation also was not new. In Mokyr's book, he describes Western technological progress from Classic Antiquity through to the Middle Ages and the Renaissance before arriving at the Industrial Revolution's "Years of Miracles." You could similarly describe an important history of innovation in ancient China, in the empires of South America up to the brutality of European conquest, in the Arab world and at some level in all human society, ever. Innovation has been with us since our ancestors on the Savannah. McCloskey notes technological change already in the Upper Paleolithic and among the proto-Australians (innovations in boats is what got them to Australia, after all), to give just a few of her examples. What was new was the *scale* of innovation and with it a new competitive process at the heart of capitalism. Sometimes, a change in degree is a change in kind and that is exactly the case here. A change in ideology spurred the gale of Creative Destruction to the historically unprecedented heights that we see today.

This image of innovation as ideologically driven is something that I encourage you to take into your further reading. It is also something that we should have some concerns about. There can be little doubt that we are living in a time obsessed with innovation. Just as you can see the signs of Creative Destruction all around you, you will also hear what some call "the gospel of innovation" and the "industrial religion of the twentieth century" (Salter & Alexy, 2014) preached and hyped by practitioners and scholars in business and management and technology, sometimes with good intentions and other times for personal profit in some form (Kärreman et al, 2021). Change, they say, is the only constant and innovation the only answer. The ideological pendulum has swung very, very far from when change was a dirty word and innovation not yet coined.

Despite this swing, three things are important to understand. One is that Creative Destruction and innovation-based capitalism are *not* something that firms enjoy or necessarily thrive on, despite all the hullaballoo. Entrepreneurs and innovators may thrive, but established and powerful firms often do not. As Schumpeter saw, Creative Destruction creates an environment of paranoid anxiety and, as we will see in our coming readings, myriad difficult challenges for firms wanting to maintain their position. Most established firms, for sure, would prefer *not* having to innovate, but do so because others do it and they therefore have to. For those established firms, innovation is a race to the bottom that they sometimes win and sometimes lose. Fortunately, that race is what makes *consumers* better off. All that struggle to expand output and reduce prices puts more, better, and cheaper goods into the hand of a greater share of consumers.

Another is the *possibility* that ideology can to some extent substitute for *actual* competitive pressure, in the Schumpeterian sense that a pervasive ideology of innovation can make firms more paranoid *and* in the sense that an ideology can make it necessary for firms to innovate in order to stay legitimate in the eyes of relevant stakeholders. A strong ideology can force firms to engage in innovation as a ceremonial, rhetorical practice. This line of thinking would bring you into a somewhat different understanding of the role of innovation in firms, which is undoubtedly a big part of the picture and the subject of much of what is called institutional theory. It is something that falls somewhat outside of the scope of this particular book but definitely is a stable of courses on organizational theory.

The third thing to understand is that the pendulum can swing again. Just as a change in ideology that nobody planned made the modern world possible, a change in ideology that nobody plans or expects can happen again and undo it. And that certainly would be tragic and dystopian. The world we live in may, in Delong's formulation, be "marvelous and terrible, but by the standards of all the rest of human history, much more marvelous than terrible" (2022, p. 1).

1.3 Chandler: The Rise of Managerial Capitalism and the Idea of Corporate R&D

It is an interesting fact of Schumpeter's oeuvre that he fundamentally changed his mind about where innovation comes from in the economy and, by implication, what type of organization is fundamentally responsible for economic growth. Living in what was then Czernowitz in what is now Ukraine, the young Schumpeter published *The Theory of Economic*

Development in 1911. In that book, he "flatly asserted ... that individual entrepreneurship held the key to economic growth in any country" (McCraw, 2007, p. 149). When he published *Capitalism, Socialism and Democracy* in 1942, he was a professor at Harvard University, having lived in the United States since 1932. In that book, he describes big business – large corporations, operating in oligopolistic markets – as the real drivers of innovation and economic development.

That is a profound change, and one that reflects the changing nature of capitalism and the changing nature of innovation in the interim period and the fact that a particular form of change happened first in the United States and only later spread to Europe. By the 1940s, a still-new form of organization had come to dominate American capitalism: the "modern," vertically integrated, multiunit business. This new organizational form brought with it "Managerial Capitalism," a way of organizing economic activities that simply did not exist a century before. It had also brought about the notion of "industrial research" and the corporate Research & Development laboratory. Originating in the German chemical industry, industrial research was developed and elaborated in the United States in the early 1900s and became, in the interwar period, the de facto way for innovation to be organized in American industry and, later on, most of the world. Profound change indeed, and a suitable occasion for a change of mind.

The emergence of the modern business – large, divisionalized, and vertically integrated – and the attendant emergence of Managerial Capitalism and, to a lesser extent, industrial research are the topics of Chandler's book. The traditional unit of production in the American economy was the "single-unit business enterprise. In such an enterprise, an individual or a small number of owners operated a shop, factory, bank, or transportation line out of a single office ... handled only a single economic function, dealt in a single product line, and operated in one geographic area" (p. 3). Prior to 1840, this was the only type of business that really existed and had existed for a long time. Its operations would have been immediately intelligible to an Italian Renaissance merchant, living four centuries earlier. The modern enterprise that Chandler describes "contains many distinct operating units and it is managed by a hierarchy of salaried executives" (p. 1). "The activities of these units and the transactions between them [are] internalized" (p. 2), meaning that many activities, disparate in nature and geography, happen within the same firm.

More specifically, this type of firm was *vertically integrated*. When a firm vertically integrates, it integrates activities that would otherwise be done by suppliers or customers into its own operations. A vertically integrated firm might consist for example of distinct divisions operating a shipping line, but also have divisions building the ships that sail for the line and divisions mining and refining steel to build those ships. It might have a division to operate the ports in which those ships dock, and another to extract and process oil to fuel them. It might also have a ground logistics division, moving over land the containers shipped by the shipping line, and a division comprised of wholesale and retail activities receiving shipments through that ground logistics company. In a vertically integrated company, goods are not (only) sold through the market the way a non-integrated shipping line might buy fuel from an oil company. Activities that might otherwise happen through the market are internalized and organized into distinct operating divisions. "By World War I this type of firm had become the dominant business institution in many sectors of the American economy" (p. 3). Such a vertically integrated firm would be comprehensible for us today, accustomed as we are to its prevalence. For the Italian Renaissance merchant, it would have been a strange beast indeed.

With the rise of this type of firm had come the entirely new idea of middle management and, more broadly, managerial capitalism. The management that happened within traditional firms was done directly, by owners who typically partook in the production process. The firm would fulfill one economic function, and then exchange the products of that function in the market. The activities of the large, divisionalized and multiunit modern business were "monitored and coordinated by salaried managers rather than market mechanisms" (p. 3), and the work of monitoring and coordinating was a new form of work, requiring new administrative innovations and ideas and a new class of workers to do it. Consequently, the rise of the modern enterprise led to a demand for middle managers, workers *specialized* in *management activities*, having received specialist training in the "science" of management and business. Middle managers would manage subordinate managers (not operating workers) and report to managers (not company owners) and considered themselves to belong to a new and distinct managerial class. Being so used to this form of organization and to the idea of managers and of getting managed, it can seem strange to contemplate that "[A]s late as 1840 there were *no middle managers* in the United States" (p. 3). By 1940, most of American economic life unfolded in ways planned and organized by managers.

Why did this happen? At the heart of the process that Chandler proposes is an interplay of the technological, the economic, and the sociological that created what Rosenberg would describe as "pressures toward bigness" (1977). First, "modern multiunit business enterprise replaced small traditional enterprise when administrative coordination permitted greater productivity, lower costs, and higher profits than coordination by market mechanisms" (p. 6). In other words, when the costs of coordinating activities internally fell below those of coordinating through the market, the road was paved for modern firms to supplant the traditional. The reduction in those costs depended on technological advances in the form of cheaper and faster communication and the advent of new managerial techniques. Second, "the advantages of internalizing the activities of many business units within a single enterprise could not be realized until a managerial hierarchy had been created" (p. 7). The availability of a cadre of workers able to undertake the economic function of coordinating and to use the new techniques available for managing was a prerequisite for the emergence of the modern firm. Third, "modern business enterprise appeared for the first time in history when the volume of economic activities reached level that made administrative coordination more efficient and more profitable than market coordination" (p. 8). This increase in volume was driven by new technology. New production techniques made possible a vast expansion of output, and railroads made possible the expansion of markets to absorb it. Once it had emerged, the new managerial class perpetuated itself. It became a source of power, became increasingly technically sophisticated, distanced itself from ownership, shaped company policy in the direction of stability, and ultimately reshaped the economy.

It is with the emergence of this new form of organization and of managerial capitalism that we see the emergence of corporate research and development and, more specifically, the "Corporate R&D Lab." Before corporate R&D, "science and technology were products firms purchased" (Dennis, 1987, p. 482) and corporate laboratories existed merely to conduct tests and ensure the reliability of purchased technology. With vertical integration, a more expansive role emerged. Just as the growing multiunit business vertically integrated to secure control of raw materials, it might also secure control over the ideas and technology that enabled its operations by internalizing the development of relevant scientific insights and relevant technological advances. Beginning in the early 1900s with General Electric, AT&T, and Kodak, major corporations began to organize their own industrial research laboratories. They took their inspiration from the chemical labs of the German dye industry (Beer, 1959) that had first developed this organizational innovation, and by the middle of the century, it had become an entirely mainstream part of large, vertically integrated firms.

With the corporate R&D lab, innovation became something that firms not just did themselves but also something that was subject to professional management and needed to integrate with corporate strategy.

1.3 Chandler: The Rise of Managerial Capitalism   13

More specifically, the *process* of developing innovations and, before that, choosing between and prioritizing innovations to develop was subjected to management. When firms *bought* innovation, the innovation could be assessed and its fit with corporate strategy could be assessed, albeit with some uncertainty. When firms had to *make* innovations, decisions about innovations were shifted forward in time and technological uncertainty increasingly taken on by firm, as opposed to independent inventors, because the firm was now undertaking research, not merely assessing its results. Moreover, the organization had to find a place within the corporate bureaucracy for inventors. Where before inventors, their psychology and their scientific ideals were considered largely incommensurable with bureaucratic organizing (Reich, 1985; Dennis, 1987), now both organizations and inventors had to accommodate a new, shared reality.

Like the modern corporation, the modern corporate R&D lab was so thoroughly successful that it ultimately spread throughout the industrialized world and became the standard model of business innovation, in the process prompting Schumpeter to revise his understanding of the nature of capitalist innovation: the largest firms with their R&D labs, not heroic entrepreneurs, were the real drivers of innovation. Today, corporate R&D is a central, if not the presumptive, site of business innovation and many challenges of organizing for innovation relate precisely to the management of industrial research and development.

2 Why Is Innovation Difficult?

> **Texts in This Chapter**
>
> Abernathy, W. J. 1978. *The productivity dilemma: Roadblock to innovation in the automobile industry* (Chapter 4). John Hopkins University Press.
> March, J. G. 1991. Exploration and exploitation in organizational learning. *Organization Science.* 2(1), 71–87.
> Rosenberg, N. 1996. Uncertainty and technological change. In *The mosaic of economic growth*, ed. R. Landau, R. Taylor & G. Wright. Stanford University Press.

Chapter 1 should have left you with an understanding that innovation is absolutely central to the functioning of the modern economy and a key strategic concern for companies. In this chapter, we will examine why innovation is also inherently difficult. We will begin with a very material understanding of this challenge, as Abernathy lays out how the nature of the production process that enables short-term competitiveness can be anathema to the development of innovation. To nuance what Abernathy calls the Productivity Dilemma, we then move on to March's analysis of how different modes of organizational learning and managerial decision-making can lead to a similar trade-off between short-term and long-term competitiveness. Finally, we emphasize the ways that innovation is made still more difficult by its inherent uncertainty.

2.1 Abernathy: From Fluid to Specific

Schumpeter made us aware of a dual challenge that capitalist economies present to firms. On the one hand, there is a short-term challenge of competing on price and quality. This is the competition that occurs at the "margin of profits," where firms seek to extend their power over existing markets by offering something slightly better than their competitors. On the other hand, there is the long-term challenge of competing with new

2.1 Abernathy: From Fluid to Specific

ideas that strike at the "center of profits." This is what Abernathy refers to as the challenge of competing *both* on productivity and incremental innovation *and* on major innovation. Why is this a challenge? Because, as Abernathy writes in his book's opening chapter, "Stated generally, to achieve gains in productivity, there must be attendant losses in innovative capability; or, conversely, the conditions needed for rapid innovative change are much different from those that support high levels of production efficiency" (p. 4). In other words, there is a *trade-off*, or dilemma, between competing in the long term and short term, the titular Productivity Dilemma. To relate this back to Schumpeter, the existence of such a dilemma is an explanation for *why* there is Creative Destruction: firms that successfully pursue production to thrive short-term will not (very likely) survive in long-term, innovation-based competition.

Two things lead Abernathy to this far-reaching argument: An observation of industry differences and an observation of organizational change over time. The first is a general observation that industries differ in what sort of innovation matters and that there is a relationship between this industry-level characteristic and how firms in those industries *organize*. Most industries are characterized by high-volume production for well-established markets. Primacy is given to a particular production process that is highly optimized and very capital-intensive, and (as a consequence) products are not only standardized but also partially defined by what is possible within the limits afforded by these production processes. In these industries, the kinds of innovation that matter most are process innovations and incremental product innovations. Some industries are radically different. In them, major product innovation is what matters and firms tend to be smaller and more flexible. Innovation often comes from new entrepreneurial firms. Products tend to be "performance-maximizing rather than cost maximizing" (p. 70), but performance criteria also "are typically vague and poorly understood" (p. 70). The production process tends to be very idiosyncratic. In industries characterized by high-volume production, organizations are highly *specific* or what Burns and Stalker have classically called "mechanistic" in their book *The Management of Innovation* (1961). In industries where major product innovation matters most, organizations are highly *fluid*, or "organic."

The second is Abernathy's own insight that these differences are *not independent*, but a result of organizations transitioning *over time* between these two states as their industry matures. The change over time from a fluid to a specific is, Abernathy argues, a systematically occurring one and a result of change in the nature of competition in an industry.

Following a major innovation in an industry, organizations tend to be fluid to accommodate the rapid speed of change and the uncertainty of the new technology. Over time, that uncertainty decreases and competition becomes more predictable and more price-focused. As price becomes more central and products more standardizable and therefore standardized (because, due to economies of scale, standardization is more profitable than customized, one-off products), organizations become more specific. They start to rely more on standardized production processes and invest in optimizing them by increasing "capital depth" (i.e., using increasingly specialized production equipment), but in doing so also sacrifice flexibility. You can think about the difference between a craft shop where everything is custom-made by hand (where efficiency is low but flexibility is high) and an assembly line (where efficiency is much greater but flexibility is very hard to achieve). Over time, the form of innovation that matters also changes. Initially, what really matters is product innovation and there tends to be a lot of it. This, however, drops over time as the product becomes more standardized. Process innovation, by contrast, hardly exists at the outset. As the product becomes standardized, process innovation can increase and with it will come increased efficiency. At a certain point, process innovation will also begin to taper off. All of this is summarized in figure 4.1, which really is the model that is the most essential thing to grasp in the chapter.

In contrast to the idea that industries have certain more or less stable characteristics, Abernathy's view is one of firms and productive units being constantly in a process of *transition*, trending away from a fluid state toward a specific one. A watershed moment in this process is the settling upon a *dominant design*. A dominant design is a more or less standard "blueprint" for how a product should be designed and function. Dominant designs exist today for most of the products that we surround ourselves with. Laptops, for instance, all follow a pretty standard design: a clamshell, foldable setup with a screen on the upper half and a keyboard in what is called a QWERTY configuration on the lower half. Cars, smartphones, hearing aids, bicycles, and other products similarly follow a standard design blueprint. "The important economic effects of a dominant design afford a degree of enforced product standardization, so that production economies can be sought, and provide a benchmark for functional performance competition, so that effective competition can take place on the basis of cost as well as product performance" (p. 75). This in turn makes possible and necessary a whole series of other changes – in organization, in production process, in marketing, and so on.

Abernathy's argument makes it apparent why we need a classification of different forms of innovation. Like Schumpeter, Abernathy recognizes that both product and process innovation matters, but also that they require different conditions, matter relatively more in different competitive situations, and seem to more or less crowd each other out. There are also other interplays between different innovation forms as firms transition from fluid to specific forms of organizing. We might imagine, for instance, that organizational innovation might be necessary to make that transition. Scaling up production might bring about a need for new methods of subdividing labor and new ways to manage and coordinate workers and units within the organization. We can also imagine that firms may seek to open up new markets over time, both to ensure that the expanded capacity that can come with economies of scale can be fully utilized and because it becomes apparent that larger and larger groups may be ready to consume the product. This raises the question of how these different sorts of innovation are supported by respective fluid, transitional, and specific structures. The larger question that Abernathy leaves us with, however, is whether the trade-off between efficiency and innovativeness *must* necessarily be a hard one, whether the dilemma is so grave and so fatalistic in its implications.

2.2 March: The Trade-Off between Exploitation and Exploration

In coining exploration and exploitation, this paper introduces what is perhaps *the* most widely used set of terms in current innovation management research, save perhaps for Schumpeter's Creative Destruction. Going forward, we are going to see this set of terms come up repeatedly as an anchor to many discussions of the challenges of innovation management. Where they do not come up directly, we will be applying them in our interpretations to make sense of many of the source texts for the book and to tie them together. These terms make explicit something about the nature of innovation and get us if not to the heart of the Productivity Dilemma, then at least closer to it. In this spirit of seeing the terms as helpful tools for understanding and theorizing, I encourage you to dwell relatively more on absorbing them than on the simulation models that March presents us with in the paper's second and third sections.

But what do the terms mean, beyond their immediate intuitive meaning? March is by intention not extremely clear and certainly this is part of the reason the concepts can get used so widely and inspire so much thinking and discussion. But in general terms, "[e]xploration includes things captured by terms such as search, variation, risk taking, experimentation, play, flexibility, discovery, innovation. Exploitation includes such things as refinement, choice, production, efficiency, selection, implementation, execution" (p. 71). Thinking about this in Abernathy's terms, exploration coincides with the emergence of new major innovations and with predominant design fluidity. Exploitation seems to reflect a much more specific form of activity.

Exploitation and exploration refer to different ways of approaching organizational learning. "The essence of exploitation is the refinement and extension of existing competences, technologies, and paradigms" (p. 85), while "[t]he essence of exploration is experimentation with new alternatives" (p. 85). Exploration deliberately has a greater element of engaging with the unknown than exploitation, but both are necessary for organizations that compete in the dynamically evolving circumstances of capitalist economies, because they speak to the dual anxiety that capitalism, in Schumpeter's view, creates for firms. Exploiting without exploring can leave the organization trapped and unable to keep up with changed circumstances. Exploring without exploiting will lead to many ideas, but too little execution to realize the potential benefits. The challenge then is one of *balance* between the two and, for Abernathy, as *fit* with the industry and the competitive dynamics that firms must engage with.

It is worth dwelling on the very different benefits from these activities. The benefits of exploitation, because exploitation tends to be applied and builds on knowledge already well understood, are characterized by "speed, proximity, and clarity" (p. 73). By contrast, "returns from exploration are systematically less certain, more remote in time, and organizationally more distant from the locus of action and adaption" (p. 73). The uncertainty and distant pay-offs of exploration are essential to understand.

Understanding these benefits is essential not only because firms must balance the two types of learning in such a way that the organization can actively compete in current conditions but does not end up trapped in those conditions once change occurs. This challenge is fundamentally Schumpeterian because the fact of capitalism is that change *will* happen. However, firms must not only engage in both exploration and exploitation. The real challenge is that there is a *strong trade-off* between the two. To say that there is a strong trade-off is to say that the two activities are mutually exclusive, that choosing between them is a zero-sum game, that doing more of one detracts from the other. This is the case between the two activities *competing for scarce resources*. Allocating resources to one means that the other will not receive resources and will not, the hypothesis would go, get pursued.

Precisely because the benefits of exploration are distant and uncertain, they also tend to be less attractive to invest in than exploitation, where benefits materialize sooner and with greater certainty. Much more than exploitation, exploration can be seen as an experiment and as a "bet" on an untested hypothesis. Exploration will often involve making choices in,

2.2 March: The Trade-Off

to borrow a term from Moore (1991), "high risk, low data" situations, while exploitation will involve "low risk, high data" situations. The two can be hard to compare, but to the managerial eye, the business case for exploitation tends to look substantially better. It will typically make better "business sense" and may even be necessary to compete in the short term. The catch-22 of that is that – to the extent that exploitative projects *do* exclude exploration – it is (put dramatically) a suicidal path long term.

There is a particularly dramatic image that can invoke the nature of this situation. Consider Ulysses, the hero of Homer's Odyssey, returning to Ithaca after the Trojan Wars. On his way, his ship must sail through the Strait of Messina. That passage – like the balance between exploitation and exploration – is far from trivial. On one side is Charybdis, a great sea monster, creating whirlpools that will pull entire ships underwater and destroy them. On the other side is Scylla, a nymph turned into a six-headed monster that will snatch sailors from the ship and devour them. The Strait is narrow and there is hardly any room for error – sail too close to either side, and the results may be dire. On the one hand, there is exploitation, to the exclusion of exploration – a seemingly safe path, but also one that leads to what sometimes gets called a "success trap" (and March himself refers to as "suboptimal stable equilibria"). That, however, sets you up for being swallowed by the whirlpool of Creative Destruction. On the other, there is exploration, to the exclusion of exploitation, where you absorb all the downsides of exploring without reaping the benefits. That is what gets called a "failure trap" and that too will destroy you, not in a whirlpool but on the rocks or between the monster's teeth. What is one to choose?[1]

That March is talking about *choice* is also essential and a difference between him and Abernathy. Due to his focus on organizations trending toward a specific state over time, Abernathy easily comes across as deterministic. Over time, industries will change, competitive dynamics will change, and organizations will have to change with them. The arrow of time points away from fluidity toward specificity. For March, it is much less deterministic. Implicitly, "buried in many features of organizational forms and customs, for example, in organizational procedures for accumulating and reducing slack, in search rules and practices, in the ways in which targets are set and changed, and in incentive systems" (p. 71), many

---

[1] At the advice of the sorceress Circe, who in some accounts was the one who transformed Scylla from a nymph to a sea monster, Ulysses chose to steer close to Scylla. While taking that path, he was momentarily distracted by Charybdis and lost six men to Scylla. His ship made it through.

choices are made that affect the balance that might be struck between the exploration and exploitation. Seemingly obvious choices to increase efficiency, for instance, might inhibit how much exploration becomes possible. Equally obvious choices to be highly flexible might inhibit how much exploitation is possible. Yet despite such implicit choices, March would think that organizations can also explicitly choose how to prioritize their activities and can make decisions about pursuing exploitative paths or exploratively seeking new opportunities. Bound of course by implicit prior choices and the limits of rationality and certainly disciplined by Abernathy's competitive dynamics, organizations and the individuals in them are in March's view "free" to explore or exploit.

Dealing with that choice is in different ways going to be at the center of what we will subsequently read. Dealing with it might be a matter of finding an optimum balance, of escaping the constraints of the trade-off, of finding ways to separate exploration from exploitation, of reflecting on implicit choices that bind explicit ones, of overcoming the challenges of uncertainty and distant pay-offs, of understanding the emergent effects of one's choices on others, and of appreciating the many limits to freedom of choice. But the nature of capitalist economies is that firms *must* deal with the choice.

2.3   Rosenberg: The Nature of Uncertainty

By March's definition, uncertainty – along with distant payoffs – is an inherent, inescapable part of the explorative learning that often forms the basis for innovation. But what precisely is this uncertainty about? What is it that is uncertain about innovation?

A "default" way to think about uncertainty is psychological or technological in nature. The psychological uncertainty of innovation relates to ideas and creativity. As opposed to many other organizational processes, creativity is deeply serendipitous, and this necessarily implies uncertainty. You might have a relatively clear impression about what can be accomplished by a skilled worker if you ask them to assemble electronics, gut fish, or drive a truck for an hour. You are unlikely to have the same clarity about outputs if you ask a skilled worker to spend an hour having a good idea. Good ideas tend to spring from flashes of insights, and insights are hard to plan for. The technological uncertainty of innovation, by contrast, relates to the viability of turning insights into inventions and inventions into innovations. Recognizing that something is theoretically possible – quantum computing, for instance – is one thing; building a quantum computer is something altogether different and whether such a leap is possible is also uncertain. This, it

2.3 Rosenberg: The Nature of Uncertainty

seems reasonable to say, is how March would think about uncertainty: we engage in explorative learning hoping that it will occasion good and viable ideas, but we do not really know.

These are very real sources of uncertainty. Consider how Kary Mullis had the insights underpinning Polymerase Chain Reaction (PCR) for which he would be rewarded the Nobel Prize in chemistry. Supposedly, the insights occurred on a 1983 spring evening as he was driving fast through Northern California toward his cabin. Like most people, he had his best idea in a very unplanned-for way (unlike most people, his best idea fundamentally changed biotechnology and enabled modern genetic sequencing). Could he have decided to sit down and have a Nobel-worthy idea? Probably not. Or consider AlphaGo, the Go-playing AI created by DeepMind Technologies that in 2016 defeated the world champion of Go. Go, till that point, had been assumed to be so complex that humans would inevitably hold an edge over AI. The defeat of course shattered that illusion. What is interesting and illuminating of technological uncertainty is that when the system was first conceived, the creators set it to playing Breakout and other games from the Atari console with the hope that the AI would be able to learn those games. Was it obvious there and then that it would improve *enough* to ultimately win the for-AI supposedly unwinnable game (see Section 3.1 for an elaboration of how technologies improve and the associated technological uncertainties)? Again, probably not.

What Rosenberg alerts us to is a form of uncertainty that tends to be afforded less attention, being somewhat less obvious. As he writes,

It is easy to assume that uncertainties are drastically reduced after the first commercial introduction of a new technology, and Schumpeter offered strong encouragement for that assumption.... In Schumpeter's view, life is easy for imitators, because all they need to do is to follow in the footsteps of the entrepreneurs who have led the way, and whose earlier activities *have reduced all the big uncertainties*. (p. 18, italics added)

The Schumpeterian entrepreneur, in other words, absorbs the psychological and technological uncertainty of bringing innovations into the world. Rosenberg continues, "It is, of course, true that some uncertainties have been reduced at that point. However, after a new technological capability of has been established, the questions change and, as we will see, new uncertainties, especially *uncertainties of a specifically economic nature*, begin to assert themselves" (p. 18, italics added). For Schumpeter, the first to bring a technology to market is the hero, and all the rest are "mere" imitators. For Rosenberg, there is nothing "mere," or trivial or straightforward, about it. What has later been called Rosenbergian uncertainty plays a fundamentally important role in determining the rate and direction of technological change, which in turn determines so much of economic growth and economic change.

Rosenberg's approach is historical and goes a long way toward showing just how non-trivial this uncertainty is. Consider, as Rosenberg does, examples like the laser, the radio, the telephone, the computer, electricity, or the steam engine. All of these technologies have found use in fields unimagined by their inventors and achieved economic impacts inconceivable to them. When the laser was developed in AT&T's Bell Labs, the patenting department of that organization refused to patent it, because it was considered irrelevant. When the radio was invented by Marconi, he imagined that it would be used for ship-to-ship and ship-to-shore communication,[2] and certainly not for mass media broadcasting. When the telephone was first patented, it was imagined as a "mere" improvement to telegraphy, the technology that it would utterly displace. The computer was imagined to be of use only for highly narrow scientific purposes. Electricity was seen as a replacement for gas lighting and the steam engine was developed to pump water out of Cornish coal mines. As Rosenberg puts it of the radio, "[t]he failure of social imagination was widespread." The same could certainly be said of all of these technologies.

We could interpret that failure as an expression of precisely limited imagination or, to give the original inventors a bit more credit, a fixation on or even obsession with solving particular problems that blinded them to the obvious. Imagination is often enormously constrained (see Section 5.2), and entrepreneurs are, in Schumpeter's description (1934), both obsessive and single-minded in their drive (see Section 9.1), so that view might be reasonable. We could also take it as an expression of the tendency for "new technologies [to] typically come into the world in a very primitive condition" (p. 20). Looking at a primitive version of a given technology, it is hard to appreciate just how useful it could turn out to be given years, or decades of improvement. The steam engine first put into use in the late 1600s is a far cry from the steam turbines that are used in today's electricity production. These explanations, however, are precisely psychological and technological in nature. Uncertainty, he argues, comes from at least five other sources that compound and interact.

First, technologies "come into the world with properties and characteristics whose usefulness cannot be immediately appreciated" (p. 22). When Edison invented the gramophone in 1877, it was not at all obvious that it could be used to scratch records and thus form the basis for the

---

[2] In what is arguably a forerunner to Instagram, you could send telegraphic "Marconigrams" via radio from the Titanic to the mainland.

emergence of hip hop 100 years later. Second, "the impact of an innovation depends not only on improvements of the invention, but also on improvements that take place in *complementary* inventions" (p. 24, italics added). Lasers in themselves might be of value (e.g., for digital storage of music on CDs), but when combined with fiber optics, they revolutionized communication. Third, "major technological innovations often constitute entirely new technological systems" (p. 25). Internal combustion engines would make possible not just carriages-without-horses, but an entire system of transportation based on cars that would have been "difficult in the extreme" (p. 25) to imagine. Fourth, "many major inventions had their origins in the attempt to solve very specific, and often very narrowly defined, problems" (p. 26). The O-ring was invented to make streetcar brakes better but turned out to crucially influence not just the design of airplanes but the viability of hydraulics-based systems in general (see Section 3.3). Fifth, "the ultimate impact of some new technological capacity ... is a matter of identifying certain specific categories of human needs and catering to them in novel or cost-effective ways" (p. 28). Even as it became obvious that radios *could* be used for broadcasting, it was not necessarily obvious that they should. That humans "needed" to hear not just sermons, but also concerts, news, and game shows through radio broadcasts was yet to be understood and depended in crucial ways on innovators who "merely" replicated the technology but replicated it in novel contexts and for novel purposes. When you saw AlphaGo besting Lee Sodol, it was not obvious one of its first applications would be reducing energy consumption in data center cooling.

These first four sources of uncertainty – the potential usefulness of properties, the dependence on complementary innovation, the implications for technological systems, and the specificity of initial application – all underscore the complex interdependencies that determine the ultimate utility of an innovation. The complexity and indeterminacy of those interdependencies make the utility of an innovation an emergent, and fundamentally unplannable, outcome. The fifth and final source of uncertainty that Rosenberg alerts us to is fundamentally different. The uncertainty here comes from the lack of clarity about *what to do* with an innovation: what human needs to address with the innovation, what markets to enter, and what value to create. This highlights the centrality of recognizing opportunities and of choices about what opportunities to pursue and how. Technology, in this way, becomes bound up with organizational processes and entrepreneurial choices, and indeed with societal developments, that are *profoundly* unimaginable and unforeseeable at the time an innovation is first introduced. When we speak of innovations, obviousness is, as Felin (2018) suggests, *not* self-evident.

3 How Do Technologies Improve?

> **Texts in This Chapter**
>
> Foster, R. 1986. *Innovation: The attacker's advantage*. Summit Books.
> Anderson, P. & Tushman, M. L. 1990. Technological discontinuities and dominant designs: A cyclical model of technological change. *Administrative Science Quarterly*. 35(4), 604–633.
> Vincenti, W. G. 1994. The retractable airplane landing gear and the Northrop "anomaly": Variation, selection and the shaping of technology. *Technology and Culture*. 35(1), 1–33.
> Adner, R. & Kapoor, R. 2016a. Innovation eco-systems and the pace of substitution: Re-examining technology S-curves. *Strategic Management Journal*. 37(4), 625–648.

In this chapter, we are going to focus on technology and how technological change impacts industries. The central metaphor for understanding technological development is the technology "S-curve." The central way to understand new technologies' impact on industries is as cyclical, as short periods of rapid and dramatic change followed by long periods of incremental improvement. We will consider both and explore how they connect to one another, to the dynamics of Creative Destruction, to the dominant organization of industrial firms, and to the balance required between exploration and exploitation.

With these basics in place, we are going to complicate the relatively straightforward story they produce. We are going to examine how technological performance at the system level is a function of sometimes highly unpredictable changes at the sub-component level and sometimes of changes at the ecosystem level. Both can render predictions of technological change and competitive dynamics more difficult and open up new avenues for innovation management action.

3.1 Foster: The Technology S-Curve

Technologies do not come into the world with their full potential performance realized or even clear. On the contrary, technologies have a life

3.1 Foster: The Technology S-Curve

cycle of being introduced, maturing, and finally stagnating and becoming obsolete as new technologies are introduced. Over the course of that life cycle, the performance of a technology is going to change. Foster's first big idea in his book is that a technology's performance is going to change in predictable ways. He writes:

Initially, as funds are put into developing a new product or process, progress is terribly slow. Then all hell breaks loose as the key knowledge necessary to make advances is put in place. Finally, as more dollars are put into the development of a product or process, it becomes more challenging and more expensive to make technical progress. Ships don't sail much faster, cash registers don't work much better, and clothes don't get much cleaner. (pp. 31–32)

In other words, the rate of technological improvement tends to be slow when the technology emerges, then more rapid as maturity is reached, and then slow again before grinding to a virtual halt. What drives improvement is *investment* and if you plot a technology's performance as a function of investment, the line you get is basically a drawn out "s" (see the curve on p. 31).

We can think about this through the concepts provided by March and Abernathy. Initially, a technology is *not* well understood, and a lot of effort is needed to figure it out. Developing it is inherently and necessarily explorative. Organizations working with the technology will tend to be fluid, essentially because there is nothing to be specific around. If the technology is poorly understood, it is hard to know *how* to organize a specific production process and what to optimize on. As investment builds up and more experiments have been conducted, exploration can give way to exploitation, especially when a dominant design emerges and sets a direction for future innovative efforts. When the industry closes around a dominant design, what Italian economist Giovanni Dosi calls a "technological paradigm" (1982) emerges and sets a trajectory for future development work. The dominant design defines a set of questions and problems to work on in order to improve the technology and a set of approaches for doing that work. What ensues is "evolutionary, incremental adaptations of existing elements, products and technologies" (Salter & Alexy, 2014, p. 33).

Toward the end of the life cycle, Abernathy would depict organizations as becoming so specific as to be almost incapable of innovation – we are beyond the point where process innovation simply crowds out product innovation, and instead in a state where efficiency simply crowds out innovation generally. March would surely think of the technology life cycle as following a pattern of, initially, "pure" exploration in the interest of discovery and then over time trending toward "pure" exploitation in the interest of efficiency and predictability and reduction of variance, with various weightings of the two learning activities in between. Foster has a somewhat different perspective in advancing the idea that technologies have *limits* at the top of the S-curve where there simply is no more innovation that can viably be done, because the cost of further improvement becomes so high. Where Abernathy would think of innovation as an effect of organizational conditions and March as one of choices and resource allocation, Foster would think of technologies as having inherent "natural" potentials that can get exhausted, much in the same way that a well can run dry. As technologies mature and reach their limit, ideas for improving them become harder and more costly to find. That is the point at which ships do not sail much faster, no matter how many masts you put on them, because physics simply constrains further improvement (for other technological paradigms, it may be other laws of natural or social science that constrain improvement).

To see that ideas indeed do get harder to find as technologies mature,[1] we can look at some of the recent evidence from Nicholas Bloom and three of his colleagues (2020). In their paper, they look at *research productivity*, which is basically Foster's improvement rate and thus an expression of how much investment it takes to sustain constant exponential growth. In semiconductors, where performance has improved roughly 35 percent every year almost since Gordon Moore in 1965 made the prediction that would become Moore's Law, research productivity is dramatically falling. Today, there are eighteen times more researchers working on developing semiconductor technology than there were in 1971. A similar pattern is evident in agriculture, where crop yields (per unit of land) have roughly doubled since 1960 with relatively constant growth rates during the period. However, it takes more than twenty times the effort that it took in the 1960s to sustain that growth rate. The pattern is less clear, but similar in medicine, where we also see that new drugs and treatments become increasingly expensive and have a decreasing impact on health outcomes. The dystopian reading of this is that we will "run out" of improvement because with decreasing productivity we will also

---

[1] The authors imply that improvement *in general* is getting harder to achieve, which, to my mind, is not at all what their data show. Rather, they look at technologies that have been subject to intense investment over long periods, have matured quite far, and *therefore* now face very low returns for further investment. Others have made the argument that improvement in general is getting harder, such as Robert Gordon (2016), but that argument has been quite convincingly rejected by, for example, Erik Brynjolfsson and Andrew McAfee (2014). The main difference between optimists and pessimists, and the reason that I think both Bloom and his colleagues and Gordon are over-dramatizing, is that they do not – in this particular work – take account of *new* technologies that are *early* in their lifecycle, that is, are not Schumpeterian enough.

run out of researchers. A Schumpeterian perspective would be much more optimistic, assuming that new technologies come along and, being earlier in their life cycles, offer opportunities for less costly improvement. From that perspective, it is an empirical question to which extent such new technologies are emerging. Such new technologies – early in their lifecycle and with potential for future improvement – are what Foster calls "technological discontinuities." It is not obvious whether you should take the dystopian or optimistic (Schumpeterian) position here. What is clear is that people almost always underestimate the potential for new technologies to come along and, consequently, prophets of the end of growth have historically always been proven wrong (Mokyr et al, 2015; e.g., Mann, 2019).

There are a few things to note before we turn to that topic, however. Do note that not all technologies follow the S-curve pattern. If you look at Foster's account of the development in tire materials (p. 124), you will see several technologies with quite different development trajectories. Note also that it is a common misconception to depict S-curves with *time* on the x-axis. When you depict improvement as an effect of time, you (inadvertently, perhaps) assume that improvement "just" happens and you end up obscuring the fact that improvement is *very much* an effect of investment and effort, that improvement cannot be taken for granted, and that organizations cannot expect to just "ride the S-curve" to success. Certainly, if investments were constant over time, this would not be much of a conceptual problem. Alas, investment in technology sometimes follows a boom-and-bust pattern of inflated expectations and shattered hopes as investors flock to and rush away from overhyped and spectacularly failing technologies, while in other cases investment can be highly directed and coordinated across different actors in an industry. Whether, in turn, consistent improvement allows for "spillovers" to occur, such that many organizations benefit from improvements in technology, can also not be taken for granted. Improvements in technology may well be proprietary, exclusively benefiting individual firms and not all potential users of a technology (e.g., Teece, 1986).

The final thing to note about technology S-curves at this point is that both the phase of rapid improvement and the eventual limit where improvement becomes hard to sustain often appear clear in retrospect, while forecasts about technology development are inherently shrouded in uncertainty. The primary source of uncertainty is where the *limit* of a technology lies. The limit of improvement in semiconductors, for instance, has been continuously debated, with repeated declarations that "Moore's Law is dead." Similar discussions surround many other technologies. It turns out to be hard to predict, because the limit is not only a function of the technologies inherent, "natural" properties, but also a function of human ingenuity. Moreover, there is an element of choice that contributes to *shaping* the S-curve. In their book on entrepreneurial strategy, Scott Stern and Joshua Gans (2017; see also Gans et al, 2020) argue that entrepreneurs when choosing to innovate on a technology can *choose their S-curve* by strategically pursuing more or less explorative trajectories. An exploitative strategy might involve quickly implementing a technology, focusing more on developing it from its current level to a particular application and thus settling for a comparatively low ultimate limit. An explorative strategy might involve a broader, longer, and more costly search process before settling into a technological paradigm, thus providing the foundations for an S-curve with a higher ultimate limit. In this way, uncertainty also becomes a function of other market actors' investment decisions, with those decisions at the micro-level creating an aggregate performance improvement, defined by the rate and direction of inventive activity.

The idea of choosing an S-curve can seem somewhat opaque, but consider the very current example of self-driving cars. While this technology is imminently close to realization, it is also clear why it has been such a difficult problem to solve. A vehicle capable of autonomous driving at high speeds in complex and erratic environments and of responding safely to that environment requires technology to have reached an extremely high level on the S-curve to be at all viable. For that reason, extensive exploration and substantial investment have been necessary, just to get *close* to realizing what could be a "minimally viable product." Now contrast this with what could *also* have happened. Instead of aiming for a fully autonomous *car*, producers could have looked at the same basic technology and taken a much more exploitative route, focused on getting a product to market much faster, if they had instead aimed for an autonomous package-delivery robot. Such a robot could suffice with driving at substantially lower speeds (say, 4 km/h instead of 120 km/h), using the sidewalk instead of the highway. Instead of having to deal with high-speed collision avoidance, it could simply stop if it encountered a situation that the software was unable to handle. Without having passengers on board, safety demands would also be much lower for this robotic mail carrier than for the autonomous car. It would, in other words, have represented the pursuit of a much less demanding minimal solution, a much more exploitative S-curve, and possibly resulted in a much lower ultimate limit to self-driving technology, because foundational and difficult-to-achieve insights might not have occurred, because they would not be necessary.

Foster's second big idea is of "technological discontinuities." A technological discontinuity refers to "a break between the S-curves" (p. 35),

3.1 Foster: The Technology S-Curve

where a new technology replaces an old one. Typically (but not always), as one technology S-curve reaches its limit and begins to be subject to decreasing returns on innovation investment, new technologies emerge. Initially, such new technologies tend to exhibit weaker performance than old ones. It is only over time that they become superior, because they start to mature and rapidly improve at a point where the old technology has effectively reached its limit. The first digital cameras were by most measures not as good as cameras using photographic film, but they improved more rapidly because photographic film had exhausted most of its improvement technology. "If you are at the limit, no matter how hard you try you cannot make progress" (p. 34), and that will set you back in competition with new solutions that *do* progress.

Technological discontinuities, Foster argues, tend to be "brutal" for established firms, because when a new S-curve emerges, its technology tends to *not* rely on "the same knowledge that underlays the old one but [on] an entirely new and different knowledge base. For example, the switch from vacuum tubes to semiconductors, the switch from propeller-driven planes to jets, the shift from cloth to paper diapers, the switch from records to tapes to compact discs …" (pp. 35–36). Each of these represents a paradigmatically different way of thinking about problems and solutions respectively for controlling electricity flows in computers, for airplane propulsion, for water absorption, and for music consumption.

This leads Foster to his third central idea, namely that when technological discontinuities arise, they tend to favor new entrants to an industry and to challenge established firms. Attackers, he suggests, tend to be afforded advantages by technological discontinuities:

When attacks are launched, they are often unnoticed by the leader, hidden from view by conventional economic analysis. When the youthful attacker is strong he is quite prepared for battle by virtue of success and training in niche markets. The defender, lulled by the security of strong economic performance for a longtime and by conventional management wisdom that encourages him to stay his course, and buoyed by faith in evolutionary change finds it is too late to respond. The final battle is swift and the leader loses. His attempts to defend his employees and shareholders fail. Doomed by doing too little, too late (p. 37).

There are lots of moving parts in that description. We will be returning to the role of niche markets when dealing with Clayton Christensen's ideas of Disruptive Innovation and the inertia of incumbents with Henderson and Clark's ideas of Architectural Innovation (both in Chapter 3). For now, consider the way this statement reflects Schumpeter's depiction of Creative Destruction. Essentially, Foster's technological discontinuities are the sort of innovative step change that strikes at the heart of profits and brings about the dynamism of Schumpeterian capitalism. For this reason, one of Dosi's observations about new technological paradigms is that they bring about the emergence of "Schumpeterian firms." The hypothesis here is that attackers, to use March's term, can pursue a purely explorative strategy and are unconstrained by having to negotiate a balance between exploration and exploitation and that this freedom for some attackers will outweigh the liabilities of competing against large, established, and efficient organizations with ample resources. In Abernathy's terms, they also do not have to undo a highly specific organization of their operations but can begin from an entirely fluid and more dynamic starting point, the assumption being that such specific organizations *are* difficult to shift.

Taken together, Foster makes us alert to the central importance that current and ultimate performance levels *and* rates of technological improvement play in determining competitive dynamics and in spurring Creative Destruction. We will return to this in Section 3.2. But perhaps more than Foster makes clear, the forecasting of these things is inherently speculative and irreducibly uncertain. Performance and improvement are both highly complex phenomena, with multiple determinants within and beyond the focal technology. This will be a continuing theme throughout the book. What is clear, already at this point, is that pursuing innovation and exploration should basically be understood as experiments, as tests of an ex ante unproven hypothesis about how technology and numerous other related factors will develop. Under certain conditions, some organizations will be better at those experiments than others and some, if not most, of those experiments will fail.

3.2   Tushman and Anderson: Technology Cycles

There is a circle to be squared in reconciling two "pictures" that we have so far encountered of innovation. One image that we have met is Schumpeter's, the other is Abernathy's. For Schumpeter, the capitalist economy is in a state of perpetual turmoil. The perennial gale of Creative Destruction constantly blows, spurred on by innovation. Innovation is the stuff that competition is made of and the result is constant change. This is the ideology of innovation at full throttle. For Abernathy, the industrial organization is perpetually seeking stabilization, specificity, and regularity. The search for efficiency drives out innovation, first by seeking a dominant design and then investing in capital deepening to the point where innovation can no longer occur. Efficiency achieved through economies of scale is the stuff that competition is truly made of and the result is a roadblock to innovation and ultimately stagnation. This is, if anything, the inverse of the innovation ideology. As it turns out, Foster's idea of technological discontinuities is a good place to begin the squaring, because it can reconcile the two opposing views into a model of "punctuated equilibrium." There is, generally, stability. And then, at "rare and largely unknowable" intervals (Salter & Alexy, 2014, p. 33), comes the Schumpeterian shock of paradigm-changing technological discontinuity.

This idea of innovation driving change through punctuated equilibrium emerges from Anderson and Tushman's analyses of three industries (cement, glass, and minicomputers) and is captured in their cyclical model. This model has emerged as the canonical way to think about how technological change brings about industrial change and drives an industry lifecycle. The model (depicted in their paper's figure 1) presents industries as transitioning between two states. Transitions between these states are driven by particular events. Eras of Incremental Change are the state that industries are in most of the time. These are long (Abernathian) periods where firms pursue increased scale and efficiency through process innovation. This is where most innovation typically happens, and most innovation is incremental and relatively unremarkable. Because the technological paradigm underlying the industry is mostly settled, development is focused on marginal improvements. This state ends with the introduction of a (Fosterian) technological discontinuity, where a new technological alternative emerges to challenge the technological paradigm. The technological discontinuity brings the industry into a (Schumpeterian) Era of Ferment, where competition is driven by innovation, intense and rife with uncertainty. The decisive event that lets the industry settle back into an Era of Incremental Change is the emergence of a dominant design. This state prevails until another discontinuity emerges, and thus the cycle continues. The model is one of long periods of evolution, interrupted by short spurts of revolutionary change. That is punctuated equilibrium.

Reading this model through March's terminology, it is apparent that Eras of Ferment are characterized by exploration. Eras of Incremental Change, by contrast, are characterized by exploitation. The emergence of a dominant design allows firms to transition from exploring to pursuing the more certain, and more proximate, gains from exploitation. The exploitative nature of eras of incremental change is evident in how competition mostly takes the form of elaborating the dominant design. That competition, however, can still be very vigorous as made clear by for instance the Cola Wars of the 1980s when Pepsi and Coca-Cola struggled for dominance of a well-established market, but competed largely *without* substantial innovation. Colored sugar water did not change much. What changed was essentially the means and intensity of persuasion: advertising, packaging, endorsements, and the like.

In eras of ferment, two forms of competition play out and innovation and exploration play key roles in both of them. The sort of competition that Anderson and Tushman, building on Foster, describe as *substitution* is competition between old and new technologies. Generally, old technologies do not go quietly into obsolescence, but rather compete vigorously with new ones. A classic example of this might be the competition between IBM and Remington Rand when electronic computers based on vacuum tubes were first introduced to replace computers based on switches. A more recent one might be the contest between Blockbuster and Netflix, when Netflix introduced DVD rental by mail to challenge physical stores, described in Keating (2012).

A less widely appreciated sort of competition is the competition that occurs between different instantiations of the technological discontinuity, what they term design competition. The classic example here is the contest in the videotape market that played out between VHS and Betamax, beginning in the 1970s, described by Cusumano et al (1992). Sony launched Betamax in 1975 and JVC launched VHS in 1976, and through to the middle of the 1980s, an intense contest played out to become the standard format, that is, the dominant design. A more recent example might be the contest between Blu-ray and high-definition DVD or the contest of Large Format Cinema between, most famously, IMAX and Dolby but also several others. An older one, described in detail in David (1985), is the contest to become the standard typewriter keyboard layout, which QWERTY won. It is an interesting feature of Anderson and Tushman's analysis of design competition that it is never the discontinuity that becomes the dominant design. This tells us something about the dynamics of design competition in Eras of Ferment and the (dis)advantages of being first to market that we will return to (see Sections 8.1. and 8.2).

It is the model that most researchers focus on as the central takeaway from the paper, but the underlying study is really admirable in its detail of following three industries over such long periods as to observe several discontinuities in each. While not quite as central as the circular model itself, there are several points to take with you going forward that deepen our understanding of technological discontinuities and add to our repertoire of theoretical distinctions. First, the kind of discontinuity that Anderson and Tushman observe differs from Foster's in an important respect. Where for Foster a new technology starts off with performance that is inferior to the old, Anderson and Tushman's discontinuities are characterized by performing *better* at the outset. The visual representation of this appears in figures 2a and 2b, where the discontinuities appear

3.2 Tushman and Anderson: Technology Cycles

as sudden bursts of increased performance. This is noteworthy not only for reminding us that Foster's pattern is a stylized one that not all discontinuities follow but also for interpreting Anderson and Tushman's findings. It appears uncontroversial that this has to lead to considerably less uncertainty at the emergence of a discontinuity than we would otherwise expect. We could, with March, expect that to make exploration of new opportunities appear less risky, and hence more attractive for incumbents than would be the case of discontinuities where the new technology is initially inferior.

Second, they alert us to the possibility that all discontinuities are not created equally. Where Foster sees discontinuities as based on new knowledge, Anderson and Tushman argue that a discontinuity can be both competence-enhancing and competence-destroying[2] and that this matters for how an era of ferment plays out, essentially by changing the relative advantages of incumbents over new entrants. This is the case, because competence-enhancing technological discontinuities essentially build on the knowledge that already underlies existing technologies, while only competence-destroying discontinuities fit Foster's model of relying on new knowledge. A discontinuity, for Anderson and Tushman, does not imply a technological paradigm shift but only a dramatic change in performance levels. That conceptual clarity can be worthwhile to bear in mind because we can see that we suddenly have two meanings related to the same term and can expect two different causal mechanisms to unfold around them.

Third, technological substitution is *not* guaranteed, again in contrast to Foster's depiction. Because the emergence of a new technology can lead to increased investment in an old one, the opportunity exists for a new technology to not improve sufficiently and sufficiently quickly to supplant an old one, even as the old one is late on its S-curve. When a discontinuity is competence-destroying, we can expect incumbents to invest heavily in competing against a new technology to keep it from gaining a foothold. This is the case, because making the shift to that new technology will be so relatively difficult for them and, we can assume, so relatively unlikely to be successful.

Fourth, what becomes the dominant design is *not* a matter of technological superiority. Rather, it is a quite complicated matter in which many elements play a part: choices between which customers to pursue most aggressively, strategic maneuvers in building alliances and supply chains, evolving customer perceptions, and so on. It is a question of

---

[2] They originally developed that argument in a prior paper, titled "Technological Discontinuities and Organizational Environments" and published in 1986.

dominant designs *emerging* as outcomes of directed human action, but not as outcomes of any particular person's intention or any particular firm's strategy. That any person or firm could actively steer the outcome is one of those interpretive mistakes that are easy to make in superficial hindsight.

Finally, the model has an alternative outcome that is not developed in the paper. It posits that an Era of Ferment ends with the emergence of a single dominant design and that the vanquished technology fades into obsolescence. Neither of those are necessarily true. An Era of Ferment could viably result in several dominant designs and an ensuing splintering of an industry into several sub-industries. A vanquished technology could also "re-emerge" after having been judged obsolete. Raffaeli's work on the Swiss mechanical watch industry (2019) is exemplary of both dynamics. In the 1980s, mechanical watch technology was widely regarded as obsolete due to the introduction of battery-powered quartz-based digital watches – a truly competence-destroying technological discontinuity. However, mechanical watches reemerged in the 2000s as a distinct market within the watch industry that largely does not compete with quartz watches. That possibility, while perhaps not frequent, is worth bearing in mind.

3.3 Vincenti: Technological Interdependencies and Performance Shifts

This paper provides a detailed analysis of a particular moment in aviation history that tells us something quite profound about technological discontinuities and eras of ferment. More specifically, it provides an account of how retractable landing gear replaced fixed landing gear as a part of the dominant design for airframes in the 1930s and does so by studying in detail the seemingly anomalous design choices made by one particular airplane designer – John Northrop. If that seems supremely obscure to you at the outset and if the details of the study seem excruciating, you could be excused for thinking so. But in that obscurity and in all those details lie, I think, some great lessons for especially management students and scholars, used as we are to more sweeping accounts of technological change, its strategic implications, and the visions of great men.

The paper has its own theoretical ambition, which is to counter what Vincenti calls "the usual view" that the transition to retractable airplane landing gear was "an essentially reasoned and ordered affair" (p. 2) and that "the desirability of the retractable gear was obvious and subject to simple and straightforward engineering assessment" (p. 4). Instead,

3.3 Vincenti: Technological Interdependencies

Vincenti wants to advance the biological metaphor, drawn from evolutionary theory, of blind variation and selective retention (elaborated on pp. 21–26). To be honest, I actually find that part of the paper to be the least interesting – many other parts are more interesting.

Read "just" as literary fiction, the historical analysis conveys something fundamentally important about eras of ferment. What it conveys so well, I think, is the incredible uncertainty that surrounds newly emerged technologies. Having read March, this would not surprise us, but Vincenti's description is interesting for how it helps us understand how an otherwise highly esteemed and talented airplane designer finds it so difficult to navigate between technological alternatives and why he is so late to transition to what *in hindsight* appears to be so obviously superior a technology. Especially when it comes to technology, this study shows us how foresight is infinitely harder than hindsight.

This caution in itself would be reason to read the paper. We can also learn something about exactly what it is about technology and eras of ferment that makes uncertainty so inherent, though. Consider, for instance, how Northrop must evaluate the relative merits of retractable landing gear over fixed landing gear. Contrary to Foster and to Anderson and Tushman, who conceive of performance as mono-dimensional, Northrop must deal with *multiple possible performance dimensions*. If we see landing gear as a *sub-system* in the larger system of an airplane, which also consists of other sub-systems (e.g., engines, wings, steering system, etc.), it is clear that the decision between retractable and fixed landing gear is a complex one with trade-offs between at least five important requirements: The sub-system must be lightweight so to not weigh down the airplane; it must be aerodynamic to avoid drag; it must be reliable to ensure safety; it must be easy to maintain; and it must be seen as competitively priced relative to alternatives.

In some cases, the balance of those trade-offs will crucially depend on technological developments *in other sub-systems*. In Northrop's case, the importance of aerodynamics *increased* over time as engines improved and airplanes consequently flew faster. That engines would improve was not obvious, but when they did, the disadvantages of fixed landing gear grew relative to retractable landing gear that folds away inside the airframe. Fixed landing gear became what Hughes (1983) calls a "reverse salient": a component that prevents the system in its entirety from achieving its performance potential. As a result, fixed landing gear was further developed to overcome this increasingly apparent disadvantage. As Anderson and Tushman show, sometimes old technologies get improved when a new technology gets introduced, in an effort to outcompete the new technology before it gains widespread adoption. This was the case for fixed landing gear, where the introduction of "trouser" covers for the landing gear (pictured in figure 4) made them appear more aerodynamic than retractable gear, but only for a certain time. When engines further improved, that advantage went away.

In other cases, change in one sub-system will compromise the performance of other sub-systems. In Northrop's case, he had developed a wing design that was for all intents and purposes revolutionary in his time. If he had implemented retractable landing gear, he would have compromised with the performance of wings, because those two sub-systems were made interdependent by competing for space within the airframe. The appearance of a trouser design, that is, relying on an elaborated version of an old technology, made it seem entirely reasonable to stay on an old S-curve for the landing gear sub-system to maintain a leading technology in the wing sub-system.

Finally, the performance of a sub-system on a particular dimension can be suddenly jolted by inventions made in fields that do not appear at all adjacent. Where Foster sees technological improvement as smooth, what Vincenti's account shows us is that retractable airplane landing gear was *suddenly* made dramatically more viable. Early versions of retractable landing gear were raised and lowered by hand, which can be somewhat problematic for a pilot who has plenty of other things to do during take-off and landing and thus reduce the desirability of moving to that new technology. A later version was hydraulic, but this relied on a wholly unreliable and maintenance-demanding system of sealing fluid within this sub-sub-system. Only when the O-ring was invented as part of developing a braking system for streetcars and later implemented in the hydraulic system did retractable airplane landing gear as a sub-system become really viable, because it made the sub-sub-system that raised and lowered landing wheels more reliable and less maintenance-intensive. "Thus did a seemingly minor component play an important role in the success of a much larger and more visible device" (p. 20).

These kinds of considerations, while seemingly obscure and far outside the domain of business and management, are crucially important for innovation and technological substitution. What is instructive about them is that "This kind of situation may be present invisibly in many cases" (p. 20), and by virtue of their invisibility be disregarded as trivial in hindsight. What we can take away from reading about them here is the understanding that innovation is, in Joel Mokyr's (1990) terms, hopelessly overdetermined: there are *so many* things that matter. In business and management research, we tend to look for those variables that are most important in explaining a phenomenon in order to get "clear" stories and prescriptions that apply across contexts. But when we immerse ourselves in the particularities of practice, it becomes clear that there are many, many dynamics that interact in order to produce particular, emergent end results.

3.4 Adner and Kapoor: Eco-Systems and the Pace of Substitution

When a technological discontinuity occurs, Foster would expect it to bring about technological substitution, and that the substitution would be quick. Recall the statement about what happens when attackers working on a new S-curve enter a market dominated by old technology: "The final battle is swift and the leader loses" (Foster, 1986, p. 37). To that, Tushman and Anderson's analysis adds that the question of whether substitution does result from an era of ferment depends on the competitive response of incumbents (e.g., do they invest heavily in elaborating the old technology) and on whether the discontinuity is competence enhancing or competence destroying. Vincenti would add that substitution depends on how the process of technological improvement unfolds, which in turn depends on developments at the level of sub-systems and components and to no small extent on unforeseeable events (e.g., the O-ring). Adner and Kapoor provide a way of thinking about the process of substitution that can systematize this. Rather than think of whether substitution happens, they focus on its *pace* and in doing so reconcile the three other views. Substitution, in this model, is bound to happen eventually and so the inherently Schumpeterian question is "just" one of when, how fast, and, by implication, how destructive for incumbents.

For Adner and Kapoor, the question is one of whether substitution begins immediately after the discontinuity emerges and, once it begins, whether it is swift or sluggish. That is the outcome they try to make sense of. To explain the outcome, they rely on two groups of concepts. The first is of an ecosystem of complements around a focal technology. A complement is a technology that increased the performance of *another* technology. A landing strip is a complement to an airplane, a light is a complement to a bicycle and, in Adner and Kapoor's case, masks and resists are complements to lithography tools in the manufacture of semiconductors. By looking at technologies *together* with their complements instead of at individual technologies, Adner and Kapoor add to Foster's understanding of technological improvement. The performance of a technology can improve without investment in that technology, provided investment in the ecosystem of the technology's complements yields improvement. Electric cars, for instance, can improve their range either by advances in solid-state battery technology (a discontinuity) or by advances in charging infrastructure (a complement). This leads to the distinction between *performance-as-developed* and *performance-as-used*. What ultimately matters, of course, is performance-as-used.

The second set of concepts are the extension opportunities for old technologies and the emergence challenges of new ones. Extension opportunities refer to the opportunities to improve the performance-as-used of an old technology. This could happen by improvement in performance-as-developed through costly investments, squeezing the very last improvement out of an old technology. Of more interest to Adner and Kapoor, it could also happen by investment in improving complements. Emergence challenges are the analog of this for new technologies: how challenging is it to improve a new technology's performance-as-developed and its attendant ecosystem to the point where performance-as-used exceeds old technology ecosystems?

If we distinguish between high and low emergence challenges and high and low extension opportunities and say that all cases of technological discontinuities will face some combination of those, we can create a two-by-two matrix. Doing so is a staple of management research and sometimes it makes perfect sense and at other times it is a ridiculous and unhelpful complexity reduction. In this case, it seems to be a meaningful distinction, and it yields the framework in the paper's figure 1, with four ideal types of substitution.

When we have low extension opportunities and low emergence challenges (quadrant 1), we would expect a "Creative Destruction"-type of substitution that is swift and decisive, much like what Foster would imagine. This is the case because there is both very little to do to improve the old technology and little to stop the new one and so superiority is achieved quickly. If, *in contrast to Vincenti's argument*, we assume that superiority on a single dimension is what matters, market dominance quickly shifts, rendering the old technology obsolete. The opposite would be the case for a situation of high extension opportunities and high emergence challenges (quadrant 4). The old technology can be improved considerably through complements and the new struggles to get off the ground, meaning that substitution does happen, but slowly. In that case, the old technology is "robustly resilient[3]" to competition. With high extension opportunities and low emergence challenges, we see some real competition between the two technology ecosystems and a drawn-out era of ferment with "robust coexistence" (quadrant 2).

---

[3] This term, as well as "robust coexistence" and "illusion of resilience," comes from Adner and Kapoor (2016b).

Rank-ordered, substitution would be fast in situations like quadrant 1, intermediate in quadrant 2, and slow in quadrant 4.

In situations like quadrant 3, where the emergence challenges for the new technology are high and extension opportunities low, incumbents can easily have the initial impression that a new technology is not a threat because it appears so hard to develop to a competitive performance-as-used, thus falling prey to an "illusion of resilience." When we assume that the emergence challenge is not so great as to be unviable, the result of this would be that the new technology enters a market but only achieves a trivial role until the point where the emergence challenge is overcome. Assuming that this challenge is indeed overcome in one decisive step and not in stages and that it is overcome before an even newer discontinuity emerges, the new technology then very rapidly transitions to market dominance. The resilience illusion is then painfully broken for incumbents, as what resembles creative destruction unfolds.

All this theory is developed up front in the paper and then studied in the context of semiconductor production, focusing on successive generations of the lithography tools that together with two complements are central to that production and largely confirm the model's hypotheses. Like Vincenti's paper, the industrial details can appear somewhat obscure, even if Adner and Kapoor trade intricacy of historical detail for a much more fully developed theory. That obscurity, however, is instructive because it is precisely in sensitivity to the details that viable strategies depart from unviable ones and that serious analyses and observations depart from those that just restate ideology. In that sense, what we should take from both Vincenti and Adner and Kapoor is an appreciation for just how much context – in this case technological context – matters for how we apply our theories, and for why having concepts that let us distinguish in finer detail is valuable.

In this case, you should take very seriously the idea that performance depends not only on a focal technology but also on an ecosystem of complementary technologies when you think about technological improvement. Just as Vincenti brought our attention to the possibility that improvement at the level of technological systems can depend on *inside* improvement in sub-systems and components, Adner and Kapoor direct our attention to improvement *outside* the technology. In this way, we can add both a micro-perspective and a macro-perspective to Foster's model and to our thinking about discontinuities. This will, in turn, shape how Eras of Ferment play out and what consequences they will have for both new entrants and incumbents. You should also take seriously the nuance of distinguishing between different levels of emergence challenge for new technologies and extension opportunities for old ones.

4 What Makes Some Innovations More Challenging Still?

> **Texts in This Chapter**
>
> Christensen, C. 1997. *The innovator's dilemma: When new technologies cause great firms to fail* (Introduction). Harvard Business Review Press.
> Henderson, R. M. & Clark, K. B. 1990. Architectural innovation: The reconfiguration of existing product technologies and the failure of established firms. *Administrative Science Quarterly*. 35(1), 9–30.
> David, P. A. 1990. The dynamo and the computer: An historical perspective on the modern productivity dilemma. *The American Economic Review*. 80(2), 355–361.

In this chapter, we are going to look at different forms of innovation, but not along the typical axes of difference. In Sections 1.1, 2.2, 3.1, and 3.2, we have distinguished between innovation in products and services, processes, and organizational practices, and between innovations that are mostly exploitative and incremental and those that are explorative and radical. The ones we will cover in this chapter are characterized by additional, complicating features that lead them to have different opportunities for new entrants, different challenges for incumbents, and different effects on industries. These features include particular aspects of marketing, organization, and uncertainty.

We are going to close the chapter by taking a slightly different angle on the relationship between technology and industries. Where we have so far taken that relationship as given, we are going to look at how technologies that are *potentially* general in nature get applied to several different industries through a process of opportunity discovery that can in no reasonable way be taken for granted and what that might imply for technological improvement.

4.1 Christensen: Disruption and Unattractive Markets

Disruption is perhaps the most ideological idea to float around in innovation management practice and – to a lesser, but nontrivial extent – research.

4.1 Christensen: Disruption and Unattractive Markets

For some reason, it seems to have become the de facto innovation strategy for entrepreneurs, the greatest fear for incumbents, and a clear and present danger for all industries. You could be excused for coming into a business school course on innovation management or entrepreneurship thinking that disruption was *all* that mattered and in shamefully many cases, you could walk out of them with that belief very much intact. If you read the more hyped-up business press, you would probably find your conviction strengthened. No sector is safe, it appears, from the tsunami wave of disruption.

Very few academic theories have this kind of impact and while it is truly fascinating to understand just why disruption has risen to this prominence in the popular imagination that falls somewhat beyond the scope of this book. Suffice to say that you need to know what people talk about when they talk about disruption, but also to know that there are pretty wide gaps between the theory and how it gets talked about, between its empirical basis and its theoretical argument, and between the claimed and actual scope of disruption.

Of all the ideas that this book presents, Christensen's idea of disruptive innovation – he does not talk a lot about disruption, but rather disruptive change, disruptive technologies, and disruptive innovation – is perhaps the most Schumpeterian of all. Schumpeter made us aware that innovation is the great harbinger of industrial change, that creative destruction is an ever-present threat for established firms. Christensen pushes this even further, focusing on "*good* companies – the kinds that many managers have admired and tried to emulate, the companies known for their abilities to innovate and execute" (p. xiii, italics in original). Christensen's argument is about how the very best companies get destroyed *by that greatness*. It is not because of the hubris of greatness, even if the story of a "fat and happy" company getting toppled makes for an excellent story, but because the very things that make a company great also make it susceptible to being swept along by creative destruction. In that sense, Christensen turns up the anxiety of capitalism that Schumpeter identified to even higher levels, but also tries to show the particular pattern that leads to this kind of destruction – there is, to his mind, a very particular recipe for it.

Disruptive innovation, in Christensen's conceptualization and in marked contrast to how disruption gets talked about, means something *really* specific. What Christensen describes as his "failure framework" is a recipe in four parts with one result.[1] The first part is that incumbents focus on a *sustaining* innovation trajectory. Along that trajectory, you can

---

[1] You can look at figure I.1 for a partial illustration of the technological and demand parts of this argument. Do not, however, focus too much on the fact that the figure presents

find all kinds of technological change: it can be both incremental and radical, it can concern products and processes, it can be competence-destroying or competence-enhancing, and it can be discontinuous or not. "What all sustaining technologies have in common is that they improve the performance of established products, along the dimensions of performance that mainstream customers in major markets have historically valued" (p. xix). The second part is that sustaining innovation trajectories *overshoot* market demand. Staying on that trajectory, established firms "give customers more than they need or ultimately are willing to pay for" (p. xx). The third part is the emergence of disruptive technologies. These technologies are often initially inferior to the incumbent technology and underperform them and mainstream market demands. These technologies *cannot* satisfy mainstream customers, but because sustaining trajectories have pushed incumbents "up market," there is space at the lower end of the market where these new technologies *can* satisfy demand. This is especially the case when new technologies can be used to address markets that are currently *unserved* (i.e., the market does not really exist, because consumers are not currently buying, much like there was no market for personal computers (PCs) during the time of mainframes).

The fourth part is that disruptive technologies make for poor investments for incumbents, for Marchian reasons. First, the development trajectory for the new technology is uncertain and the current performance is certainly low. It is clear that it is inferior. Second, the market that it serves is certainly unattractive, because the market is small and margins are low. How the market may develop is highly uncertain. When technology improves, these elements (sustaining innovation, market overshoot, a technological change, unattractive markets) come together in a particular way. Suddenly, the new technology rapidly increases in performance (possibly along a new performance dimension) and becomes relevant for a much larger share of the market, thus pushing incumbents into a progressively smaller market niche. Incumbents are unable to react before it is too late, because "the very processes and values that constitute an organization's capabilities in one context, define its disabilities in another context" (p. xxvii). The result is the creative destruction of the incumbent. *That* is what disruption means *in a technical sense*.

It is worth knowing that Christensen's theory has been challenged quite convincingly in recent years after some twenty years with almost no critical reception. Historian Jill Lepore (2014) has argued that disruption is overhyped as a theory and woefully poorly grounded in data. She

---

developments as linear. That is, for all intents and purposes, just a more pedagogical way to represent what is more likely exponential change at different rates.

contends that Christensen's failure framework fails to explain the development of the disk drive industry on which it is actually based. King and Baatartogtokh (2015) have gone even further. Examining in detail seventy-seven examples of innovations that are held out as examples of disruption by Christensen himself, they contest that Christensen's recipe only fully explains 9 percent of them. In the remaining 91 percent, other processes seem to explain technological change much better. Shih's (2016) account of Kodak's demise – a widely touted example of disruptive innovation – shows in fine detail how that demise resulted from a much more complex process than what the theory of disruptive innovation lets on. These critiques, I think, are true and should give us pause in thinking about disruption and, at the very least, have us dial down the hype around it. We should recognize it for what it most likely is: one recipe for creative destruction, but one of many possible.

To me, the short-hand way to understand this particular recipe is as a technological change *combined* with the application of the technology in an unattractive market. The combination of these two elements does not imply, as we sometimes think, that incumbent firms are obnoxiously blindsided by change, even though that story may nicely fit a "fat and happy" or "bloated bureaucracy" storyline of corporate demise. Contrary to the conventional stories, in-depth histories of incumbents being "disrupted" sometimes show that incumbents *do* know about the emerging technologies, they *do* in some cases understand them and are able to replicate them, and they *do* to some extent understand how markets are developing. Incumbents may *underestimate* these developments (see Section 5.3) or their own ability to respond (see Section 3.1), but the problem also often seems to be that incumbents struggle to *justify* engaging with disruptive innovations. Christensen suggests as much in the second chapter of his book: "although entrants led in *commercializing* disruptive technologies, their development was often the work of engineers at established firms, using bootlegged resources" (p. 43; italics in original; we return to the issue of "bootlegging" in Section 7.3), but

managers [in the particular case that Christensen examines] made *an explicit decision* not to pursue the disruptive technology. In other cases, managers did approve resources for pursuing a disruptive product, but, in the day-to-day decisions about how time and money would actually be allocated, engineers and marketers, acting in the best interests of the company, consciously and unconsciously starved the disruptive project of resources necessary for a timely launch (p. 44, italics added).[2]

---

[2] ChatGPT is one example of this. The technology underlying this product was originally developed inside Google but was only fully commercialized by OpenAI.

As Christensen makes clear, engaging with disruptive innovations is often in direct contradiction with what are widely considered "best" business practices and can be difficult because incumbent firms typically depend on their investors' good graces to operate. Violating best practice can jeopardize investor support, which can destabilize firms in various ways. Add to that that investors often prioritize consistent, short-term return on assets rather than what often appears to be high-risk, long-term, explorative projects, especially when investing in incumbents that are meant to be relatively more secure than early-stage ventures. When exploration and exploitation compete for scarce resources and allocation decisions must be justified, exploitation often crowds out especially the very explorative activities that are needed for dealing with disruptive innovation. Rather than have firms undertake this kind of diversification, many investors prefer to manage that portfolio risk themselves. The story of the demise of Blockbuster is especially instructive in this regard (Keating, 2012).

That said, why is it necessary to know about disruption if the theory does not hold water? The straightforward answer to that is that if you intend to be knowledgeable and conversant about innovation, you need to be familiar with the idea. Knowing the concept, knowing that it is heavily ideologically infused, knowing what it *actually* means, and knowing that it does not hold water are all going to be helpful in and of themselves. To talk meaningfully about a topic, we do not just need to know what is true about it, but also sometimes what is *not* true.

The more operational answer is that Christensen's recipe and its reception still do teach us something. For entrepreneurs, there is a way to think about disruption as a playbook for market entry. Zuckerman (2016a) lays out the conceptual argument for this, while Gans et al (2020) provide a concise and very practical way to think about the disruption play as one of several entrepreneurial strategies, albeit one that is probably more romanticized than it deserves to be. At the heart of these interpretations is the idea of entering at the low end of a market and scaling up from there, actively speculating in the dynamics of technological improvement (it may be Fosterian improvement, low-end market dynamics, or "architectural change," as we will return to in Section 4.2) and in the myriad different difficulties that incumbents may face in moving to unattractive markets.

For incumbents, it is best read as a warning, *not* a prediction, and certainly not a law-like description of how industries function. Disruptive innovation is something that can happen and that firms should be aware of and possibly even anxious about. That said, if one wants a good sense of what that warning is for incumbents (and what might be done about it), Gans' treatment of the Disruption Dilemma (2017) is both more nuanced and, I believe, more helpful than Christensen's (in part because it incorporates organizational insights that we will cover in Section 4.2).

Read this way as a cautionary tale, disruptive innovation runs into the interesting facts of social science that our object study not only changes over time but also actively gets shaped by our theories. Social science theories are not just neutral depictions of the world but "performative" ideas that contribute to producing and changing that world (Mackenzie, 2008). Consider Google. In many ways, this is a company of the admired sort that might be ripe for being disrupted. But arguments that the company does several things to actively avoid that, to avoid competitors entering even low-end or niche markets, are increasingly emerging in popular media. One thing the company does, it appears, is to actively block competitors from appearing in Google searches, effectively rendering them invisible to consumers. Second, it seems to actively copy disruptive innovations and give these copies preferential treatment in Google searches, making them highly visible. These two tactics together make market entry by potential disruptors tremendously difficult (e.g., Duhigg, 2018). Third, it actively buys up would-be competitors early on to the extent that "getting bought by Google" is replacing "disrupting Google" as the preferred end-game plan for many entrepreneurs in the industry. To see why this might be the case, look up the list of mergers and acquisitions by Google's parent company, Alphabet. Fourth, and somewhat in a different league, there are suggestions that Google works to actively suppress studies of these business practices (Stoller, 2017). The only good thing to say about that is that Google at least has had the common decency to stop using *Don't be evil* as a corporate motto.

These issues all speak to a larger question of antitrust and government intervention in curtailing the formation of monopolies that fall beyond the scope of this book. For now, note that they are exemplary of how a social science theory can *shape* what it purports to *study*. When a theory like Christensen's becomes widely popularized and gets interpreted as a warning, chances are that the warning may be heeded and that incumbents start actively working to prevent disruption, thus making the theory *less* true over time – irrespective of how true it actually was in the first place. It can become a self-defeating prophecy. When, as is the case with innovation, we are dealing with a phenomenon where today's inefficiencies can be tomorrow's opportunities, this is doubly the case.

4.2 Henderson and Clark: Product Architectures and Organizational Architectures

Foster alerted us to how technological discontinuities can devastate incumbents in an industry. With Christensen, we saw how "disruption" can come from the combination of technological discontinuities and low-end markets. This kind of innovation has a certain dramatic flair in many ways. Discontinuities grab headlines because their novelty is obvious. But other, less dramatized forms of innovative change can – through a different set of mechanisms – bring about *equivalent* change in industries. In Henderson and Clark's paper, we are going to look at another way for innovation to play out that is much more subtle than what we have previously seen: "architectural innovations." An architectural innovation is a "reconfiguration of an established system to link together existing components in a new way" (p. 11). Architectural innovation leaves "the core design concepts (and thus the basic knowledge underlying the components) untouched" (p. 10). Harkening back to Vincenti's treatment of landing gear designs, we are operating at the level of components and sub-components here, but not looking at change *in* the components. We are looking at how those components are put together, at the product architecture. It is emphatically not about new systems, new components, or new S-curves. It is altogether more mundane, focusing merely on the *reconfiguration* of systems and components that already exist. As it turns out, such reconfigurations can bring about the same kind of industrial change as more bluntly novel solutions. Why that is is going to tell us a lot about organizational dynamics around innovation.

It can be a little difficult to wrap your head around what precisely an architectural innovation is, and there is a good reason for that: it is something that we are unlikely to experience directly as consumers of technology. Henderson and Clark's example comes from semiconductor photolithography, as was the case with the paper by Adner and Kapoor that we read in Chapter 3. Their argument is that the machines that are used to make semiconductors have undergone substantial changes, some of which have been architectural. As a consumer, you will never feel a change like that and if you did, you would never do it with the kind of intensity that industry insiders do. That contributes to the relative obscurity of what is studied here. Henderson and Clark mention some more popular examples, though, like portable transistor radios emerging in the 1950s. A more recent example of an architectural innovation that many may be familiar with is the GoPro camera. The main innovation in that case is not the components (all of those were well understood before the GoPro and were not developed further in any dramatic way). It is the way they are put together to produce a novel functionality.

For all its seeming obscurity, there are two reasons to spend time thinking about this concept. First, it adds an important nuance to our thinking about different kinds of innovation. Second, it challenges incumbents in a way that is somewhat profound, perhaps even puzzling.

Thus far, we have talked about different types of innovation. There can be innovations in products or production processes, in marketing and organizational practices, at the level of components or systems. Innovations can also be incremental or radical, perhaps even so Schumpeterian that they strike at the center of profits. These distinctions, as also previously covered, are important because innovations of different types operate in different ways – they are part, if you will, of different "recipes" for different kinds of change in organizations, industries, and societies. Henderson and Clark add two concepts to our repertoire of distinctions, with one being much more central to them than the other, and they do this by moving from a one-dimensional to a two-dimensional distinction of innovation novelty. In a one-dimensional distinction, an innovation can lie on a spectrum from incremental to radical. However, if you think about novelty in two dimensions – whether *core concepts* change and whether *linkages* change – what you get are four types of innovation: incremental and radical innovations that we have already dealt with, modular innovation (which is not the topic of this paper but is important in other ones), and architectural innovation (which is what is central here, as the title gives away). This is what is summarized in the paper's figure 1 and well-illustrated with the example of fans (pp. 12–13). Core concepts describe the components or sub-systems that are part of an innovation. Linkages are how those core concepts are linked together to form a system.

Why does this distinction matter, then? What separates an architectural innovation from an incremental and radical one?

To answer that question, we need to detour a little bit into what happens to firms once an industry settles on a dominant design. Before settling on a dominant design, Henderson and Clark argue, there will be multiple competing designs that each consist of a set of sub-systems and components, and a particular way for those components to be put together – a particular product architecture. Once a dominant design emerges, the architecture of products becomes largely taken for granted and attention shifts toward improvement in components and sub-systems. With the dominant design, for example, smartphones largely settled, firms now compete to make better smartphones with better screens, faster processors, better cameras, and so on, while largely taking for granted how those components will interact. This has an effect on how firms innovate, Henderson and Clark argue, taking their cues especially from ideas around "organizational routines" (most notably Nelson & Winter, 1982). With a dominant design settled, firms stop exploring alternative designs and begin exploiting the dominant one. This means that their knowledge about alternative designs withers away[3] and that the dominant design begins to shape organizational routines.

The organization comes, in subtle ways, to mirror its product through its development of routine ways of working. The organization moves from fluidity to specificity, not in its production apparatus (as Abernathy would imagine it), but in its innovation processes. Communication channels in the organization come to mirror how the product is designed and the kind of interfaces that the product architecture introduces, both formally and informally. With increasing specificity, development work tends to get organized around the particular components that people work on (e.g., a car's engine, suspension, steering, etc.) and people from different departments tend to interact around the problems that occur where their sub-systems interact (e.g., windshield developers might talk more to window designers than to engine designers). Communication filters emerge to economize on the amount of information that people need to deal with. If you work on engines, maybe you do not need to spend time hearing about the latest developments in paint application techniques. Efficient strategies for solving problems start to develop because a product architecture tends to create problems of a particular sort that can be dealt with using solutions of a particular sort. Just like how a dominant design creates specific production systems in the interest of increased efficiency, so does it create specific, routinized, and efficient innovation development systems.

As it turns out, architectural innovation creates several problems for this specific, routinized, and efficient innovation system. Henderson and Clark describe "the Kasper Saga," noting how an incumbent (Kasper) failed to recognize that a competing product (offered by Canon) actually differed from their products because they looked only at components and failed to notice how a subtle change in the relationship between components allowed the competing product to outperform their own. In this way, the incumbent underestimated the novelty of a solution based on new architectural knowledge, considering the competing product to essentially be a copy of their own – "Kasper conceived [the new product] as a modified [old product]. Like the incremental improvements to the [old product] before it, design of the [new product] was managed as a routine extension to the product line" (p. 25). Relatedly, they also underestimate the difficulties of delivering new products of their own to compete with those of their competitors, misunderstanding the reasons for why their own product could not perform at the level of competitors.

---

[3] We will return to the idea of knowledge withering away when we cover Cohen and Levinthal's concept of absorptive capacity in Section 6.3.

As a result, they focused on the "wrong" things as they sought to improve product performance.

What is interesting to note here is that this underestimation of new entrants and new competing products does not, as was the case with disruptive innovations for Christensen, come from an underestimation of how technological improvement might make unattractive markets attractive. It also does not come from underestimating the rate of technological improvement, as would be the case for Foster, or the relative development potential of old and new technologies, as would be the case for Adner and Kapoor. Rather, here we are dealing with what seems to be an actual failure, an actual organizationally induced blindness of sorts.

There are at least two ways to think about that. One is the knowledge that would be necessary to appreciate the novelty and implications of an architectural innovation that *simply does not exist* and is very hard to build up in an organization. By implication, it would also be costly to develop and so firms might tend to prioritize it less when not engulfed in an era of ferment. Instead, they might prioritize more exploitable forms of learning. That would be the Marchian interpretation. It would imply that firms would need to continuously explore alternative designs, even if this is potentially inefficient and costly. An alternative interpretation, which is what Henderson and Clark seem to suggest, is that the kind of knowledge that would be necessary to identify an architectural innovation is beyond any one person and thus depends on cooperation between individuals with different knowledge bases. The problem is that this cooperation is impeded by formal and informal communication channels, information filters, and problem-solving approaches. The implication would be that the firm would need to work to keep these routines at bay and to remain fluid. This would certainly come at the price of lowered efficiency and slower development times.

In both cases, the need to be efficient in the short term is what forces an organization to accept, respectively, a certain level of forgetting and a certain level of inertia. This, in turn, renders it potentially vulnerable to competitors and new entrants. To stay on top of the heap, organizations (mostly implicitly) accept the risk of getting caught blindsided and being relegated to an altogether less attractive heap, namely the ash heap of history.

4.3 David: General Purpose Technologies and Their Reach

So far, we have looked at technologies and innovations that shape and, in some cases, transform their industries. Many of them can be important. But some technologies have much deeper implications: they change *many* industries, bring about industrial (sometimes social) revolution, and even change the human condition. These are what we call general-purpose technologies, or foundational technologies. They are watershed innovations, like the wheel, steam engines, electricity, the concepts of mass production and factories, computers, or the internet. Today, technologies such as blockchain and artificial intelligence are poised to become tomorrow's general-purpose technologies. Just by looking at these examples, it is not hard to imagine that these innovations *must* be conceptually different from those that we have previously met in terms of their characteristics, their effects, and especially how those effects are brought about. Those are what David's paper illuminates.

The background for his analysis is what is called the "productivity paradox." This term was quite prevalent in economics in especially the 1970s and 1980s and it is, just to be clear, not the same as the Productivity Dilemma that we talk about in management studies. Rather, the productivity paradox refers to what was a genuine puzzle at the time. On the one hand, computers were being widely adopted and were beginning to change people's everyday work in quite dramatic ways. On the other hand, national statistics were showing a *slowdown* in productivity improvement.[4] In aggregate, everyone appeared to be getting *less, not more, efficient* by working in new ways and investing sometimes heavily in new technology. Robert Solow (who we encountered in passing in Chapter 1) famously captured the sentiment of the paradox when he stated that "what everyone feels to have been a technological revolution, a drastic change in our productive lives, has been accompanied everywhere, including Japan, by a slowing down of productivity growth, not by a step up. You see the computer age everywhere but in the productivity statistics" (Solow, 1987). As I mentioned in Chapter 1, we usually associate innovation with precise productivity improvements, so you can see why this would be puzzling, even alarming. In the least gracious and curmudgeonly interpretation, maybe computers were just a (really expensive) fashion. We now know that they were not, but we do also have the advantage of hindsight.

In David's 1990 argument, he posits that computers belong to a special class of innovations – they are a *general-purpose technology* – and therein lies an explanation for the puzzle. To make that clear, he puts the (lack of) effects of computers into historical context by comparing them to the effects of the dynamo. The dynamo and the computer, it turns out, follow broadly similar patterns or, as David puts it "… each of the principal empirical phenomena that make up modern perceptions

---

[4] Indeed, rates of productivity improvement have been historically low from the 1970s up to today (Gordon, 2016).

of a productivity paradox had its striking historical precedent in the conditions that obtained a little less than a century ago in the industrialized West.... In 1900, contemporary observers might have remarked that the electric dynamos were to be seen 'everywhere but in the productivity statistics!'" (p. 356).

When electricity was first introduced, it was overwhelmingly used for lighting. Edison invented the electric lamp in 1879, but by the turn of the century only 3 percent of households were using electric lights and – more importantly for productivity concerns – only 5 percent of the power used in manufacturing came from electric sources. The real bottleneck in increasing productivity was the slow pace of adoption of electricity in factories. There are some basic economics of when one might replace a well-functioning machine with a newer one that explain some of this, but the really profound part of the explanation is that electricity did not just mean that a machine shifted from one power source to another. With electricity, the whole idea of what a factory was could change. Factory buildings could change, production lines could be designed in radically different ways, work on the line could change, and in turn management practices had to change. "Although all this was clear enough in principle, the relevant point is that its implementation on a wide scale required *working out the details in the context of many kinds of new industrial facilities, in many different locales*" (p. 358, italics added). This required a learning process that was distributed across geographies and people and was highly dependent on costly experiments being undertaken to apply this new and still uncertain technology. That, David posits, explains why general-purpose technologies take time and that is why computers took a long time to have discernible impact – they were general purpose by nature and depended on follow-on innovation to achieve their real impact. What mattered was not replacing a typewriter with a computer. What mattered was using a computer to do things that were impossible to do before. Figuring that out required forms of experimentation and learning that were not obvious at the outset.

To put this into terms that are familiar, general-purpose technologies exhibit strong characteristics of exploratory innovations and tend to follow an exaggerated S-curve. While the potentials of a technology may be clear[5] (at least in principle), there will often be deep uncertainty about whether those potentials can be practically realized and how that may happen. It will also often depend on the (uncoordinated) choices of many distributed actors. As a result, there will be considerable distance

---

[5] As we will cover in the subsequent sub-chapter describing Shane's ideas of entrepreneurial opportunity discovery, they often are not particularly clear.

in time between first investments and far-reaching benefits materializing. That means that we will see an S-curve that is drawn out across the x-axis. However, the performance improvements that can accrue directly from a general-purpose technology will also tend to exceed those of more conventional technologies dramatically. Relying on these performance improvements is what you will sometimes hear talked about as "riding the S-curve." This tends to refer to companies leveraging improvements in technologies without directly driving that improvement themselves. The S-curves that get ridden are often those of general-purpose technologies.

Much more dramatically than conventional technologies, general-purpose technologies have indirect benefits as well. These primarily come in the form of what are sometimes called "innovation complementarities" (Jovanovic & Rousseau, 2005), which describes how a technology enables follow-on innovation. It is generally the case of technology that they build on one another, but a defining characteristic of a general-purpose technology is the dramatic extent of follow-on innovation. Consider, for example, the staggering amount of innovation that has been built on top of the internet. While important, the original use of the internet for connecting respectively military and academic networks together is largely eclipsed by the way innovations in internet technology have transformed (and will probably continue to do so for decades) virtually all aspects of life and commerce in greater and greater parts of the world. This is precisely because of the opportunities of innovation complementarities. A more current example of this is the (at the time of writing) highly hyped Blockchain technology, which is also poised to enable follow-on innovation in a just astounding range of areas (Iansiti & Lakhani, 2017).

Through their direct and indirect benefits, general-purpose technologies often get described as important "engines of economic growth," driving whole eras of economic progress (Bresnahan & Trajtenberg, 1995), albeit with considerable lag between their invention and impact. In this sense, all the ways we make use of general-purpose technologies end up shaping our lives. But the impacts of general-purpose technologies actually extend even further, shaping even the human condition, as I somewhat prosaically claimed at the opening of this sub-chapter. As Rosenberg and Trajtenberg show in their study of the Corliss Steam Engine, this particular general-purpose technology not only transformed how production happened but also *where* it happened (2004). Before the steam engine, factories had been dependent on water for power and thus factories tended to be located outside of urban centers, close to large rivers. With the advent of the steam engine, this constraint was lifted. When it was, it became possible to locate factories closer to consumer markets and closer to thick labor markets. Suddenly, cities could be centers not only of trade but also of large-scale production. Industrial work changed from being something that farm girls did before getting married to being something that women and men moved to towns to do for all of their working lives. The impact of that change is hard to overstate: increased urbanization is one of the defining points of the industrial revolution and it played a massive role in the emergence of new political ideologies and social classes that still matter today. Later, this urbanization would play a central role in many other changes that shape how we live today.

5 How Does Knowledge Shape Ideas?

> **Texts in This Chapter**
>
> Galenson, D. W. 2009. Old masters and young geniuses: The two life cycles of human creativity. *Journal of Applied Economics*. XII(1), 1–9.
>
> Ward, T. B. 1994. Structured imagination: The role of category structure in exemplar generation. *Cognitive Psychology*. 27(1), 1–40.
>
> Shane, S. 2010. Prior knowledge and the discovery of entrepreneurial opportunities. *Organization Science*. 11(4), 448–469.
>
> Jones, B. F. 2010. Age and great invention. *The Review of Economics and Statistics*. XCII(1), 1–14.

Technology is often a crucial input to innovation, but so are knowledge and ideas. Indeed, technological change emerges out of ideas and, as we will see, knowledge stands in an interesting relationship to the generation of the novel ideas that you could say are essential raw materials for innovation. First, Galenson's work provides some nuance to the nature of ideas and of knowledge, suggesting that knowledge can be both a prerequisite for and an impediment to the development of ideas, depending crucially on what kind of ideas we are dealing with. Then, the papers by Ward and Shane present two contrasting views of how knowledge can shape imagination, highlighting how one's prior knowledge might overstructure, enable, or narrowly focus ideation. Finally, Jones' paper zooms out to the macro level, inviting us to think about why it appears to be getting harder and harder to have ideas early in life.

5.1 Galenson: The Life Cycles of Creatives and Two Types of Creativity

There is a long tradition in the psychological study of creativity of studying highly creative people. This is intuitively appealing. It seems sensible to go where "the action is" to study that action. Alas, there are a number of methodological problems with this approach. Looking at how highly

5.1 Galenson: The Life Cycles of Creatives

creative people work creatively does not necessarily tell us very much about how people *generally* work creatively, and may unduly romanticize their uniqueness. The things that make highly creative people creative, for instance, might make people generally less creative (losing a parent in childhood is just one example). Highly creative people do not work alone but are dependent on collaborators, technologies, and ecosystems that allow them to be creative. Absent these things, highly creative people might have produced fewer, and less creative, creative outputs. They are dependent on many factors outside of their direct control. To be counted as creative in posterity, painters need curators to include their work in prestigious exhibitions. Absent timely curation, painters may be no less creative in their process, but a lot less visible in their outputs and a lot less recognized for the actual creativity of their process. Moreover, what is counted as creative in one time and place is not the same as what is counted at others (a creative Kalahari bushman is doing something different from a creative Renaissance painter) and changes over time (posterity may appreciate some artists that were disregarded in their time).

These caveats aside, Galenson's study of artistic innovation is interesting precisely for what it tells us about the lifecycles of those individuals who achieve recognition for their creative works, how that lifecycle relates to the process through which they create, and what role knowledge plays in it. While it is clear that creativity can take many forms and occur in many domains (some of which are underappreciated and some of which are unduly romanticized), some individuals nonetheless have an outsized impact on the fields in which they work – be that in art, science, innovation, or entrepreneurship – and understanding that impact can surely tell us something useful about the creative individuals, the fields in which they create, and the role that knowledge may or may not play in innovation.

The main problem in studying creative output is to find a reliable way to gauge when something is creative. To overcome it, Galenson looks at books on art history. In them, he looks for the paintings that are reproduced as illustrations. The logic behind that is that art history is largely a history of innovation, focused on when new styles ("-isms"), approaches, and ideas are introduced and by whom. Those paintings that are reproduced, as opposed to just being mentioned, are reasonably enough assumed to be those that the art historian authoring a book considers most important. And while any one art historian may disproportionately favor one painter, looking across multiple volumes can confer a general sense of what paintings art history as a discipline considers to have been central works and, by implications, decisive innovations. Based on these illustrated paintings, he compiles a list of painters whose work made it into the textbooks, and the age of the painter in the year when they produced *most* of the work that was ultimately illustrated.

This exercise reveals that there is considerable variation in *when* painters create their most creative work. Some do so early in their career, with Picasso being the prime example that Galenson highlights. While Picasso created a wealth of famous works throughout his career, including "Guernica" when he was in his mid-fifties, his major innovations were created when he was just twenty-six. By contrast, some do so quite late. Paul Cézanne also created famous works throughout his career, including "The Murder" in his late twenties, but is recognized primarily for the work he did in his sixties. Only very few artists make their major contributions midway in their careers, it seems. They create, but not the works that posterity evaluates as seminally innovative.

In and of itself, this might be an interesting finding. The most interesting insights, however, come from Galenson's subsequent inquiry into how these artists work and the kinds of works they create. He has the good fortune that eminent creative artists (because they are eminent) tend to attract considerable attention from art history. There are biographies and analyses of these eminent individuals' lives documenting how they lived and worked, and evaluations of the nature of their creative contributions. These sources allow Galenson to discern two "archetypical" images of the creative artistic process, and of creative output, and these seem to track with the age at which the artist was most creatively productive. And these two images are of "young geniuses" making conceptual contributions and "old masters" making experimental ones. Old masters make their innovations based on extensive knowledge and experience accumulated over a lifetime. Young geniuses do so from a more limited knowledge base. They rely instead on *insight* and a particular vision that breaks sharply with established ideas.

Consider the two different processes through which old masters and young geniuses create their innovations. Old masters work "by trial and error, cautiously and incrementally" (p. 2). The goals they pursue are vague and ill-defined, and they tend to stick with the same problem over long periods. "Their uncertainty about their goals means that these artists rarely feel they have succeeded, and their careers are often dominated by the pursuit of a single objective. They repeat themselves, painting the same subject many times, gradually changing its appearance" (p. 2). The execution of the creative work is central to their process. Young geniuses work from plans, emerging from the particular vision they are pursuing. That vision tends to lead them to very precise goals, and once those goals are achieved (they often are – if they had not been achieved, the artist would not have achieved renown and would not have entered into Galenson's dataset), they move on to different problems. As such, they do not repeat themselves. Picasso, exemplary of the young geniuses, pursued numerous different styles rather than refining any one over an extended period. Execution of the artwork plays a less central role, because when the artist sets out to actually paint the painting, extensive preparatory work has already been done to ensure that the execution will realize the artist's vision.

From these different processes emerge two quite different kinds of innovative work. Young geniuses make *conceptual* innovations. They depart from ideas that diverge dramatically with the status quo, and the novelty lies in the very idiosyncratic nature of the idea itself. Old masters make *experimental* innovations. Their ideas are refined, elaborated, and extended over repeated trials, and their contributions come from practiced mastery. The radicalness of the innovation comes not from one flash of inspiration, but from a series of incremental advances. The novelty of their innovation comes from the aggregation of many incremental steps. A young person could not conceivably make an experimental innovation, and an old one may struggle to make a conceptual one. Experimental innovations require knowledge and practice that could not conceivably be built up without a lifetime of work, and conceptual innovations require a willingness to part with knowledge and practice that may for all kinds of reasons be difficult for an older one.

This suggests that knowledge can play different, almost diametrically opposed, roles in the creative process. It may be an impediment to certain forms of creative action and a precondition for others. The popular trope that creativity is a young person's game where industry experience and technical understanding are liabilities may, in some cases, be true. In mathematics and physics, most very creative contributions are made early, because those fields consider conceptual innovations most important. The same seems to be the case in poetry. In other cases, however, that trope may be decidedly wrong, and creativity may be dependent on deep knowledge that can only be built up over decades. Those fields may hold experimental innovations in higher regard. And in some fields, there is room for both. There are novelists, economists, scientists, and entrepreneurs that peak early and some that peak late, because those fields can be importantly advanced by both experimental and conceptual novelty. Whether knowledge is an impediment or precondition for creativity is contingent on the nature of the creative output.

We might imagine, for instance, that the reasons we see young founders leading firms that introduce disruptive innovations because disruptive innovations are often based on idiosyncratic insights about the potential size of the market. Firms based on advancing the state of the art in their field through experimentation might be led by more seasoned founders but also make for less spectacular news stories. They may also, interestingly enough, be more likely to succeed (Azoulay et al, 2020). By the same token, firms might decide to hire younger workers in explorative subunits (a topic that we return to in Section 6.1), if those subunits are tasked with developing what are essentially conceptual innovations. Youth and inexperience might in those cases be valuable assets because they might allow for novel insights. By contrast, we might imagine that working at the cutting edge of technological understanding – a precondition for making creative contributions in certain fields – requires a depth of knowledge that is unachievable without years of immersion in the field and contemplation of its problems (an issue that we return to in Sections 6.2 and 6.3). In such fields, the proposition that you are better off not knowing what you are doing is not only counterintuitive, but preposterous. It would be a recipe for moving fast and breaking things not meant to be broken.

5.2 Ward: Structured Imagination, or the Downsides to Knowledge

It is easy enough to understand how knowledge might be an asset when creating experimental innovations. While it is easy to get ideas, it is much harder to get ideas that other people find interesting and valuable. It is also hard to execute on those ideas and realize their potential. Knowledge and experience would clearly be helpful in both regards. It is less easy to understand why conceptual innovations can be created, apparently, without much knowledge and experience and how knowledge might actively impede people's ability to think in particular creative ways. And yet, if we look at start-up founders (or at least the ones that are most newsworthy, as we will return to in Section 9.4), we see a similar pattern. Newsworthy start-ups are often those that break dramatically with established industry approaches and their founders are often young and occasionally university dropouts. They also frequently highlight how *not* knowing very much about the industry they entered was actually an asset, something that allowed them to approach challenges in a novel way.

Ward's paper presents an explanation for this, showing how knowledge might impede people's ability to make conceptual creative leaps. More specifically, he shows how categorical representations structure imagination, how what we already know structures how we think and what we are able to imagine. As it turns out, people generally struggle to break away from the categories they know, even when encouraged to do so and to use their wildest imagination, and most creativity is therefore not so much about creating something new as it is about *re*creating something and combining elements of existing exemplars in new (or not so new) ways. That goes some way toward explaining why most innovations are in fact incremental and minor variations on existing solutions (e.g., Rosenberg, 1982; Basalla, 1998). Conceptual leaps are rare, and rare for the reason that they are immensely hard to generate cognitively when our imagination is so heavily structured.

The study reported in the paper is composed of five parts, and the first four are laboratory experiments. The first is straightforward, asking participants to imagine an animal living on another planet, looking for whether these imaginative creations might be structured by existing categorical representations (i.e., whether they resemble animals living on Earth). The second nuances this, asking participants to imagine an animal on another planet that has a certain property (e.g., having feathers) and looking for whether the imaginative creation has attributes that correlate with that property in Earth animals (i.e., whether an animal with feathers will also have a beak). The third experiment tries to force people "outside the box," asking them to imagine animals living under conditions explicitly *not* found on Earth (e.g., "the planet's surface is made up of molten lava and food is only available on scattered islands in this sea of deadliness"). The fourth experiment is primarily intended to eliminate the possibility that people are providing less creative ideas than they could because they believe experimenters would consider their most creative ideas silly. The fifth experiment is not really an experiment but a study of animals imagined by science fiction writers who are reasonably assumed to be very creative people (the participants in the prior studies were all college students). This is done to rule out the possibility that the findings in the prior experiments were driven by quirks in the study participants.

The findings suggest precisely that imagination is structured, that people rely extensively on categorical representations that they already know as opposed to idiosyncratically imagining novelty out of thin air and inspiration. When imagining creatures on other planets, people imagine what are essentially animals on Earth with minor tweaks along a limited set of dimensions and consequently their imaginings are easily recognizable as Earth animals with a twist (see the paper's figure 1). It is particularly noteworthy that people's imagined extraterrestrials rely on *clusters* of attributes, such that if an imagined animal has feathers, it is often imagined to also have a beak and wings and to be in effect a bird in space. This reliance on known categories persists even when people are forced to imagine creatures with no known earthly precedent, when asked to imagine wildly, and when we look at the work of people who should, for all intents and purposes, be really creative. It seems, in other words, to be the case that our cognitive process of being creative necessarily relies on categories that we know and that we necessarily assemble novel solutions out of what we already have access to. We do not create *de novo*. For better and for worse, we mix and remix.

While laboratory experiments of this kind seem immensely definitive, there are good reasons to approach them with care. Psychological experiments, it has recently become clear, appear much more well-controlled and replicable than they actually are (Simmons et al, 2011; Aarts et al, 2015). Moreover, laboratory experiments suffer from very low levels of "ecological validity." That is to say that the behavior that experimenters observe in the laboratory may often be an effect of the laboratory setting and the circumstances of the experiment, and not reflect human behavior "in the wilds" of everyday life. Given the very short timeframe afforded by the first four experiments in this study, people may end up developing less creative ideas than if – as would be the case in a real-life situation – they had more time to think and more time to look around for inspiration that might allow them to break free of salient categorical representations. Given low incentives to exert themselves and create something very novel, why should they? It would hardly be surprising to observe people doing silly things when given silly tasks in silly situations.

Nonetheless, the study offers an interesting hypothesis for thinking about how knowledge might impede us in the effort to make creative leaps. Knowing something, we might infer, provides us with categories and those categories structure how we cogitate as we attempt to create something new. "The normative tendency in using imagination is to base creations on the central features of a predictable, highly related knowledge base" (p. 38). If you have a knowledge base that is highly related to the creative task at hand, you invariably draw on it, Ward suggests.

This suggests that we reconsider for instance the role played by dominant designs in industries, as well as why certain types of innovation can have outsized consequences. In addition to structuring how firms invest in innovation and how competition unfolds (cf. Section 3.2), dominant designs may also contribute to "closing" the range of creative thinking that designers can cognitively do, because the dominant design comes to structure how they are able to conceive of new ideas. As decision-makers evaluate innovations that may or may not turn out to be disruptive, they may be unable to gauge whether it is worth pursuing low-end market customers, because they are cognitively trapped by available categorical representations of their product and its use (cf. Section 4.1). And when technical specialists analyze products based on alternative linkages between known components, the inevitable reliance of available representations may explain why highly skilled people can simply be "blind" to new configurations (cf. Section 4.2). When we evaluate these behaviors with the benefit of hindsight, all of the failures of imagination appear almost implausible. If, however, people are as blinkered by available knowledge as Ward suggests, we can see why these failures are reasonable and even to be expected.

What the study does not tell, however, is what happens when people do not have a related knowledge base, or when that knowledge base varies. What would happen if a person had no related knowledge base? In the case of imagining animals, this is a silly question to ask, but what if we were asked to imagine applications for a new technology or to imagine alternative approaches to solving a practical business problem, neither of which you knew anything about? What categorical representations would you then draw on, if any? We can imagine – as the popular advice goes – that this would allow a person to be unconstrained in their imagination, and provide you with a fresh perspective. On the flipside, a lack of categories to draw from could also leave you paralyzed and unable to find ideas to sample. Both are possible implications of Ward's ideas. Indeed, to the extent that we think of innovation as being fundamentally *recombinant*, in the sense that all ideas are more or less novel recombinations of already existing ideas (e.g., Schumpeter, 1911; Hargadon & Sutton, 1997), we might well actually fundamentally reinterpret Ward's findings. It would, if innovation is recombinant, be the case that prior categories are what in fact make it possible to be innovative, not what constrain creativity.

What would happen if a person had a broader knowledge base than others, accrued from experience in a different domain? Would they be able to sample from that knowledge base to make conceptual leaps that others would not? Some work suggests that this is the case (e.g., De Cruz & de Smedt, 2010; Duggan, 2013), but we could also easily imagine that the conceptual transfers from distant domains – the kind of creativity that broad or idiosyncratic knowledge would enable – would be very likely to miss the mark and, for all their originality, be of very limited value. As would be the case of highly explorative learning, the variance in solutions inspired by distant domains ought to be very high. There would be many low-value solutions, but also the potential for very high-value ones to occur at rare intervals.

And what would happen if a person had a much deeper knowledge base than others? Would that constrain you more than a shallow knowledge base, or would a deeper understanding allow you to make more abstract leaps than people with a shallow understanding? Galenson's idea of experimental innovators suggests that deeper knowledge is of little value in those situations, but we could imagine that there are fields where you need to get above a certain threshold of knowledge to even be able to make a contribution (see Section 5.4). Without a requisite depth, you might well make a leap, but not in a forward direction.

As a final consideration, it is worthwhile to recall that both Ward and Galenson are looking at individual innovators and to speculate on what their ideas would mean in less individualized creative settings. After all, a lot of the innovation that happens in society happens in organizational settings where people specialize and then collaborate in order to integrate effort (cf. Section 1.3). Sometimes that collaboration involves *really* large teams, which seems to impact the kind of ideation and innovation that becomes possible (Wu et al, 2019). Such settings could under certain circumstances exacerbate the problems of relying on an established and unduly limited set of categories, but they might also allow people to overcome the limitations of their individual cognitive processes by compensating for any one person's failure of imagination (e.g., Melero & Palomeras, 2015). Which of these effects dominates, however, is likely to be determined by a complex interplay of factors at many levels of the organization.

5.3 Shane: Prior Experience, or the Upside to Narrowness

All the forms of innovation that we have covered in Sections 1.1, 2.1, 3.1–3.3, and 4.1–4.3 depend on opportunity recognition, on someone recognizing that a new solution can somehow create value. This is most clearly the case for general-purpose technologies. When a general-purpose technology emerges, the full extent of its applicability is not known. The "killer app" for a particular technology is often not the one that the inventor envisages, as we preempted in our reading of Rosenberg. Rather, the full range of applications that turn a technology into a general one has to be discovered and figured out. It is also the case, but perhaps less clearly, with disruptive and architectural innovations. A disruptive innovation depends on someone recognizing that a particular early-stage technology can be used to create value for a particular group of "low-end" customers who are currently overserved by established solutions and could be satisfied with a poorer-performing one. An architectural innovation depends on someone recognizing that additional value – whether in the form of new functionality or increased performance – can be created by reorganizing a set of known components in a novel way. These are issues of Rosenbergian uncertainty and the issues that motivate Shane's study of *how* those opportunities get recognized. They are also issues of, fundamentally, creative insight: to generate the hypothesis that value could be created is inherently creative, and thus it becomes worthwhile to understand

5.3 Shane: Prior Experience, or the Upside to Narrowness

how these hypotheses emerge. Shane's paper sets out to understand how entrepreneurs come to recognize the opportunities afforded by the technologies, and what determines their ability to recognize them and execute on them. The answer, as betrayed by the title, is that knowledge about particular usage contexts amassed prior to encountering the technology plays a key role in making this creative leap, affording the entrepreneur a form of tunnel vision that enables recognition of particular opportunities, but obliviousness to others.

Shane's study pits three competing views against each other. The baseline assumption of mainstream economic thinking ("neoclassical equilibrium theories") is that markets are composed of maximizing agents and that markets function well. In this world, there is little opportunity for entrepreneurship: "no one can discover a misalignment that would generate an entrepreneurial profit because, at any point in time, all opportunities have been recognized and all transactions perfectly coordinated" (p. 449).[1] What drives entrepreneurship is instead personal preference, typically those with a greater preference for risk or uncertainty or, perhaps less conventionally, greater disutility from subordination to managers. The baseline assumption in the psychological position on entrepreneurship is not unrelated. The view here is that there are stable human traits and that these are what determine the decision to enter into entrepreneurship.[2] It is not so much a question of preference, but rather a question of "enduring human attributes" (p. 449) or "superior information processing ability, search techniques, or scanning behavior" (p. 449). The baseline assumption of Austrian economic theories is that "markets are composed of people who possess *different* information (Hayek, 1945). The possession of idiosyncratic information allows people to see particular opportunities that others cannot see, even if they are not actively searching for such opportunities" (p. 449).[3]

Shane's argument is that the third view, Austrian theories, provides the most compelling answer. His argument is that opportunities get

---

[1] This – as we have explored in the context of general-purpose technologies – is *empathically* not a realistic assumption to make. Economists tend to have more nuanced views than Shane gives them credit for, even if those views do not always filter into the way their theoretical models work. It is more fair to say that mainstream economists assume that opportunities can be discovered through investment in "search." They may exist on "rugged landscapes" (Levinthal, 1997), but investment will uncover them.

[2] The view that human traits are stable is, to be clear, not a position that is shared across *all* of psychology. There seems to be agreement that *some* traits are relatively time-stable, but also that many are not. Some will also argue that traits are highly context-dependent and subject to change given appropriate "stimulus," rejecting much of the assumption of stability.

[3] A range of other assumptions are embedded in Austrian economic perspectives aside from distributed information.

discovered largely through *serendipitous insights* (i.e., without much deliberate search) by people who possess particular prior knowledge *relevant to that particular opportunity* (i.e., knowledge makes only *certain* opportunities obvious) and that people's decision to exploit a particular opportunity depends *on the opportunity* (i.e., it is not a feature of people's inherent mental attributes). The knowledge needed to recognize an opportunity, in other words, *is* highly unevenly distributed and brings about a narrowness of vision that impedes alternative opportunity recognition. That has considerable implications for how we think about entrepreneurship and about innovation management as an intra-organizational phenomenon. Leaving that for the future, we will now examine *how* Shane arrives at this conclusion.

Because he starts out with a clear intention to demonstrate that Austrian theories do a better job of explaining opportunity recognition than mainstream economics and psychology, Shane initially draws out a set of propositions based on an Austrian perspective and in disagreement with alternative ones. These are: (1) All individuals are not equally likely to recognize a given entrepreneurial opportunity; (2) people can and will discover entrepreneurial opportunities without actively searching for them; (3a) people's prior knowledge about markets will influence their discovery of which markets to enter to exploit a new technology; (3b) people's prior knowledge about how to serve markets will influence their discovery of how to use a new technology to serve a market; (3c) people's prior knowledge of customer problems will influence their discovery of products and services to exploit a new technology (pp. 451–452, graphically summarized on p. 453). It may spoil the plot somewhat, but those propositions all turn out to be supported by the analysis.

To test these propositions, he examines the entrepreneurial opportunities identified for 3D printing which is, at my time of writing (2018), depending on your temperament, possibly a general-purpose technology right about the point of having "all hell break loose" (Foster, 1986, p. 31). Basically, he looks at every entrepreneur that contacted the owner of the patent on this technology with an interest in commercializing it. We know that general-purpose technologies can be a long time underway, but it is interesting to note that in the ten years after the technology was developed, only eight companies sought to apply it to commercial ends. The opportunities range from printing conceptual models for architects to artificial bones for surgery to ceramic molds for industrial metal casting.

Interestingly (and in accordance with Shane's propositions), the individuals who did pursue entrepreneurial opportunities around the technology were highly limited in their opportunity recognition. They recognized only the particular opportunity that they pursued and did so largely because they possessed some relatively idiosyncratic experience, typically from work experience in the market that they intended to address with their particular solution (i.e., their former professional selves are their current customers). Because of this knowledge, they "just" recognized the opportunity. The alternative way that you could think about how technology gets commercialized through systematic search largely does not happen: no one started the technology and investigated different applications by doing market research of various kinds. They largely know the markets that they will address in advance and that is what makes an opportunity appear and appear attractive. And of course – this being the death knell to the mainstream economic argument – no one can possess enough knowledge and enough experience to identify all possible, or even relevant, "Need-solution pairs" (Von Hippel & Von Krogh, 2015).

In itself, this is interesting mostly as a bit of trivia from the history of technology. The wider implications of the argument, however, are what is truly interesting. They concern the way that innovations are evaluated and the way that different people are going to see different potential and value in different innovations, because those evaluations are going to shape what decisions get made.

If we think about potential new entrants to an industry, it makes it plausible to think of innovation as eminently *likely*. There are, in Shane's Austrian conception of the nature of entrepreneurial opportunity, vast opportunities. You will sometimes hear the advice, originating I believe with Peter Thiel (2014) and now pervasive in tech jargon, that you should look to build "the valuable company that nobody else is building." In a world of perfect information, it is per definition hard to imagine that you could realistically be the first person to identify an opportunity and a solution to it – if that company does not exist, it would probably be because there is no way to build a profitable business around it. But in an Austrian world, your insight might actually just be that unique. You may be the first person to have the combination of prior knowledge, insight in a technology, and an idea for exploiting it. The same prior knowledge that affords an advantage in recognizing one particular opportunity, however, can also easily create a disadvantage in recognizing *alternative* opportunities, because it creates a "knowledge corridor" (p. 452) that both enables and constrains opportunity recognition.

In a more organizational sense, the effects of this "corridor" seem more one-sidedly constraining. Imagine that an idea originates somewhere, anywhere, in a large organization. The person who originates it sees tremendous value in it, possibly because it solves a problem that she has herself experienced or because she works with a new technology that others have yet to fully understand. For that innovation to have far-reaching impact, it will have to be shared with many others who will have to see similar value in it (the same thing would be the case for our entrepreneurial start-up earlier, which will often have to find venture capital funding for the idea). Now, almost per Austrian definition, others will *not* see that value because the knowledge required to appreciate it is *not* going to be available to them. In an organizational setting where cooperation and coordination and resource allocation require many more people to have a shared evaluation, in an Austrian view, innovation may well be very likely but recognition of that innovation by others highly unlikely, leaving many ideas underdeveloped relative to their potential. We will return to this conundrum in Sections 6.1–6.3 as we look at opportunities for organizations to "work around" the Productivity Dilemma and at the challenges of managerial control over innovation processes.

5.4 Jones: Is (Great) Invention Getting Harder?

Whether knowledge enables or impedes innovation may be contingent on the nature of the innovation. It can enable experimental innovation and impede conceptual innovation. Established knowledge can structure imagination by cognitively limiting the kinds of innovation that a person can generate. Idiosyncratic knowledge can allow individuals to make conceptual leaps unavailable to others, but only within narrow "corridors." This is what we summarily take from the previous three readings. What they largely disregard is the context, or (for the purpose of this chapter) the nature of the knowledge base of the field creativity unfolds within. Given our understanding of technologies and industries as continually evolving, this should certainly concern us. We might expect, for instance, that the kinds of creativity that unfold in an industry up to and right after a technological discontinuity to be fundamentally different from what happens in contexts with widely accepted and largely unchallenged dominant designs. Knowledge would play different roles in those two contexts.

What Jones' paper documents is the role of changing knowledge bases in scientific fields over time. The knowledge underlying a field is not stagnant, but rather growing and accumulating over time, and sometimes upended by radical change in the field. This corresponds, with slight fudging around the edges, to how technologies evolve over time (Dosi, 1982). In both technology and science, knowledge accumulates as problems (be they scientific or technical problems) become progressively better understood and that leads to improvement. When discontinuities happen, that knowledge is upended and replaced by a new knowledge base. In science, such discontinuities are referred to as "paradigm change" and periods of incremental change "normal science" (Kuhn, 1962). This process dramatically impacts how invention progresses in the field, including who does it when.

Jones looks specifically at two data sources. First, he looks at the individuals who receive Nobel Prizes for their scientific work (i.e., recipients of the Nobel Prizes in physics, chemistry, medicine, and economics[4]), and can therefore quite safely be assumed to have made very significant scientific inventions – Nobel Prizes are not lifetime achievement awards, but rather awards for *specific* inventions or discoveries.[5] This allows Jones to find the age of the recipient in the year that specific discovery was made. Second, he looks at technological almanacs. "The technological almanacs compile key advances in technology, by year, in several different categories such as electronics, energy, food and agriculture, materials, and tools and devices" (p. 2). While these may not be advances on the scale of Nobel Prizes, the discoveries and inventions they chronicle are substantial advancements of their field. As with prize recipients, the age of the individuals at the time they innovate can then be assessed. For both data sources, then, Jones is able to track over time the age at which great innovation occurs.

From this analysis, he observes two striking things. The first and central observation is that great scientific innovators are making their innovations later in life. "The mean age at great achievement for both Nobel Prize winners and great technological inventors rose by about six years over the course of the twentieth century" (p. 1), and the shift in and changing shape of the age distribution of inventors can be seen very clearly in the paper's figure 2. Inventors are making their inventions at later stages in life. The second observation, more peripheral to the overall argument but very notable for its implication, is that fundamental change in a field can reverse this trend. Looking at figure 5 in the paper, you can see that over time the age for great invention is increasing in every Nobel discipline, except for physics. The age for great invention actually fell in physics in the early 1900s, only to then increase again from the 1930s and onward. While there may be many factors at work

---

[4] The Nobel Prize in Economics is, of course, not a Nobel Prize in the sense that it was not established by Alfred Nobel in 1895, but by the Swedish central bank in 1968 and is therefore correctly referred to as the Sveriges Riksbank Prize in Economic Sciences in Memory of Alfred Nobel.

[5] This is explicitly the case for the prizes in Physics, Chemistry, and Medicine. For economics, this is less systematically the case.

here, there is a "remarkable coincidence between the quantum mechanics revolution and the unusual behavior in the age data. Many historians chart the specific period from 1900 to 1927 as the time when *the entire worldview of physics changed*" (p. 10, italics added). The Newtonian worldview that underpinned pre-1900 physics was not cast aside, but lots of progress in the discipline would from then on happen within the space of quantum physics.

As we think about what to make of these findings, it is worth noting that the fields in Jones' study are not easy to access. On the contrary, there is a considerable burden of absorbing knowledge that people must necessarily bear if they want to make notable contributions and this usually happens through education. This is how Jones explains the first observation. As the stock of knowledge in a field increases, the time it takes to get to the knowledge frontier where discoveries happen, "the bleeding edge of scientific understanding," increases because there is simply more to understand about the field. To paraphrase Newton, you need to stand on the shoulders of giants to make a scientific advance, but to do so you need to first climb up the giant's back. When more and bigger giants have come before you, there is more climbing to be done and more time to spend doing, and so each generation would need to invest more time in education.

This has a bearing on the productive lifecycle of innovators, but before turning to this, it is worth noting that Jones assumes that there is really only *one* lifecycle for scientific innovators. This is the lifecycle of the young genius: Jones' innovators acquire the knowledge in their fields while young, have an explosion in productivity, plateau, and then see their productivity decline toward the end of their careers. While this is very much the prevalent model in physics where conceptual innovation is highly valorized, especially economics seems to have space for both conceptual and experimental innovators (Weinberg & Galenson, 2019).

If, however, we work from Jones' assumptions, the increasing age at which great inventions and discoveries are made has an important implication. In his model, innovators (and this is true of conceptual innovators in Galenson's presentation) need youth to innovate, but youth is a very finite resource. They also need to get to the knowledge frontier to actually innovate, but growth in knowledge means that you need to spend more time on education to get there. If more of that youth is spent on education, there is less of that finite resource, less time for actually innovating, before the sclerosis of age and structured imagination sets in. Consequently, those most capable innovators are innovating less and, by implication, there will be less innovation. To put that another way, the more the knowledge base in a field grows, the more impossible it becomes for people to help grow it. Growth in knowledge, then, would undermine the conditions for future conceptual innovation. For individuals, a growth in knowledge might mean that would-be conceptual innovators simply cannot make their innovations, because the time spent on education might completely crowd out the time for innovating.

Jones' second observation suggests that this trend is not irreversible. Discontinuities, or "paradigmatic change," that render prior knowledge obsolete can allow young geniuses back into the game that normal science might otherwise push them out of, by reducing the time required to get to the relevant knowledge frontier. Rather than just introducing new problems to solve, as Foster might have suggested, a discontinuity might allow a fundamentally different kind of innovator to make fundamentally different kinds of innovations than would otherwise be the case. In this sense, fundamental changes in a field's knowledge base can open the doors to further conceptual innovation, until all that innovation creates a new mountain of knowledge that must be climbed. That climb, however, may favor the would-be old masters and an experimental kind of creativity.

This raises two key questions. First, would there be a way to get to the knowledge frontier faster? Anyone taking education knows from experience that you learn many things that are not in your interest and that give you a broad basis of knowledge, so surely it would be possible to get to the knowledge frontier faster by simply *specializing*. In this sense, the answer to the question is clearly "yes," but this may well have consequences for what you can do once you get there. Conceptual leaps and idiosyncratic insights may after all depend on having broad knowledge from which to sample in order to create those novel remixes of ideas, at least for people working alone. The "Renaissance Man" may very well be killed off by the growth of knowledge and innovators in the future forced to compensate for the narrowness of their own specialization by collaborating with others (Jones, 2009). This, of course, makes great invention a much more organizational issue than it has ever been before.

Second, what does it mean for a society and an economy driven forward largely by innovation and scientific discovery that both are getting harder? Irrespective of whether you think we need more Schumpeterian economic growth (cf. Section 1.2) or to re-orient the global economy toward de-growth and environmental sustainability, there is no doubt that innovation and the scientific discovery that underpin it are absolutely central and in this regard it should certainly be deeply concerning. In both scenarios, we need scientific progress and we need scientists to be productive, not to spend their potentially most productive years catching up to the knowledge frontier. It may well be that innovation is simply getting harder, and that should trouble us. But it could also be that innovation is simply getting harder in *established* fields, and that new disciplines are cropping up and that those new disciplines are where young geniuses increasingly go to explore promising opportunities, leaving old disciplines to old masters.

6   Can Organizations Exploit *and* Explore?

> **Texts in This Chapter**
> Adler, P. S. et al. 2009. Perspectives on the productivity dilemma. *Journal of Operations Management.* 27(2), 99–113.
> Brown, J. S. & Duguid, P. 1991. Organizational learning and communities-of-practice: Toward a unified view of working, learning, and innovation. *Organization Science.* 2(1), 40–57.
> Cohen, W. M. & Levinthal, D. A. 1990. Absorptive capacity: A new perspective on learning and innovation. *Administrative Science Quarterly.* 35(1), 128–152.

In this chapter, we are going to look at how organizations can combine exploitative and explorative learning. If they can it would after all challenge some of the theoretical preconceptions that Abernathy and March would give us and raise serious questions about whether Creative Destruction is in fact the inevitable threat that Schumpeter made it out to be. As it turns out, there are multiple "recipes" for how to effectively combine exploration and exploitation, based on a variety of empirical observations, that might make us less confident in the generalizability of the Productivity Dilemma. Zooming in on Communities of Practice, we are also invited to think through whether at some levels of the organization the distinction between exploration and exploitation even makes sense while Cohen and Levinthal's work invites us to reconsider whether it is actually a problem that firms specialize in *either* exploration or exploitation. After all, they could always collaborate with other organizations that do well what they themselves do not.

6.1   Adler et al: Re-thinking the Trade-Off between Exploration and Exploitation

Up to this point, we have accepted Abernathy's idea of the Productivity Dilemma and March's related one that there exists a "hard" trade-off between exploration and exploitation as meaningful descriptions of what might be called organizational reality. We have done so for two reasons. Both ideas are foundationally important to understanding innovation management as a practice and as a body of academic knowledge. As we saw in Chapter 1, they contribute key insights as we try to appreciate that most foundational of ideas in our field, namely Creative Destruction. Both ideas also seem to have some empirical currency. Organizations do seem to generally struggle to achieve high levels of efficiency and excel in their current operations, while also dealing with at least some forms of novelty and change, as we saw in the work of both Christensen and Henderson and Clark in Chapter 3.

Accepting the ideas put forward by Abernathy and March as *too* true, however, can be quite problematic. Empirically, there are organizations that do manage to both be highly efficient and innovate. Anthropomorphizing the organization, the term used to describe this ability to reconcile apparently mutually exclusive activities is *ambidexterity*. An ambidextrous person, in the word's original usage, is someone who writes equally well with both hands. In an innovation context, the term is used to describe the ability to both explore and exploit. It has been in use since Duncan (1976) introduced it but rose to conceptual prominence following a later study by Tushman and O'Reilly (1996). They defined ambidexterity as "The ability to *simultaneously* pursue both incremental and discontinuous innovation" (p. 24, italics added), thus suggesting that firms could engage in both exploitation and exploration at the same time (i.e., a positive-sum situation), rather than having to balance in a trade-off (i.e., a zero-sum situation). The idea is that there are certain things you can do, certain recipes you can follow, that allow you to have *synergies* between exploration and exploitation. Some firms appear able to pull that off, being both very innovative and very efficient. The prototypical example of the achievement is Toyota, celebrated for having reached industry-leading productivity levels and very high innovativeness through its use of what tends to be called lean principles. The recipes that allow for such a synergy would, for readily apparent reasons, be very attractive: overcoming the Productivity Dilemma might reduce the risk of Creative Destruction. It may be overly prosaic, but ambidexterity is in principle an elixir for corporate immortality.

As this paper – which really is not a paper in the way we usually encounter them, but rather a collection of six short essays by different scholars summarizing their respective ideas on the issue – demonstrates, there are different reasonable ways to think about ambidexterity and thus different reasonable ways to disagree with Abernathy and March. The disagreement comes in different degrees of severity and is based on

6.1 Adler et al: Re-thinking the Trade-Off

a quite diverse set of justifications. Even if it might be a bit simplistic, you might think of them as representing a continuum of disagreement with the idea that efficiency trades off against innovation.

Tushman and Benner represent the softest disagreement. They depart from a study (Benner & Tushman, 2002) examining how efforts to standardize organizational processes impact the nature of innovation in organizations, which found that increased standardization does not lead to *less innovation*, but rather to more exploitative innovation, and that exploitative innovation and explorative innovation do trade-off against each other. They

> argue that process management techniques stabilize and rationalize organizational routines, while establishing a focus on relatively easily available efficiency and customer satisfaction measures. While increased efficiency results from these dynamics in the short run, they also trigger internal biases for certainty and predictable results ... while exploitation and inertia may be functional for organizations within a given technological trajectory or for existing customers, these variance reducing dynamics stunt exploratory innovation. (pp. 100–101)

In this sense, they are in quite close agreement with both Abernathy and March. They claim that process standardization makes organizations *tightly interrelated*, because it aligns "a firm's structure, rewards, culture, competences, and identity, as well as in the demography of the senior team" (p. 101) so well, with the downside being that this can "impede anything but *internally consistent* change" (p. 101, italics added).

To Tushman and Benner, however, this does not mean that there is not a way to soften the trade-off and that is where they differ with Abernathy and March. The way to do that is through structural change in how the organization operates. Instead of thinking of entire organizations as making the choice between exploration and exploitation, they suggest that for the purpose of overcoming the trade-off, the organization is better thought of as comprised of different subunits that are either explorative or exploitative. The core of this idea, typically labelled *structural ambidexterity*, is to separate explorative activities from exploitative ones and, once that separation has been achieved, to ensure integration across those activities such that synergies between them can be realized. The "recipe" for succeeding with this is to internally align each subunit to be optimized for either exploitative or explorative activities, and hence to be differentiated from each other. One can think of this as an established firm having a mainline legacy business and, at the same time, a small, entrepreneurial, start-up-like subunit pursuing novel opportunities (possibly following what is sometimes called a "skunkworks" model). To ensure that this can become a positive-sum activity, Tushman and Benner emphasize the importance of having a top management team in place that can oversee the integration between these very inconsistent subunits. It stands to reason that neither of those components is easy to do right. Moreover, while in any given industry it may be clear what to exploit, there is also bound to be uncertainty about when and what to explore and hence what explorative subunits to establish, meaning that both technological forecasting and opportunity recognition are central precursors to even talking about structural ambidexterity.

Brunner and Staats similarly accept that efficiency crowds out variance and innovation, thus agreeing with the basic ideas of March and Abernathy. Instead of responding to that crowding out by structural means like Tushman and Benner, their suggestion is to use managerial interventions to re-introduce variance and to do it at the level of otherwise efficient processes. This is done through *deliberate perturbations*. In exploitative organizations, managers[1] can identify those processes that have potential for improvement and deliberately "disturb" them by proverbially throwing a wrench in the machine. If (and that is a nontrivial *if*) the process around such disturbance can be managed correctly, they can bring about what Brunner and Staats describe as exploratory interpretations of the disturbance and its causes, and such interpretations can generate learnings among workers. In turn, this can lead to new and more efficient ways of working. While this sacrifices short-term "static" efficiency to some degree, the overall result is increased "dynamic" efficiency.

The form of ambidexterity thus achieved is not simultaneous like that proposed by Tushman and Benner. Rather, it is achieved by shifting between exploration and exploitation over time – it is a matter of specific processes being, at one time or another, committed to either exploitation or (often more rarely) exploration. Like Tushman and Benner, however, it does see management as key to achieving ambidexterity, because management is tasked both with deciding when to shift from exploitation to exploration and with ensuring that integrative learning happens. The central challenge that this poses is that it presupposes that management is able to efficiently recognize which processes are sensible to perturb

---

[1] Brunner and Staats suggest that managers do not need to necessarily intervene "mindfully," in the sense that they do not need to choose on a case-by-case basis which processes to intervene in. Instead, they can set up systems that themselves trigger "a constant stream of perturbations that employees are tasked with interpreting" (p. 105). I find this choice of words particularly unfortunate, because it invites the ill-advised interpretation that perturbing "mindlessly" can be a good idea. The right way to interpret the suggestion to not intervene mindfully is to think about setting up what Adler and Borys (1996) describe as "meta-routines," that is, routinized ways to bring about change in otherwise routinized work processes.

and which are better left alone. Confusing the two will lead to a situation where managerial efforts to introduce variance simply become annoyances and where the result is dynamic *in*efficiency. It is an open question whether managers who observe work processes, but do not partake in them, can know them well enough to recognize such opportunities (an issue that we will return to in Section 5.2). The other challenge is to ensure that perturbations are not dealt with too quickly but used to generate valuable learning. How to orchestrate that opens up a range of other questions branching into psychology and pedagogics.

Turning to Adler, we see a different form of disagreement with Abernathy and March. While Adler recognizes that a highly specific and bureaucratic organization of work is necessary to exploit and achieve efficiency, he problematizes whether such organization necessarily hampers exploration and innovation. More specifically, he suggests that bureaucracy can lead to both exploitation and exploration, and hence to ambidexterity, given the presence of high levels of trust and within-firm community. The Productivity Dilemma, in other words, is a dilemma only to the extent that trust and community are absent. If it were present, the dilemma would cease to be a dilemma. What Abernathy and March find to be true is not generally true, but only true under a given set of circumstances.

Given high levels of trust, the kind of ambidexterity that Adler describes is what is typically referred to as *contextual ambidexterity*. When Adler imagines that exploration can be combined with exploration, it is by the two being integrated at the level of the individual worker who – while engaged in a work process that is highly specific, structured, and efficient – is able to think creatively about how that process can be innovated upon in order to become more efficient. The more structured the process, the hypothesis goes, the *easier* it is for workers to ideate around it (for a discussion of the relationship between structure and creativity, see Chapter 4). Innovative workers can then in various ways be supported to have their ideas implemented into formal practice. This stands in marked contrast to both Tushman and Benner, who imagined that exploration would not occur within tightly coupled exploitative units. It also contrasts with Brunner and Staats, who imagine that variance must be (re-) introduced by management to contribute to dynamic efficiency. As we will return to, there are conditions under which workers at various levels have more or less leeway to introduce variance on their own initiative and there is often the possibility – even under conditions where workers have little ostensible discretion – for workers to introduce variance more or less covertly (e.g., Bernstein, 2012; Hartmann & Hartmann, 2023). The challenge that this raises is that a wellspring of unmanaged, working-level initiative might compromise the opportunities for management to coordinate effort within the organization and that may compromise overall efficiency, even if the individual innovation seemingly improves it.

This proposition places center stage the question of which circumstances make the Productivity Dilemma either real or not, by sustaining or undermining the trust and community that Adler points to. In Adler's analysis, the economic system in which the firm is embedded is central to answering that question. Specifically, he argues that capitalism introduces a conflict into the organization that makes trust and community very precarious: both can exist within a firm and thereby make ambidexterity possible, but the profit pressure inherent in capitalism (especially finance capitalism) can easily lead to them being quashed, resulting in a hardening of the exploration-exploitation trade-off.

This is a difficult argument to engage with empirically, given that most of the modern world's economies are organized as (more or less purely) capitalist and so it is hard to find a good counterfactual in which to examine the exploration-exploitation trade-off. The same firm does not exist at the same time in both a capitalist and noncapitalist economic system. It is, however, interesting to note that one of the most lauded cases of ambidexterity is Toyota, a firm that emerged and grew under a Japanese system of labor law in which lifetime employment was strongly enforced, leading to reduced internal job security and therefore potentially a softening of some of the conflict that capitalism prompts (see, e.g., Repenning, 2000). However, even in Toyota, as Adler argues, the achievement of ambidexterity is precarious and not the result of simply applying a given managerial recipe. There are many moving parts in making Toyota ambidextrous and a range of contextual factors in play at multiple levels.

With MacDuffie's argument, we move on to more fundamental problematizations of the Productivity Dilemma. All the previous arguments see the Productivity Dilemma as true, at least to some extent. They also all propose a path to achieving ambidexterity *in some form*. Those forms may differ in the level at which ambidexterity should be manifested and whether it should be achieved through differentiation or integration (Raisch et al, 2009) – structural ambidexterity through organizational design, sequential ambidexterity[2] through managerial intervention,

---

[2] The term sequential ambidexterity is often used to describe a process of shifting *the organization* back and forth between explorative and exploitative. Essentially, this can be thought of as the transition from fluid to specific that Abernathy describes and then back again to fluid when exploration is called for. This way of thinking about ambidexterity is the way that it was first described by Duncan (1976). I find this relatively implausible as an approach, because it defies so much of what we know about how difficult

contextual ambidexterity through the creation of enabling contexts. MacDuffie's argument, while seemingly similar to Adler's suggestion of involving workers at all levels of the organization in innovation, is based on the idea that Abernathy and March actually *misrepresent* the nature of what they are trying to describe. The point is not that there are ways around the Productivity Dilemma and the hard trade-off, but that these terms are poor descriptions of reality.

For MacDuffie, the core of the misrepresentation is in the depiction of exploration and exploitation. It is wrong, he suggests, to assume that "[P]rocess improvement is the handservant of exploitation and the enemy of exploration" (p. 107), and hence to accept March's description of exploration and exploitation as trading off against each other. Instead, we are better served by thinking of exploitative and explorative activities as "different outcomes *from the same process*, dependent on how problems are framed" (p. 108, italics added). Exploration and exploitation, in other words, are the same process ascribed different meanings and achieving outcomes of different scales. We are just blinded to this because of an infatuation with inventors, invention, and product innovation, possibly owing to a particular ideology of innovation (see Section 1.2).

This process that can give rise to both explorative and exploitative outcomes is *continuous learning*, which, MacDuffie argues, is pursued in every aspect of Toyota's operations. Rather than thinking of learning as the preserve of technical specialists, Toyota expects all organizational members to be "active cognitive contributors," implying that all workers are intended to not only learn about the work they do but also to ideate and contribute new solutions to the organization. This stands in some contrast to the impulse implicit in Abernathy's argument that workers, as they become more specialized, should follow prescribed processes to the point of doing so mindlessly. Abernathy's view, MacDuffie would argue, harkens back to the tenets of late-1800s Scientific Management (Taylor, 1911), according to which managers design and specify the production process and workers function essentially as machines (or adjuncts to them) and are afforded no role in improvement.

The Toyota production model turns that logic on its head, based on the assumption that those best equipped to identify improvement potential are those engaged in the working practices (which we will return to in Section 5.2). As such, not only are workers engaged in ostensibly exploitative processes expected to innovate, but they are also supported

---

organizational change is. Sequential ambidexterity is, in my reading, much better applied as a description of what Brunner and Staats describe, where *work groups* shift back and forth between exploitation and exploration.

by a range of organizational mechanisms – a valorization of "kaizen," an ability to "stop the line," etc. – that make it possible for them to not only ideate but also have those solutions implemented. Workers should in this context be understood broadly, encompassing the manufacturing employees on the shop floor, but also those in support functions and indeed those in the R&D functions that we usually associate with exploration. Everyone, at least in principle, is expected and empowered through formal mechanisms for suggestion of ideas, experimentation, and implementation to learn and innovate, even if the results of that process are different forms of innovation.

Superficially, there seem to be a lot of similarities between this argument and the one made by Osono and Takeuchi. Like MacDuffie, Osono and Takeuchi suggest that Toyota relates to the Productivity Dilemma in a nonconventional way and that it is this different relating that allows the firm to engage in both exploitation and exploration and thereby to be ambidextrous. An important difference in the arguments, however, is in their description of *how* Toyota relates to the Productivity Dilemma. For MacDuffie, the focus was on continuous learning and putting in place a system, a set of managerial techniques, that allow for capturing the value of this ongoing learning, based on the idea that exploration and exploitation are not fundamentally different processes. For Osono and Takeuchi, what Toyota does is to *transcend* the distinction between the two. By adopting a fundamentally different philosophical position on the dilemma, Toyota becomes able to dissolve the trade-offs between exploration and exploitation, between organizational fluidity and specificity. As they phrase it, "[Toyota] actively embraces and cultivates contradictions instead of passively coping with them. Toyota actually thrives on paradoxes; it harnesses opposing propositions to energize itself" (p. 105). These contradictions are dealt with not in the dualistic form in which they are described by Abernathy and March. They are dealt with through a set of philosophical approaches that bring about particular types of change (driven by "forces of expansion") within a framework of stability ("forces of integration"). What is at stake, in their account, is not so much that it is *practices* that allow for ambidexterity, but rather *understandings*. It may sound like something out of a self-help book, but the underlying idea is that understanding the world differently changes the world.

Winter's argument also contests the dualism between exploitation and exploration, but from the standpoint of the role that *routines* play in especially exploration, which may at first brush seem slightly out of context to the rest of the discussion. Winter's seminal work in what is called evolutionary economics (Nelson & Winter, 1982), which suggests thinking of competing firms as living organisms operating under selection pressure from the competitive environment in what is effectively a form of "generalized Darwinism" (Aldrich et al, 2008) that seems a natural continuation of Schumpeter's description of capitalism. In that very influential description of economic behavior and change, Nelson and Winter posited that routines "play the role that genes play in biological evolutionary theory. They are a persistent feature of the organism and determine its possible behavior ... they are selectable in the sense that organisms with certain routines may do better than others, and, if so, their relative importance in the population (industry) is augmented over time." (Nelson & Winter, 1982, p. 14). It is in this capacity – as determinants of organizational survival over time – that they are brought into this discussion of the Productivity Dilemma and of the trade-off between exploitation and exploration, which is also precisely about survival over time in changing environments.

Routines, Winter argues, are too often misunderstood. They are erroneously linked conceptually to exploitation and specificity. It is true, he argues, that routines are persistent and recurrent and thereby represent reductions in variance, which would make them inherently specificity-increasing and exploitative. It is not true that this means that routines and routinization trade off against exploration and fluidity. Routines are instead best viewed as essential to exploration, because really routines represent (and are essential to) the accumulation of *skills* and a disciplined approach to progress. The disciplined cultivation of routines is important *both* to exploitation and exploration, and indeed the two are complementary. To make this argument, Winter makes use of the metaphor of the skilled performer and generalizes that metaphor to a description of how organizations function. Performers develop skills based on repeated practice, which is essentially the cultivation of a routine, and a rich set of well-honed skills enables a performer to better learn new things. Well-honed skills also allow for higher-quality improvisation than poorly honed ones, as will be immediately apparent if you compare what a three-year-old and a concert pianist do when you ask them to improvise on a piano. Reasoning by analogy, Winter asks, "Why should it be surprising or paradoxical to find a highly disciplined organization at the forefront of world competition in its domain?" (p. 103), that is, why should a highly routinized organization not be able to both be highly efficient and highly innovative?

The argument, in my reading, is potentially true, but the metaphorical basis is somewhat tenuous and quite typical of the way that metaphors are used in management research, especially strategic management research. Likening an organization to a person and putting "the conscious mind [...] in the role of top management, deliberating and setting directions" (p. 103) seems to afford top management a level of control over organizations that is not really reasonable, because it implies that those outside of this "organizational brain" are just "neuronal patterns [that] do the implementation" (p. 103) and implicitly have almost no agency, which is a brazenly poor description of how organizations actually function and of what managers actually do (e.g., Mintzberg's [1971] classic study of managerial work). Organizations, like society at large, are filled with individuals planning and acting to realize those plans, each acting according to the information available to them.

Returning to the issue at stake in the paper, how can we make sense of this diversity of perspectives and all the ways that Abernathy and March can, it seems, be refuted? One way to approach this would be to look for differences in what the arguments address and use those differences to navigate the arguments' respective relevance. To this end, one could claim that the six perspectives are more or less implicitly describing *different* Productivity Dilemmas, *different* forms of exploration which we that (somewhat clumsily) describe as capital-E Exploration and small-E exploration. Small-E exploration is what Adler and MacDuffie are primarily describing and that form of exploration happens almost invariably as an integral part of individuals engaging in their daily work, as we will return to in Section 5.2. It is not exploitation, because it does not lead to reduced, but to increased, variance in the organization's operations: it increases the diversity of approaches used and increases organizational flexibility and adaptability. It happens because learning is nigh inevitable in work and that learning, given appropriate contexts, can be a basis for innovations that can be implemented into the working process. Such exploration most likely happens best through some form of contextual ambidexterity at the individual or working-group level. It might well happen both with and without formal mandates and formally allocated resources (Hartmann & Hartmann, 2023). One might also refer to this as "tweaking" or "micro-invention" and think of it as distinct from "major innovation," considerably more common and quite possibly of equal effectual magnitude (Meisenzahl & Mokyr, 2012).

Capital-E Exploration, by contrast, refers to the major innovations that Tushman and Benner are concerned with and there are reasonable arguments for why that might *not* be achievable through contextual means. Capital-E Exploration – the learning required to deal with technological discontinuities, new product architectures, low-end markets, novel business models, and so on – might require differentiation between established and novel business units, simply because learning on this scale requires resources and thereby inevitably brings the Explorative activity into competition with exploitative ones, a competition that exploitative activities often win, as March suggests. Differentiation according to the structural ambidexterity recipe could conceivably protect exploration from that competition, given appropriate, but difficult-to-orchestrate, top management efforts to coordinate and integrate (see, e.g., Gans, 2017, Chapter 6). One could imagine that structural solutions are required during eras of ferment, in addition to contextual ones that are relevant, especially during eras of incremental change.

In another sense, it is hardly surprising that there are diverse responses to the challenge posed by the Productivity Dilemma. Given the incredible diversity of organizations in which the dilemma plays out, it would be incredible (possibly even suspect) if there was agreement on *one* answer, *one* way to fix the problem that purported to have universal relevance. Some answers, following this line of thinking, will work better in some contexts and not so well in others, simply because of organizational heterogeneity. If you accept this line of thinking, the challenge becomes one of knowing enough about the context in which you might be operating to understand and to judge what will be appropriate there, given the particulars of that context. This approach would call less for evidence on what works and instead suggest that one cultivates a qualitative intuition or, as Dunne would put it, "a 'nose' for what is salient in concrete situations" (1993, p. 368) and based on that sort of "practical wisdom" (Flyvbjerg, 2001), makes decisions about what sort of solution might reasonably be expected to work (see this point elaborated in Chapter 13). Sometimes the solution might be structural, sometimes sequential, and sometimes contextual. Sometimes even transcendental.

6.2 Brown and Duguid: Organizational Learning and Inevitable Innovation

In Section 5.1, there were several arguments about the potential of workers outside of R&D functions to engage in innovation, especially small-e explorative process innovation. In several cases, it was even suggested that innovation was to some extent inevitable. That idea owes a lot to Brown and Duguid's idea to view working, learning, and innovating as inherently unified.

The authors base their argument on an empirical study of photocopier repair technicians in Xerox, conducted by Julian Orr and described in his book *Talking about Machines* (1996[3]). Orr's work was ethnographic, based on in-depth participant observation of these technicians as they worked to fix malfunctioning Xerox machines. Superficially, that sort

---

[3] You might ask how Brown and Duguid's paper from 1991 can be based on a book from 1996. There is no time travel involved. Orr's book is based on his PhD thesis, completed in 1990.

of technical work is relatively banal. Technicians receive three weeks of training and are then sent into the field, armed with repair manuals, and expected to do the job. On closer inspection, that account falls apart. Technicians' working practice is more like "continuous, highly skilled improvisation within a triangular relationship of technician, customer, and machine" (Orr, 1996, p. 1). It is both technically and socially complex in a way not immediately apparent to nontechnicians. The technical problems that they must solve are highly idiosyncratic and the problems must be solved in ways that also manage customers' relationship to Xerox. "Work in such circumstances is resistant to rationalization, since the expertise vital to such contingent and extemporaneous practice cannot be easily codified" (p. 2). Technicians are not "low-skill" workers following manuals, but over time and through experience build up high levels of mastery that is valued in the professional community and serves as a basis for skillful and resourceful improvisation.

What Brown and Duguid do is to "re-purpose" these findings, by reading them through a particular set of theoretical lenses. The most important of these is the idea of *communities of practice*, developed by Lave and Wenger and most famously described in the book "Situated Learning: Legitimate peripheral participation" (1990). Situated learning, as a concept, is a way to account for learning as it happens through practice and should be seen as a counter to the idea of learning as a transmission of knowledge. It is empirically based on observations of apprenticeship and how it makes learners become capable knowers. In Lave and Wenger's description, learning is a process of coming to participate in particular communities of practice. Initially, when the learner is starting out, participation is peripheral, but if it is legitimate to be peripheral to the community (i.e., if the community is accepting of novices and helps them into the community), the learner can over time partake in the process of knowing that occurs within the community. This kind of learning is about more than "knowing things." Knowledge is tied up with practices, professional culture, and personal identity.

The implication of this view of knowledge is that it is per definition hard to understand work if one does not partake in it. Knowledge exists within communities and may flow easily within it but is very hard to transfer to nonmembers. In part, this is because knowledge is often "tacit" (Polanyi, 1966) and hard to account for, but also because it is so interwoven with community membership. What this suggests is that the knowledge that matters to an organization is likely to be both highly heterogeneous within its boundaries and at the same time widely distributed beyond them. That makes it inherently difficult for managers to plan and make decisions, because they *cannot* have detailed knowledge of the things they are planning and making decisions about. There is more than passing resemblance between this view and the Austrian ("Hayekian") view that underpinned Shane's argument about how the ability to identify opportunities and problems was highly distributed across the economy. The Hayekian view emphasizes that knowledge is intimately tied to the particulars of time and place and extremely difficult to aggregate and make available for centralized decision-making (Hayek, 1945). To see just one illustration of why this matters, consider the viability of Brunner and Staats' idea of deliberate perturbation: if you think that knowledge of working processes is only very imperfectly unavailable to people who do not partake in those processes, it is hard to imagine that managers would be able to effectively identify what processes to perturb. You could also consider the viability of Tushman and Benner's model of structural ambidexterity: if the ability to identify opportunities to explore is widely distributed, how likely is it that top management can effectively make decisions about what explorative business units should be exploring? Conversely, if you took a different view of knowledge, both those ideas become viable and arguably more viable than the kinds of ideas proposed by Adler and MacDuffie.

In the view of work that Brown and Duguid develop, work has both a formal ("canonical") and informal ("noncanonical") component, both in terms of what actually gets done and how it is organized. The canonical part of work involves doing what the job formally entails and doing it in prescribed ways. For Orr's technicians, this meant repairing machines according to manuals. The noncanonical part involves all the other aspects of work that are important, but not explicated. The technician not only repairs the machine but also manages a customer relationship, among other things. Technicians encounter problems that are not covered by manuals, because "real" problems are unpredictable and more complex than manuals assume. And technicians organize themselves in ways that allow them to learn from each other, even as the organization views it as unnecessary. Paradoxically, such noncanonical work is often crucially important and wholly underappreciated. "Many organizations are willing to assume that complex tasks can be successfully mapped onto a set of simple, Tayloristic, canonical steps that can be followed without need of significant understanding or insight (and thus without need of significant investment in training or skilled technicians)"[4] (p. 42). As organizations become more specific, in Abernathy's terms, the gulf between actual practice and canonical practice widens because work becomes more tightly specified and ostensibly less mindful and more de-skilled. This can

---

[4] By Tayloristic, Brown and Duguid are referring to the ideas of Scientific Management as developed by Frederick Taylor (1911).

"actually make ... work more difficult to accomplish and thus perversely demands more, not fewer, improvisational skills" (p. 42).

Improvisational skills develop from learning-in-work. This kind of learning happens to the extent that workers not only immerse themselves in *doing* work but also have access to communities of practitioners to engage with and become encultured into. "Workplace learning is best understood, then, in terms of the communities being formed or joined and personal identities being changed. The central issue in learning is becoming a practitioner not learning about a practice" (p. 48). It is from this idea that we can begin to see why you could consider learning almost inevitable: it is hard to imagine anything but the most isolated forms of labor that do not entail *some* element of community, especially given that people will often intentionally seek out community where there is none immediately available (whether in physical or online forms). Community participation may be unplanned, highly emergent, invisible to outsiders, and highly noncanonical, but nonetheless highly impactful in the kinds of learning that it fosters.

When learning occurs in communities of practice, innovation can result. This kind of innovation, which is best thought of as small-e exploration, represents an expansion of practices beyond the canonical, driven by community members improvising solutions to noncanonical problems, experimenting with and refining those solutions, and diffusing them to other members of their community. We can think of this as improvisation aggregating imperfectly into a repertoire of diverse, novel practices. The organization might then try to put in place systems to surface these novel practices, and possibly support them. One way to read the Toyota case is that Toyota succeeds *not* in making their workers innovative but in having those innovations that they develop revealed and refined. The alternative is that such novel practice simply lives on in informal ways and that production processes, beneath a veneer of specificity, are in fact highly fluent and adaptive. The empirical possibility here is that "small, self-constituting communities ... [can] evade the ossifying tendencies of large organizations" (p. 50) and that organizations that *appear* to be non-innovative do, in fact, innovate and continuously develop what appear from a distance to be completely stagnant processes. It is not all that hard to imagine how that can lead managerial decision-making to have many, many unexpected consequences.

6.3 Cohen and Levinthal: Absorptive Capacity and the (Other) Effects of R&D

In addition to the different forms of ambidexterity previously covered – contextual, structural, and sequential – there is another variety that deserves mention: *network ambidexterity*.[5] In contrast to those forms that all saw the achievement of exploration and exploitation as something that should occur within the same organization, network ambidexterity refers to the ability of a *dyad* or *cluster* of organizations efficiently exploring and exploiting as a collective. Some firms might specialize in efficient production and exploitative process innovation, while others[6] specialize in exploration, and through knowledge flows *across* organizational boundaries, the firms jointly achieve ambidexterity in their network. Much like how structural ambidexterity would suggest specialized business units, network ambidexterity suggests specialized firms. Unlike structural ambidexterity, which would suggest integration through a hierarchical mechanism, network ambidexterity achieves integration through collaboration or some form of market mechanism. This approach to innovation as something that happens not solely within the firm is on the ascendant and has been gaining in importance for some time (e.g., Powell et al, 1996; Lundvall, 2010).

As is the case for all forms of ambidexterity, network ambidexterity has distinct challenges. For it to function, organizations have to integrate knowledge developed outside their boundaries and to understand that challenge, Cohen and Levinthal's concept of *absorptive capacity* becomes central. Absorptive capacity refers to the ability of an organization to "recognize the value of new information, assimilate it, and apply it to commercial ends" (p. 128). Benefiting from outside knowledge, in other words, depends on three – at least analytically – distinct processes. It involves identification: looking beyond the frontiers of the knowledge that the firm already possesses and making judgments about parts of the knowledge that reside "out there" is of potential value. It involves assimilation: the members of the organization need to acquire that knowledge (i.e., learn), such that the knowledge is brought "into" the organization. And it involves application: working with that knowledge to make it useful for innovative and commercial ends. All those processes are challenging in their own ways, as will be familiar to any student trying to attain some mastery of a new academic field. Being able to do all three things well, as an individual and an organization, is what Cohen and Levinthal describe as having high levels of absorptive capacity.

---

[5] Solon Moreira provided helpful feedback on this chapter. I am grateful and of course claim full responsibility for errors and misinterpretations.

[6] These others need not only be firms but should be thought of as "knowledge producers" in a broad sense of encompassing firms as well as, for example, independent inventors, universities and research institutions, customers, suppliers, "crowds," and others. We will return to this issue in Chapters 10 and 11.

The paper's main claim is that absorptive capacity at both the individual and organizational level depends on *prior knowledge*.[7] For individuals, having a stock of prior knowledge makes it less cognitively demanding to acquire new information, provided that the new information is *related* to what is already known. Learning about a new development in aerodynamics would be easier for an aeronautics engineer than for an electrical engineer, and easier for an electrical engineer than for a historian, because their stock of related prior knowledge *ceteris paribus* is very different. As Cohen and Levinthal summarize it, "learning performance is greatest when the object of learning is related to what is already known" (p. 131). Under conditions of uncertainty about *what* to learn, however, the individual's absorptive capacity is not just a function of expertise, but also of the diversity of knowledge. "[A] diverse background provides a more robust basis for learning, because it increases the prospect that incoming information will relate to what is already known" (p. 131). Saying that absorptive capacity at the individual level depends on prior knowledge thus in effect means saying that it depends on the depth and breadth of prior knowledge. This ought to mean that what is important is not just the stock, but the nature, of prior knowledge.

From the individual level, Cohen and Levinthal shift to the organizational. In doing so, they argue that "[a]n organization's absorptive capacity will depend on the absorptive capacities of its individual members ... a firm's absorptive capacity is not, however, simply the sum of the absorptive capacities of its employees ... it also depends on transfers of knowledge across and within sub-units that may be quite removed from the original point of entry" (p. 131). This places center stage three issues: how the prior knowledge of individuals aggregates into organizational prior knowledge, how information is communicated through the firm, and how absorption is organized for.

The issue of aggregation involves thinking about the optimal level of sameness and diversity of knowledge within the organization. To the extent that the members of the organization share similar (individual)

---

[7] It is worth noting that Cohen and Levinthal are discussing an emphatically *different* kind of knowledge than what Shane (Section 3.4) refers to, despite both papers using the term prior knowledge. For Shane, prior knowledge referred to experiences with problems that could serve as a basis for applying a technology. For Cohen and Levinthal, prior knowledge refers primarily to experiences with technologies or bodies of academic knowledge that can then be applied to problems. One can distinguish between the two as "need"-related or "solution"-related knowledge (Schweisfurth & Raasch, 2018). Less centrally, for Cohen and Levinthal, prior knowledge also refers to knowledge of where to search for new information. You might expect that knowing a lot about a topical field would correlate with knowing where to search for information that is related to the field. Note also that for Shane, prior knowledge is an individual-level construct.

prior knowledge, they may (in aggregate) be able to discover, acquire, and apply new related information very efficiently. However, that sameness may also compromise the ability of the organization to search more widely and more exploratively for new information. A team of very specialized chemists might with relatively few resources recognize the value of and learn about a new photosensitive compound to add to photographic film, but might struggle to recognize the value of a new software-based technology for improving digital image sensors. An interdisciplinary team with heterogeneous prior knowledge might be more efficient at identifying valuable external knowledge from a wide range of scientific fields, but less efficient at collectively acquiring that knowledge in order to bring it into the firm. This implies, as Cohen and Levinthal phrase it, "that the ideal knowledge structure for an organizational subunit should reflect only partially overlapping knowledge complemented by non-overlapping diverse knowledge [which] suggests an organizational trade-off between diversity and commonality of knowledge across individuals" (p. 134).

The issue of communication involves thinking about the formal and informal processes through which communication flows through the organization, that is, the networks[8] along which information travels. "The firm's absorptive capacity depends on the individuals who stand at the interface of either the firm and the external environment or at the interface between subunits within the firm" (p. 132). The way that individuals fulfill this "interface function" of passing on knowledge between potentially very disparate actors, and whether they engage in such knowledge sharing, becomes essential for how knowledge, once recognized, is assimilated and, once assimilated, applied. The problem here is twofold. First, it is hard to know what technical knowledge to supply without a complete understanding of what problems solutions are demanded for, because knowledge essentially becomes valuable when needs and solutions are paired. Second, the fulfillment of the interface function depends not just on the prior knowledge of the individual sharing information but also on the prior knowledge of the receiver. Sharing too much and sharing without common prior knowledge may be wasteful, while sharing too little will compromise firm-level absorptive

---

[8] Understanding networks and how they function is the subject of that branch of social science known as social network analysis. It turns out that both formal and informal networks play key roles in explaining a whole range of social outcomes, pertaining also to organizational and innovation-related issues. This work, however, is so expansive as to fall beyond the scope of this book. For further general reading, see, for example, Granovetter (1973) or Burt (2004). For readings related specifically to absorptive capacity, see, for example, Tsai (2001) or Moreira et al (2018).

capacity. This points to "a trade-off in the efficiency of internal communication against the agility of the subunit to assimilate and exploit information originating from other subunits or the environment" (p. 133).

The issue of organization deals with the decision of how to assign the work of scanning the environment for new information. One could imagine that the interface function could be centralized in an organizational subunit that is particularly specialized in searching for novel knowledge, much like how one might centralize R&D efforts in the reasonable belief that this will allow for a more efficient innovation process. Such a specialized "search and absorb" unit could then also develop routinized ways of communicating novel technological opportunities to the relevant subunits. In the pharmaceutical industry, for instance, it is very common to have "technology scouting" departments tasked with searching for new technological opportunities or firms with which incumbents might partner for technology development. Alternatively, one could imagine a highly decentralized interface function where everyone is tasked to search for new information in addition to their regular work. That might bring "more eyeballs" to the firm's search efforts but might increase the efforts required to transfer knowledge and to find relevant receptors for the knowledge. What is most meaningful is, most likely, a function of the nature of the knowledge to be absorbed, but it is questionable whether that can be known, and hence organized for, in advance.

That said, the nature of the technological environment that the firm finds itself in may shape the optimal organization of environmental scanning: As Cohen and Levinthal phrase it,

[a] difficulty may arise under conditions of rapid and uncertain technical change, however, when this interface function is centralized. When information flows are somewhat random and it is not clear where in the firm or subunit a piece of outside knowledge is best applied, a centralized gatekeeper may not provide an effective link to the environment. Under such circumstances [e.g. in eras of ferment], it is best for the organization to expose a fairly broad range of prospective receptors to the environment. (p. 132)

How the prior knowledge of individuals aggregates into organizational prior knowledge is, in fewer words, far from straightforward. There is a wealth of complications that matter for how absorptive capacity actually develops and enables the firm to successfully benefit from external knowledge and, by implication, allows it to achieve network ambidexterity. That, however, is not all the paper suggests.

The notion of absorptive capacity as something that firms can invest in developing through engagement in explorative R&D changes the economics of engaging in such R&D. While an innovation project may fail, it may lead to an increase in prior knowledge because something is learned in that project. That prior may at *a later time* prove valuable for identification, assimilation, and application of external knowledge, provided that what is learned is related to that external knowledge. "We may therefore consider a firm's R&D as satisfying two functions: we assume that R&D only generates new knowledge, but also contributes to the firm's absorptive capacity" (p. 138). Those additional effects may be substantial and justify more investment in R&D than would otherwise appear to be reasonable. Yet they are also inherently uncertain because it is difficult to foresee both what learning a project may (serendipitously) give rise to and whether that knowledge may turn out to be useful in the future.

Investments in R&D at one point in time may also shape the technological uncertainty that a firm experiences in future periods. "In an uncertain environment, absorptive capacity affects expectation formation, permitting the firm to predict more accurately the nature and commercial potential of technological advances" (p. 136). Recall that while mapping the shape of S-curves is straightforward in retrospect, predicting it is inherently uncertain: it cannot be known a priori when a technology will begin to rapidly improve and when improvement rates will taper off. That makes committing to emergent technologies inherently risky. What Cohen and Levinthal suggest here is that high levels of absorptive capacity may correlate with the ability to forecast technological improvement, which means that the uncertainty associated with emergent technologies may be heterogeneous across firms. In this way, it may be meaningful to think of uncertainty as composed of both subjective elements (that are idiosyncratically experienced, perhaps also as a function of prior knowledge in Shane's sense) and objective ones (that are commonly shared). Investing in R&D in order to build up absorptive capacity at one point in time may thus also make exploration appear less explorative to some firms than to others.

Investments in R&D and thus in absorptive capacity can also create particular trajectories that shape the real options available to firms in the future. This is what Cohen and Levinthal refer to as "an extreme case of path dependence in which once a firm ceases investing in its absorptive capacity in a quickly moving field, it may never assimilate and exploit new information in that field, regardless of the value of that information" (p. 136). This may be a function of the inability both to predict that potential developments and value of a new technology and to detect signals from the environment about others' predictions. It may also be that investing in absorptive capacity may become increasingly costly as a technology develops, such that while early investments would be low, later ones would be prohibitively high. The extreme result of such path dependence is "lock-out," which can "confine firms to operating in a particular technological domain," potentially placing them at risk of Creative Destruction by more proactively investing competitors.

The main value of the paper lies in this wealth of theoretical propositions and all the hypotheses that they create for future work to explore. They are, however, propositions and most of the most interesting ideas in the paper are actually *not* dealt with in the empirical analysis that the paper also contains. The empirical analysis in the paper, for instance, is wholeheartedly at the organizational level and makes no effort to measure individual-level phenomena. In part, this is reasonable enough. Many of the concepts that the paper mobilizes are hard to observe, let alone measure, and the kind of multi-level theorizing that it engages in – in which individual-level attributes and behaviors shape higher-level outcomes – is tremendously hard to grapple with irrespective of the methods one might apply. That is why it can feel like the analysis "loiters" around many of the ideas that the paper presents without really getting to them in any particular detail. The same lack of meaningful detail comes through (somewhat less reasonably) when the incredibly complex phenomenon of *what a firm knows* is collapsed into a measurement like R&D spending normalized for firm sales.

That said, the conceptual and most interesting part of the paper has its own limitations. The most pressing of this is the unfortunate use of metaphor that was also discussed in connection with Winter's contribution to "Perspectives on the Productivity Dilemma." The use of the terms "absorbing" and "absorptive capacity" invariably conjures up the image that the organization absorbs external knowledge like sponges absorb liquids, and yet organizations are not sponges or even particularly sponge-like (Fiol, 1996), and knowledge is not liquid or liquid-like in the way that it is "acquired" or in how it "exists" (as discussed in Section 5.2). It stands to reason that metaphors guide theory generation in the social sciences, and that metaphors distort the nature of what is being described. The question is whether that distortion illuminates more than it obscures, and with what consequences it is applied. And that is ultimately a matter for further empirical study.

7 Should Innovation Be Managed?

> **Texts in This Chapter**
>
> Cooper, R. G. 1990. Stage-gate systems: A new tool for managing new products. *Business Horizons*. 33(3), 44–54.
>
> Mouritsen, J., Hansen, A. & Hansen, C. Ø. 2009. Long and short translations: Management accounting calculations and innovation management. *Accounting, Organizations and Society*. 34(6–7), 738–754.
>
> Criscuolo, P., Salter, A. & Ter Wal, A. L. J. 2014. Going underground: Bootlegging and individual innovative performance. *Organization Science*. 25(5), 1287–1571.
>
> Foss, N. J. 2003. Selective intervention and internal hybrids: Interpreting and learning from the rise and decline of the Oticon Spaghetti Organization. *Organization Science*. 14(3), 331–349.

Even as a romantic conception of innovation – emphasizing its uncertain and serendipitous nature, for instance – might suggest that it is inherently hard to manage, the brute fact of the matter is that most innovation, in most organizations, *is* managed. In this chapter, we look into what happens to innovation when it is subjected to management, paying particular attention to the unintended and second-order consequences of those efforts to manage. Management can surely "get things under control," but the interesting questions relate to what happens next, to what *also* happens when things do get under control. The first three readings provide three different angles on that. In the first, we read about a pretty neutral-looking management technique and think through why it might not be so neutral. In the second, we are shown how innocuous things like accounting numbers can drive innovation strategies. In the third, we are introduced to the dynamics of hidden innovation projects and think about what formal management actually gets to manage and the limits of managerial influence. The final reading zooms out and asks what happens when organizations actually lean into the unmanageability of innovation and attempt to be less organized and to manage innovation less.

7.1 Cooper: Innovation through Stages

When innovation happens in organizations, it is not just something that is organized at a general level but also something that is actively managed. It is not merely a matter of structuring the organization, its boundaries, and its processes in a way that enables innovation to occur. Instead, individual innovations are subject to management. As is the case of almost everything else that formally happens within the context of (Chandlerian) firms, decisions about what innovations to invest in, to commercialize, to prioritize, and to abandon are made by managers, not by the individuals "doing" the innovation. In this sense, innovation is assumed – *has* to be assumed, to some extent – to be *like* everything else that happens within firms, which it is generally not. March would insist, for instance, that innovation may involve explorative learning and be characterized by greater uncertainty and variance in outcomes than other organizational processes (e.g., a highly specific production process) and in that sense be a very different beast to manage.

Nonetheless, there is no shortage of ideas and concepts about how to manage innovation and especially to make innovation more efficient, and new ones come along regularly in what resembles a fashion cycle (Abrahamson & Fairchild, 1999). Cooper's concept of Stage-Gate Systems as an approach to managing innovation is, although somewhat dated, both still standard fare in many innovation management contexts and exemplary of many of these ideas and concepts. It promises to accelerate and "drive new ideas to market faster and with fewer mistakes … to reduce cycle time yet improve […] new product 'hit rate'" (p. 44) and to ensure alignment between the innovation project and organizational priorities and market needs. To achieve this, stage-gate systems impose a structure on what might otherwise be highly unstructured, force certain questions to be answered earlier than they otherwise might be, and introduce decision points in the innovation process where managers can enact management, that is, monitor progress, make choices, allocate resources, and ensure integration of effort. This may seem onerous if you construe innovation as a more or less freewheeling creative process, but the point is clear: to ensure that the innovating organizations does not "suffer the costs of experimentation without gaining many of its benefits … [by having] too many undeveloped new ideas and too little distinctive competence" (March, 1991, p. 71).

The challenges with systems and concepts for managing innovation are twofold. They are situated within organizational processes that may be much messier than the systems account for. They also imply trade-offs, the precise nature of which are not always made clear. Before we elaborate on these two challenges, it is worth dwelling slightly longer on the precise way that Stage-Gate Systems purport to operate.

Stage-Gate Systems, Cooper asserts, "recognize that product innovation is a process. And like other processes, innovation can be managed. Stage-gate systems simply apply process-management methodologies to this innovation process" (p. 45). It does so by removing variance from the process of innovation. The innovation process is broken down into a set of standardized steps, referred to in the system as stages. All innovations go through the same standard stages, and each stage is characterized by a defined set of activities that must be completed. "For example, the 'Validation' stage might entail a list of mandatory or optional activities such as in-house prototype tests, field tests with customers, pilot or trial production, and test marketing" (p. 46). Each stage ends with a gate that is simultaneously the entrance to the next stage. "These gates control the process.... Each gate is characterized by a set of deliverables or inputs, a set of exit criteria, and an output" (p. 46). In other words, each time a project has progressed through a certain stage, the participants need to produce certain documentation of their process (e.g., a business case for the idea). This documentation is evaluated according to preset criteria (e.g., the expected return on investment for the project) and results in a decision to proceed to the next stage, to abandon the project, to stall the project, or to have the project repeat the prior stage. This is what Cooper refers to as the "Go/Kill/Hold/Recycle decision." The envisioned process is depicted in figure 2, albeit the particular sequence of stages is intended to vary by organization.

The fixed time frames, the focus on evaluable deliverables, and the opportunities to terminate projects are, in theory, what make Stage-Gate Systems "better" at innovation. These are the mechanisms that turn a largely unstructured process into something faster and more structured, and into something that managers can "manage, direct and control." The fixed time frames ensure that a project progresses over time and ideally does so at greater speed than in an unstructured process. The deliverables do two things. Frontloading certain required deliverables (e.g., market research) can protect against costly investments in projects that turn out to not meet a market demand. Deliverables can also ensure that a project that may be both complex and uncertain as regards both the market and the technology can be monitored and held to a common standard, assessable by individuals without the technical or market expertise. Finally, the opportunities to terminate projects are what afford managers control over what might otherwise be at the discretion of research scientists and allow for potentially unsuccessful products to be funded excessively long.

It stands to reason that the *effects* of Stage-Gate Systems and the way that they impact organizational innovation processes are highly contingent on the particular ways that those systems are designed. Organizations might, for instance, make choices about how to sequence activities, what deliverables to require at each stage, and how deliverables are evaluated and these choices could conceivably make Stage-Gate systems have radically different effects (consider, e.g., Azoulay et al's [2011] comparative study of how different funding program designs impact scientists' creative work). Decisions about whether to engage in technological exploration before market tests, or whether to gauge the fit between a product idea and the firm's product portfolio, clearly condition what forms of innovation become viable within the organization. A requirement for a strongly grounded business case may favor projects with known markets and clear value propositions, but challenge more explorative projects. Conversely, deliverables emphasizing radicality and "disruptive" potential may lead to the termination of exploitative ones. And policies about *who* evaluates projects at various stages can enable or undermine ideas based on idiosyncratic insights and hypotheses (cf. Section 5.3).

Irrespective of the particularities of their design, Stage-Gate Systems assume an *orderliness* that may not fully reflect organizational processes. Project managers and evaluators may, for instance, not follow the prescribed procedures. The Stage-Gate System assumes simplistically that they work on their projects, submit them for evaluation, and then await judgment in a relatively disciplined fashion when, in practice, they may actively promote their projects, work to persuade evaluators through informal channels, and ensure that evaluations are more rituals than actual decision points (e.g., Christiansen & Varnes, 2007). They may actively work to politicize a process that Cooper assumes to be capable of driving out such politicking. The Stage-Gate System similarly assumes that decision-makers allocate their attention to the "right things" and in fact hold projects to similar standards. In practice, they may attend more to, for example, novel projects than those in more dire need of attention (e.g., Bentzen et al, 2011). The "complete" process (p. 48) that Cooper envisages may have very many incompletenesses, loops, and loopholes, even as it ostensibly appears "complete." For Cooper, such incompleteness is the problem that Stage-Gate Systems are intended to solve. In practice, it is the reality that the systems must contend with.

Stage-Gate Systems might also introduce trade-offs that are not immediately visible. Most obviously, they may bias organizations toward exploitative projects. A focus on early assessments of technological and commercial viability may push out projects where those questions are highly uncertain. You cannot "cut off" one side of a distribution, getting

7.1 Cooper: Innovation through Stages

only the upside variance and doing away with the downside. Less obviously, particularly projects targeting novel or potential markets that cannot be easily analyzed (an essential component of disruptive innovation) are likely to be terminated, leaving companies vulnerable. Recall that Christensen observes many of the innovations that turn out to be disruptive originate within incumbent firms that choose not to invest in them, only to ultimately be outcompeted. Second-order consequences of managing innovation processes tightly, such as the effects on personnel selection, might also matter. Certain innovation workers may leave companies following particular processes, or choose against working there in the first place, conditioning what kind of creative ideas are even available for the organization to make decisions on. Efforts to manage and to manage in particular ways, in other words, have costs.

It would be wrongheaded to read this as an argument for *not* managing innovation, for simply dismissing the means and intended ends of the Stage-Gate System. It seems wholly unreasonable (most of the time, at least) to simply throw money at an R&D department and to leave innovators to their own devices, hoping that brilliant ideas emerge from the creative anarchy. It is also not a rejection of the elements of a Cooperian Stage-Gate System. There are certainly good reasons to have an early focus on market viability, to place low-cost activities ahead of high-cost ones (this may also allow firms to test out more innovation ideas, as opposed to committing only to very few), and to try to create a forward progression in projects. It is rather to say that potential adopters of a Stage-Gate System (or similar, more recent concepts and systems) should approach that adoption in an immensely reflexive manner, with considerable sensitivity to local contexts and needs (Kärreman et al, 2021). It is also to say that the *value* of such a system is highly contingent on the organization. For some, it may be valuable, for others immensely counterproductive (e.g., Annosi et al, 2020). Certainly, managers should have very well-grounded hypotheses about *why* they should be applied, because they are de facto not a panacea.

You might be right to object that it is somewhat unfair to judge Cooper and the complex system he proposes on the basis of a short and summary description. It is, after all, more of a sales brochure extolling the merits of a new management concept than a piece of disinterested scholarship. It cannot be assumed to explicate the insufficiencies and problems of the solution, much like how a car salesperson is unlikely to tell you that a competing manufacturer's offerings may serve your needs better. It is hard to blame Cooper for painting a positive image of his product, you might say. But recognizing that management ideas are sometimes products to be sold does place the onus on the consumer of this and other management ideas to be a critical consumer of those ideas, to do more than simply reading "what it says on the tin" and being lured by skillfully marketed promises.

7.2 Mouritsen et al: Management Accounting and Justifications for Innovation Projects

What does accounting have to do with innovation? If that were the first question that came to mind when you saw this chapter's title, it would not be unreasonable. Accounting, after all, is often depicted as a somewhat dreary affair that has little to do with the altogether more flamboyant and romantic image that people (occasionally rightly, most often wrongly) associate with innovation. In that common view, innovators are heroes in the Schumpeterian mold, and accountants are something closer to Chandlerian bean-counters. For all the romance of innovation, everyone seems to agree that creative accountants are *not* what you would generally want.

Alas, as is often the case for popular wisdom, this view misses something crucial: accounting plays a very considerable (often underappreciated) role in how organizations manage innovation. Accounting calculations, more specifically, can shape the nature of the innovation that an organization does. Accounting practices produce the kinds of *calculations* that make it possible to assess innovation projects and their performance relative to other projects and investment opportunities, both prospectively and retrospectively. In Cooper's Stage-Gate System, for instance, the assessment of R&D costs and production costs are integral to project evaluation (Cooper, 1990, pp. 51–52). While such costs *appear* "neutral" (such is the nature of accounting), they are often the result of particular choices that could have been vastly different. Tushman and Benner's recommendations for how to achieve structural ambidexterity (Section 6.1) also emphasize that explorative and exploitative subunits may need to be managed by different metrics, precisely because *metrics* and other accounting numbers condition decision-making processes. For all its apparent neutrality, accounting exerts considerable organizational influence. Without being obviously authoritative, accounting numbers and calculations have a lot of authority. When managers manage "by the numbers," the numbers are doing a lot of the management. Calculations, like theories, are *performative*. In describing innovation, they shape innovation. They are engines, not cameras (MacKenzie, 2008) of the innovation process.

This can seem somewhat obscure, but Mouritsen et al very helpfully illustrate the dynamics of how accounting choices, calculations, metrics, and numbers come to shape innovation processes. Their study examines three firms and how they use accounting numbers in the management of their innovation process. All three firms are innovative firms in innovative industries, but their approaches to innovation differ. All three firms use management accounting numbers when evaluating the performance of innovation projects, but the kind of numbers they use differ. As it turns out, management accounting numbers play an important role in what kind of innovation projects and development activities innovation workers and innovation managers can *justify* as economically reasonable and it is by enabling certain justifications and challenging others that numbers shape innovation. Numbers, so to speak, enable rational decision-making and make some activities rational while others appear to be in excess. Different numbers, different rationality, different innovation.

SuitTech produces bespoke scientific instruments. These are highly technical solutions for corporate and university research labs, with sales engineers collaborating closely with customers in the development and design of novel, one-off solutions. Engineers spend considerable time on each development process, have considerable flexibility in how they approach problem solving, and make use of a wide variety of externally sourced components, allowing them to meet very specific customer demands. The "authoritative performance measure" (p. 741) in SuitTech is *sales performance*. The number used to assess innovation was related to the *revenue* generated, but not the direct costs of producing a solution (e.g., the cost of components).

HighTech produces health care measurement systems. Again, these are highly technical products, but they are not bespoke solutions like SuitTech's. Each product is based on considerable R&D work done in-house, and products are intended to be "market-driving" technological developments. Innovation projects could freely draw resources from the firm's research unit, based on the assumption that learnings from one project might spill over and create value also on future projects, and this allowed the resultant products to be at the forefront of the relevant science. Those products would, however, have to fit within an existing product program. In HighTech, the key metric to assess performance was the *contribution margin* for each product, that is, the revenue generated by the product minus the direct costs of producing it. Indirect costs (e.g., the cost of firm-wide R&D) were not included, meaning that innovation project managers functionally "can get technological advice for free" (p. 744).

LeanTech produces products for video and audio transmission to telecom companies and broadcasters. These would appear to be customized solutions, but because they were based on a limited set of standardized hardware modules, standard software packages, and software developed in-house, customization was primarily a question of integrating components to specific needs. Focus lay not just on innovativeness but also on manufacturability and the ability to respond quickly to customer demand. LeanTech relied on *activity-based costing*, a method of allocating indirect costs to specific projects and visualizing how particular projects and activities would draw on shared resources. Capital costs (e.g., the costs of financing inventory) and depreciation (i.e., the calculated reduction in the value of assets over time) were, however, not allocated to specific innovations.

While these cases by no means imply a causal relationship between particular accounting practices and particular approaches to innovation, their data do show how different accounting practices *motivate* different approaches by making them easier to justify. In SuitTech, "sales performance motivated a strategy of tight customization through liberal use of externally sourced special and customized components" (p. 742). Because sales engineers do not have to justify using expensive components and do not have to justify the time they spend working with clients to create customized products, they can focus solely on product performance. In HighTech, the focus on contribution margin means that direct costs come into focus and innovation managers rely on R&D (an indirect cost), as opposed to components (a direct cost), to drive product quality, because "the costs of R&D were not allocated to new product development" (p. 744). Because innovation managers do not need to justify their use of R&D resources, R&D can pursue "detours" and explorative learning. In LeanTech, the use of activity-based costing means that indirect costs are brought into the evaluation of innovation projects, raising awareness of, for example, set-up times in production and making it more "rational" to reduce the range of standard components.

By shaping the innovation process, accounting methods have other knock-on effects. They shape what kinds of customers and markets it becomes reasonable to focus on. The focus on sales performance justifies focusing on customers with idiosyncratic needs, while activity-based costing suggests pursuing customers with needs that can be serviced through minor variations on standard solutions. By implication, they shape what competitive strategies appear viable. Niche and differentiation become easier to justify and to pursue when accounting numbers are closer to the "top line," while cost leadership is motivated by a "bottom line" focus. Supplier relationships and the decisions about the boundaries of the firm are also shaped by accounting. When innovation managers can disregard direct costs, the firm can have loose relations with a wide range of suppliers, while a disregard of indirect costs justifies keeping R&D in-house.

Activity-based costing can make extensive outsourcing and tight relationship to select suppliers easy to justify. In this sense, the choice of accounting method can implicitly drive choices that would ordinarily be thought of as strategic and central to firm competitiveness.

Thinking of this in terms that we have used before, you might say that explorative learning is facilitated by "shallow" calculations (focused on revenues, absent costs) while "deep" calculations (focusing on the bottom line and seeking to make innovation managers aware of and account for more costs) motivate more exploitative learning. A bottom-line focus might drive organizations away from fluidity and toward specificity, and this might in principle jeopardize organizations' ability to adapt to changing circumstances and novel competition. This might be especially so if accounting metrics extend even deeper than to the allocation of indirect costs. Alas, a "top line" focus might risk justifying "failure trap" behavior, where learning and experimentation take precedence over execution. If organizations emphasize even more shallow metrics (e.g., number of customers, as opposed to actual revenues), it may motivate what is essentially economically unsustainable growth. In this way, we can think of organizations as choosing not just between explorative and exploitative projects, but also at the meta-level choosing between calculations that make explorative and exploitative projects systematically more justifiable.

If this is true, it is particularly noteworthy that we see a similar dynamic across all three cases, irrespective of their differences. In all three, calculations are problematized and that problematization consistently involves management accounts advocating for deeper calculations and greater conscientiousness about more costs amongst innovation managers. In SuitTech, accountants push for focus not on revenues, but on contribution margins. In HighTech, accountants push for awareness of indirect costs. In LeanTech, the push is for awareness of financial costs. Nowhere (at least as reported by the authors) is there a push in the opposite direction. This would uniformly imply a less explorative approach to organizational learning and a more specific form of organizing. Surely, such changes should be strategic choices, based on an understanding of industry developments and competitive dynamics. They surely should not be unintended consequences of something as innocuous and neutral as a number.

7.3 Criscuolo et al: Bootlegging

There is a baseline assumption in systems like the State-Gate System that management "works" in the sense that managers can observe their workers, identify desirable and undesirable behavior, and get workers to change their behavior. This has been true of management generally throughout the modern history of the idea (Bernstein, 2017), and while workers may struggle to change their behaviors, change only slowly, reluctantly, or when properly incentivized, may not like the change, or may need to be told in particular ways, management is still considered capable of shaping subordinates' actions. For management to work, workers need at a basic level to comply with (or at least respond to) management. To do as they are told, as it were.

Alas, people do *not* always do as they are told, as will be perfectly obvious to anyone who has ever been told to do something. Management does not always work and does not always work very well when it actually works. Managing people may not be quite as bad as herding cats, but it is certainly not like herding sheep. People are difficult.

Bootlegging is a particularly acute example of this. Bootlegging describes the situation where innovation workers "take the initiative to work on ideas that have no formal organizational support and are often hidden from the sight of senior management but are undertaken with the aim of producing innovation" (p. 1288). It involves innovation workers doing work that avoids managerial observation and thereby also eschews managerial evaluation and direction, but not to subvert organizational goals. On the contrary, as Augsdorfer has documented, while bootlegging innovation workers do work around organizational procedures, they do so with the *intention* to support organizational goals of successful innovation. They do this work with limited resources – necessarily so because no formal resources are allocated for the activity – and yet manage to increase their innovative outputs because of it. Most of their activities also seem to be aligned with organizational interests. While bootlegging involves innovation workers *not* doing as they are told, the outcomes of bootlegging tend to be good. The main observation of Criscuolo et al's study, after all, is that bootlegging allows innovation workers to achieve higher levels of innovation performance. Bootlegging, essentially, is innovation without innovation management, but within innovation strategy. Good innovation, *pace* Cooper.

In this way, bootlegging stands in an interesting relation to formal innovation management of the kind we see exemplified in the Stage-Gate System, because it shows how people might adapt and react to being managed. First, it "allows individuals to explore divergent research directions that fall outside the remit of formal projects" (p. 1288). It is a way for people to engage ideas that may be more explorative than what formally managed processes allow for. Organizations may seek to corral employees' exploration through stages and gates, and employees may work around those efforts by simply keeping their work hidden.

They have discretion in deciding *what* goes into the Stage-Gate system. Second, it "allows individuals to delay the moment of monitoring and assessment by the organization until the idea is reasonably developed" (p. 1288). People might anticipate how their innovations will be evaluated at a particular stage and, especially for very early-stage ideas, avoid revealing them until they are quite certain that evaluations will be positive. In this way, there is also discretion in determining *when* something goes into the system. In other words, it is only a selected set of ideas that are subjected to management, and they are revealed at tactically opportune moments. Formal management and formalized innovation management procedures may direct innovation workers' efforts, but not directly. Innovation workers do not just let innovation management happen to them.

To understand how bootlegging impacts innovation, it is worth first considering why innovation workers might want to bootleg in the first place. One hypothesis would be that innovation workers are simply motivated by exploration and discovery. There is, after all, evidence to suggest that some scientists willingly "pay" (by foregoing higher compensation) to do science (Stern, 2004; see also Roach & Sauermann, 2010) and programmers accept lower wages in return for working with interesting IT systems (Tambe et al, 2020), and we can imagine that they willingly accept the risks associated with unsanctioned projects because of the intrinsic rewards those projects might bring. They may be personally invested in their ideas and be reluctant to simply get a "Hold" or "Kill" evaluation. Or, for projects that have already been "killed," workers may continue developing ideas in order to subsequently submit them for managerial evaluation. Another plausible hypothesis would be that innovation workers feel stifled by formal rules and claim autonomous, unstructured spaces for themselves. They might "need" that space, in a psychological sense, and may go out of their way to create it for the intellectual freedom that Stage-Gate Systems suppresses. It may increase motivation to have some amount of worktime set aside for engaging their own interests, and that might spill over into a better work environment that can attract more talented innovators.

Alas, given that both of those hypotheses have some real drama to them, it seems the answer is somewhat more mundane, if all the more telling for it. For Criscuolo et al, the central motive for bootlegging is simply to increase one's innovation performance: innovation workers want to do well (as assessed by their organizations), recognize that formal management of their work impedes their innovative performance, and hide some part of their innovation work to get a chance to perform better (in stark contrast to Cooper's equating of "better" with more tightly managed).

Bootlegging might allow them to have fewer projects rejected, because they shepherd their ideas into favorable positions. It might allow them to generate more variance in the quality of their ideas and select only high-value ideas to present. Or it might allow them to refine ideas so that they are more favorably evaluated than would have been the case if they had followed formal procedure. There are, in other words, good reasons for why innovation workers might benefit from hiding some of their innovative projects some of the time. They are in effect protecting the organization from itself and can do so given two conditions: the assessment of their performance is agnostic to *how* they develop innovations, and their innovations are generally aligned with organizational interests.

Bootlegging, then, is quite clearly a socially complex phenomenon. There are many intentions at work, many trade-offs to be considered, many interpretations of people and contexts being made, and so on. It is therefore not at all surprising that Criscuolo et al find that the effect of bootlegging on innovation performance is very sensitive to contingency. The innovative performance of the bootlegger's unit matters. People who bootleg in a highly innovative unit will be *more* innovative than people who also bootleg but do so in a less innovative unit. This may have to do with highly innovative units being given more discretion in their work, while lower-performing units may also be managed more closely. The level of bootlegging by others in the unit matters. People who bootleg in units where many people bootleg will be more innovative than people who bootleg in less bootlegging units. This may have to do with bootleggers being able to get more peer support in pursuing informal projects and more advice on how to (politically) transition an informal project into formal processes. The formalization of the innovation management process also matters. When innovation management is increasingly formalized (e.g., when a Stage-Gate System is implemented), people who bootleg do not benefit as much from doing so. This may have to do with bootlegging being more difficult to do, with bootlegged ideas getting valued lower, and with higher opportunity costs.

Alas, the complexity of bootlegging also extends to its study. It is not easy to study, or even observe, bootlegging behavior precisely because it is secret. "Capturing individual bootlegging efforts poses significant challenges for researchers because of the nonprogrammed and often secretive nature" (p. 1296). Why, after all, should people tell you their secrets? Secrets are secret for a reason, and promising people anonymity may remove some reluctance to share a secret (to the extent that people believe your promise of concealing their identity), but it hardly provides a motivation. To be more poignant: If innovation workers are willing to keep a secret from their managers and colleagues, why should they disclose it in a survey from a researcher that they do not know and have no reason to trust? The issue, then, is to consider the kinds of biases and distortions that the nature of the phenomenon introduces into the data about it. We might, for instance, expect some nontrivial element of nondisclosure, leading to many false negatives (i.e., people who bootleg, but do not disclose it) in the data set. We might expect that people who believe that they benefit from bootlegging will more readily reveal that they engage in the activity, leading to an overly positive assessment of bootlegging's influence on performance because failed bootlegging efforts are underreported – those who pursue ideas in secret, only to have them fail, may be reluctant to disclose that they bootlegged. We might also expect that those who do disclose (true positives) to be either in more supportive contexts or hold a more positive view of their organizations. Both situations might impact the moderating effects studied.

Irrespective of the methodological problems of studying it, the notion of bootlegging shows us something interesting about formal management of innovation. People can often work around formal processes – including formal innovation management processes – in different ways, and formal management can elicit informal counter-efforts, which may lead to unforeseen organizational effects. Innovation workers can, it seems, carve out autonomy to work on self-directed projects and may well engage also in other forms of "constructive disobedience" (Rennstam & Kärreman, 2020), rendering management somewhat less potent than assumed by, for instance, Cooper.

That said, formal management efforts may work in indirect ways, such as by making certain informal processes more difficult to engage in or benefit from or disciplining workers' expectations of what they might be able to get away with in the future. Formal systems do happen to workers, but workers also happen to systems and the outcomes of that interaction are very contextually contingent. As Bernstein (2017) puts it in his overview of observation and its effects in organizations, "[w]hen it comes to a battle between transparency and hiding, human ingenuity tends to defeat even the best system design. The result: increased transparency can actually decrease the observer's accurate awareness of the observed, due to the latter's hiding behaviors, and thus result not in more learning and control for the observer, but less" (p. 45).

7.4 Foss: Letting Emergence Reign (or Not)

Earlier in this chapter, I claimed that it would be unreasonable to simply throw money at R&D departments and hope for the best. But perhaps it would not be quite as unreasonable as it appears. It is, after all, hard to manage people, and getting them to stick to formal processes often does not work. It seems to be the case that *not* managing may actually work quite well, such as when people engage in unsanctioned innovation and turn out to be more efficient innovators for it. And management can be done in more indirect ways, such that for instance management accounting numbers can exercise considerable influence on decision-making, possibly substituting formal intervention under certain conditions (see also Kunda, 2006). You might, out of those claims, come to the hypothesis that nonmanagement might not be altogether bad, that it would (or could) perhaps be better to not manage innovation workers and innovation processes at all, or to do so only in very "light" ways. We could actually imagine replicating the logic of academic science and giving R&D departments a budget and an otherwise free rein.

Just as systems for managing innovation come and go, so do variations of *this* hypothesis. There are, as we have discussed, serious challenges with formal management of the innovation process and sometimes management concepts come along that seek to overcome those challenges by, in some form or another, setting innovation free and *not* managing it. Concepts like that tend to be launched with great fanfare and they are typically surrounded by adjectives such as "organic," "bossless," "nonhierarchical," and "flat" and a slew of buzzwords. As a genre, they tend to be heavy on utopianism (Ten Bos, 2000). A company like Google famously dedicated 20 percent of all employees' working time to projects that they themselves defined. Valve, the computer game company, has a "rule of three" where, if three employees think an idea is worthwhile, they are allowed to pursue it (Felin, 2016). Companies such as GitHub, Medium, and Zappos committed to a "Holacracy" model that allows workers to essentially self-organize around what they consider important (Bernstein et al, 2016). As so often happens for fashions, however, many organizations end up abandoning the free-wheeling concepts and retreating to something more classically Chandlerian (the abandonment of anti-managerial concepts often happens more quietly than the embrace of them). In doing so, they effectively seem to be suggesting that management of the innovation process, for all its discontents and challenges, is preferable to the alternative.

While we can pass off such adoption-and-then-abandonment as just another consequence of management fashion, it stands to reason that there is a deeper lesson to be learned here. Surely, understanding what goes awry with nonmanagement of innovation will help us to appreciate the value of management and managed approaches to innovation.

Foss' study of Oticon's "Spaghetti Organization" helps us understand the adoption and abandonment of a radically "flat" approach to

7.4 Foss: Letting Emergence Reign (or Not)

innovation management. Oticon was and is a Danish hearing-aid manufacturer. In 1991, the organization abandoned most of its hierarchical layers and switched to a project-based mode of organizing. "Development projects could be initiated by, in principle, any employee, just like entrepreneurs in a market setting" (p. 335), "employees would basically decide themselves which projects they would join" (p. 334), "there were no restrictions on the number of projects employees could voluntarily join" (p. 334), and "[p]roject managers were free to manage projects in their preferred ways" (p. 334). The little standardized management that was done was done by a "Products and Projects Committee." This committee approved or rejected projects. The only evaluation criteria were "that the relevant project relate to the business areas of Oticon and yield a positive return over a three-year period and with a discount rate of 30%"[1] (p. 337). This switch was accompanied by several complementary changes related to the physical layout of the organizational headquarters, the introduction of new IT to enable information sharing, a push toward a particular organizational culture, and the implementation of employee stock ownership.

Foss' study is couched in theories and framings from organizational economics. From this perspective, the Spaghetti Organization represents a radical case of what he terms an "internal hybrid." Production, this perspective suggests, can be coordinated through markets or hierarchies. Hierarchies have the advantages of "superior ability to perform coordinated adaptation to disturbance ... and share knowledge" (p. 336). Markets tend to be inherently fluid, offer superior incentives for good performance, allow for better use of heterogeneous knowledge, and enable autonomous adaptation and experimentation. An internal hybrid between a market and hierarchy is a hierarchical organization infused with elements of market control, and a radical internal hybrid is one that infuses the hierarchy with extensive market-like dynamics and allows for extensive unplanned emergence. In this way, the Spaghetti Organization sought to combine "the superior abilities of a hierarchy to build knowledge-sharing environments and foster a cooperative spirit with the flexibility and creativity of a market-like project organization" (p. 336). Many other concepts for nonmanagement of innovation are, in effect, variants of such internal hybrids.

The Spaghetti Organization seemed to deliver on these aims. A new paradigm of hearing-aid design (in-the-ear aids, as opposed to previous

---

[1] Having read Section 7.2, you should immediately recognize such a metric as altogether less neutral than it appears in Foss' description. You should feel prompted to ask what kind of learning and innovation this calculation is going to privilege and, a little more abstractly, how project initiators might go about creating the calculations that make their projects fit the criteria.

behind-the-ear aids) had recently pushed the industry into an era of ferment, and Oticon seemed at the outset unable to adapt. Some commentators suggested that "Oticon was locked into a competence trap that was reinforced by strong groupthink" (p. 333). Following the introduction of the Spaghetti Organization, Oticon broke through that trap and caught up to the technological discontinuity, aided by the discovery that (not altogether unsurprisingly, cf. 4.1) "Oticon already had embarked upon development projects for in-the-ear hearing aids as far back as 1979" (p. 335). Many new products were rapidly introduced, and development project time was cut in half. The numbers looked stellar: company revenues shot up and profit margins increased by an order of magnitude. In the slightly longer view, Oticon exists today as one of the world's leading hearing-aid providers. Before Spaghetti, it looked to be headed the same way as other victims of Creative Destruction. With Spaghetti and the tearing down of corporate hierarchies, it survived.

While it seems clear that the internal hybrid did work in this case, the question is *why* it worked or, more precisely, why Oticon was suddenly able to innovate so rapidly. Most centrally, the Spaghetti Organization allowed Oticon to make better use of its existing knowledge. The rediscovery of prior projects with in-the-ear solutions is one example of this. The knowledge of these projects had, we might infer, simply been lost to top management through some combination of information filtering (cf. 4.2) and organizational forgetting. More broadly, knowledge could be used better because of more efficient allocation of competence to problems. Innovation workers, in this case, seemed better able to determine where they might best contribute than their managers. In this way, the Oticon case is essentially a confirmation of the Austrian proposition that knowledge is highly dispersed and hard to aggregate, and a repudiation of the assumption that "managers are, on average, more knowledgeable with respect to what actions subordinate employees should optimally take than these employees are themselves" (pp. 338–339). Many other factors came into play, as Foss also outlines, and pulled in similar or different directions, but the ultimate, albeit overdetermined and emergent, outcome was rapid innovation, that customers turned out to value more than competing offers (over which Oticon, of course, had no control).

In light of how well Oticon performed, it can seem surprising that it ultimately abandoned the Spaghetti Organizations that supposedly "saved" it. In 1996, only five years after the introduction of the internal hybrid, it quietly transitioned away from the model and adopted an altogether much more conventional form of ("matrix") organization used in many other R&D contexts. That surprise raises another question: Why was the highly efficient model abandoned?

7.4 Foss: Letting Emergence Reign (or Not)

There could be many explanations for why such an organizational form might fail, because simply *working in them* could itself be quite complex (e.g., Kellogg et al, 2006). In Foss' explanation, the problem – theoretically foreseeable, but practically less so – that would ultimately make the Spaghetti Organization unsustainable was *selective intervention*. In internal hybrids, managers delegate decision rights and autonomy to subordinates. In doing so, they signal to subordinates that they will refrain from intervening, that is, that they will respect those subordinates' decision-making and not overrule it by intervening. However, because internal hybrids remain embedded in a hierarchical setting, managers still have the right to intervene. They may promise to respect subordinates' decisions *ex ante*, generally uphold the promise, but in certain cases break it. That is what we refer to as selective intervention: that managers manage in a hands-off fashion and intervene only occasionally (Williamson, 1996). Those occasions would, we might expect, be when they believe that positive gains will result from their interventions or when they are themselves pressured by superiors. "It is," Foss argues, "hard for [managers] to commit to a noninterference policy because reneging on a promise to delegate will in many cases be extremely tempting" (p. 341). In Oticon's case, workers were given far-reaching autonomy, but management was still enacted through the *Projects and Products Committee*. The conceptually foreseeable consequence was extensive politicking (i.e., "influence activities"). Also, "those to whom rights are delegated will anticipate [selective intervention]. Loss of motivation results" (p. 341).

For Foss, taking his cue from economic research comparing economic systems, the Projects and Products Committee comes to take on a role similar to the planning boards found in socialist planned economies.[2] For all the autonomy of Oticon workers, "[t]he fact that the Projects and Products Committee could veto a project ex ante suggests that it was the real holder of power in Oticon. Frequent intervention on the part of the Committee ex post project approval confirms this.... Thus, it became increasingly clear that the Committee could at any time halt, change, or even close projects" (p. 337). Irrespective of how much autonomy workers were ostensibly granted, the Committee retained the right to intervene and when intervention happened, workers perceived it as both unjustified

---

[2] It stands to reason that if you think this is reasonable, you should also find it quite reasonable to think of an organization as a sort of authoritarian dictatorship. If Oticon's Projects and Products Committee is metaphorically equivalent to the USSR's planning boards, surely Oticon would be equivalent to the USSR? That might sound farfetched, but see, for example, Anderson (2017) for an argument about why organizations are in fact best understood as a (private) form of communist dictatorship. Delong's chapter on really-existing socialism makes a similar argument (2022).

and arbitrary meddling in what was supposed to be self-organizing processes, and as a violation of the espoused value base. Consequently, promises of autonomy are not trustworthy. Knowing in advance that managers can intervene in projects leads workers to adapt their behavior, as they anticipate that management may intervene and when this is particularly likely. As tended to be the case under socialist planning, this "diluted incentives and badly harmed motivation" (p. 342).

This suggests a simple remedy and a "quick fix" for getting nonmanaged innovation to actually work. Managers, you might say, should commit to nonintervention and simply refrain from meddling. But can you really expect managers to sit idly by? When they perceive that unwise decisions are being made, unpromising opportunities pursued, and fruitless exploration undertaken? Generally put, the problem for Oticon's Spaghetti Organization, and possibly for other concepts of flattened hierarchies and nonmanagement, is that organizations *are* organizations, not markets. They are managed by managers whose job is managing *and therefore interfering*. There cannot really be formalized nonmanagement of innovation as long as that innovation happens within a formal organization. It is, as Foss quotes von Mises, hard to "'play[] market' inside hierarchies" (p. 341), and it remains something of a pretend game. The simple remedy is not so simple.

Perhaps a better, albeit more socially complex, remedy is to not attempt to formalize nonmanagement, but to embrace the hypocrisy of managing without managing, to accept that talk does not have to reflect action all the time (Brunsson, 1989). It is clearly the case that formal management of innovation is difficult *and* that formal nonmanagement is also difficult. At the same time, innovation workers who independently carve out a space for experimenting and innovating seem to do better than those who do not (see also Bernstein, 2012). Perhaps, then, the most efficient way to manage innovation is to embrace the rhetoric of formal management and to attempt to direct innovation processes, while at the same time making it less difficult for innovation workers to *informally* "do their own things," to pursue contrarian ideas and explorative learning with only those resources that they can informally gain access to, and to allow those ideas to liberally percolate into formal innovation projects (Augsdorfer, 2005). This is clearly another form of pretend game, but such is perhaps the nature of organizations?

There is an additional lesson to be gleaned from the Oticon case. Beyond Foss' analysis, the company also seems to represent a quite successful example of the sequential ambidexterity that I broadly disparaged in an earlier chapter. It was an organization "stuck" in an exploitative, highly specific state. In-the-ear designs ushered in an era of ferment. The organization was radically reorganized, transitioning rapidly to a highly fluid state and becoming in turn able to adapt to the technological discontinuity. When the era of ferment came to an end, the organization transitioned back to something more exploitative and specific, capable of elaborating the two (now coexisting) dominant designs. This is the essence of sequential ambidexterity. The Spaghetti Organization was, in this narrative, the right solution *in a particular time and place*, the right fit to a certain set of contingencies. When those contingencies changed, the concept was abandoned.

Perhaps, then, it is wrong to view it as a solution that had to endure and that could not be sustained for any number of reasons. Perhaps the Spaghetti Organization, or any other form of formalized nonmanagement, cannot be made to work well permanently, but that does not necessarily imply that they cannot be made to work for a time, and that interesting things cannot be accomplished with them in that time.

8 How Are New Technologies Brought to Market?

> **Texts in This Chapter**
>
> Moore, G. A. 1991 (2006). *Crossing the Chasm: Marketing and selling disruptive products to mainstream customers.* Collins Business Essentials.
>
> Lieberman, M. B. & Montgomery, D. B. 1988a. First-mover advantages. *Strategic Management Journal.* 9(S1), 41–58.
>
> Navis, C. & Glynn, M. A. 2010. How new market categories emerge: Temporal dynamics of legitimacy, identity and entrepreneurship in satellite radio, 1990–2005. *Administrative Science Quarterly.* 55(3), 439–471.

So far, we have looked at the challenges of generating new innovations, but that is of course not the end of the story. To bring about, or defend against, Creative Destruction, the product innovations that firms develop need to get into the market or otherwise diffuse. In the first reading, we look at how diffusion tends to happen and how, from a company's perspective, high-tech products might follow slightly different dynamics and call for substantively different strategies. Then, we address the question of *when* to enter an industry and bring a product to market, exploring the advantages that firms can try to capture by being a "first mover," and the disadvantages that they will have to grapple with along the way. Third, we explore what it means to bring innovative products to the market when those products are not yet understandable to their users and why markets for new technologies sometimes behave in very peculiar ways.

8.1 Moore: The Chasm, and Finding Beachhead Markets

Consider Morison's (1966) account of the invention and curiously slow diffusion of Continuous-Aim Firing, invented by Admiral Sir Percy Scott around 1900 and introduced to the American Navy by Lieutenant William Sims. Because it happened from a moving platform and without good sights, gunfire at sea was notoriously imprecise before Scott's invention. Naval artillery was simply not expected to hit anything unless firing at point-blank range. With Scott's invention, the accuracy of his gunners improved dramatically, some 3,000 percent. Sims encountered Scott's invention, recognized the value, and immediately wrote a report to inform his Navy superiors of the invention. Did they leap at the opportunity to dramatically improve an essential subsystem of the naval battleship, catapulting forward its functioning? No. Sims' report was brushed off as noncredible nonsense and filed away, literally to be eaten by cockroaches (p. 29). Sims persisted. The Navy relinquished, testing out the continuous-aim firing system. Alas, the test was done on dry land and found to *not* work (unsurprisingly, because it was done on land!), confirming to the Navy that Sims was definitely wrong. Sims persisted. He was dismissed as a "crackbrained egotist" (p. 31). Only when Sims wrote to the American president was the innovation implemented. Were it not for the presidential intervention, the innovation would surely have languished in obscurity.

Were it not for the ultimate success that Sims enjoyed, this story would seem bleak and disheartening to any innovator, but precisely for its bleakness, it speaks to a broader issue. "Many technologists believe," writes Rogers, "that advantageous innovations will sell themselves, that the obvious benefits of a new idea will be widely realized by potential adopters, and that the innovation will diffuse rapidly. Seldom is this the case" (Rogers, 2003, p. 7). On the contrary, it is often the case that the innovations – even those with obvious technical benefits for specific application – fail to diffuse, leaving technologists, futurists, innovators, entrepreneurs, and their investors disappointed (and poorer for their efforts). Why is this the case?

If we are to understand the dynamics of why some innovations diffuse, why some diffuse widely, and why some do not diffuse at all, *Diffusion of Innovation* (the book, first published in 1962, where the Rogers quote earlier is taken from) is the seminal place to begin. It lays out how the diffusion of innovations depends on characteristics of adopters and their social systems and also documents the process through which diffusion happens. There are lots of moving parts in the theory, but most famously Rogers advances the proposition that individuals who adopt at different times differ in fundamental ways from one another. There are, Rogers argues, five categories of adopters: innovators, early adopters, early majority, late majority, and laggards. The bell curve distribution of these categories and especially the idea of early adopters has diffused quite widely in popular discourse (pun intended).

The five adopter categories make up different shares of the total market and adopt for really different reasons. Innovators make up 2.5 percent of all adopters (assuming that the innovation fully diffuses), and they are the very first adopters of an innovation. They adopt primarily because of fascination with technology and tolerate high levels of risk that the innovation will not ultimately work. Early adopters (13.5 percent) adopt after innovators. They adopt not because of fascination with novelty, but because they expect substantial benefits from the technology. Their willingness to pay for a new product is typically high, as is their tolerance for working with and learning about new technologies. The early majority (34 percent) adopts after early adopters. These adopters postpone adoption until prices have fallen and technological uncertainty reduced (e.g., through the emergence of a dominant design) and base adoption decisions on the practical and proven value of the innovation. The late majority (also 34 percent) adopts after the early majority. These adopters are inherently skeptical about innovations. They want prices lowered, uncertainty all but eliminated, and ease of use improved before committing to adoption. Laggards (16 percent) adopt at the very end of the innovation's lifecycle and do so only reluctantly.

This is where Moore enters into the discussion. Rogers, Moore argues, is right about many things, but wrong about one really important thing, at least when the innovation to be diffused is a high-technology product. Moore readily accepts Rogers' five categories. Indeed, there are five psychographically different groups that adopt at different times across the lifecycle of a technology. Moore accepts the importance of *referencing* as crucial to the adoption decision. Rogers asserts in his book that the objective performance of a technology matters less to the adoption decision than the subjective experiences of near peers, transmitted to the potential adopter through word of mouth. What Moore does *not* accept is Rogers' claim that there are no breaks between the adopter categories. For Rogers, the five categories are ideal types, overdramatized distinctions. In empirical reality, the distinctions blur and "pronounced breaks in the innovativeness continuum do *not* occur between each of the five categories" (2003, p. 282, italics added). For Moore, there *are* breaks and they are significant. So significant, in fact, that overlooking them as Rogers does will trap you in the High Technology Marketing Illusion (and yes, this is only the beginning of the rhetorical drama that Moore uses to color his argument).

For Moore, there are two minor breaks that introduce nontrivial, but benign, challenges for high-tech marketing. The first break, a "crack in the bell curve" in Moore's parlance, is when firms shift from innovators to early adopters. "It is a gap that occurs when a hot new technology product cannot be readily translated into a major new benefit" (p. 17). To be adopted by early adopters, the new technology has to be shown to enable "some strategic leap forward ... which has an intrinsic value and appeal to the non-technologist" (p. 18). Unlike innovators, early adopters will not adopt simply because of the novelty of a technology, and so compelling applications need to be identified and explored. This is not easy (cf. 5.3), but it is doable. The second "crack" is when the firm shifts from serving the early majority to serving the late majority. "The key issue now ... has to do with demands on the end user to be technologically competent" (p. 18). Unlike the early majority, adopters in the late majority are not willing to have to work to become technologically competent. A product must be easy to get, implement, and use if the late majority is to adopt. While not straightforward, this is again a challenge that can be overcome.

The real challenge is the transition from early adopters to the early majority, and this transition represents a veritable chasm for high-tech firms. Early adopters, Moore asserts, are visionaries who will pay for, and accept the risk of, a new and unproven technology. They are "betting" on that great leap forward promised by new technology. By contrast, adopters in an early majority are pragmatists. They "are prudent souls who do not want to be pioneers ('pioneers are people with arrows in their backs'), who never volunteer to be an early test site ('let somebody else debug your product'), and who have learned the hard way that the 'leading edge' of technology is all too often the 'bleeding edge'" (pp. 41–42). They do not want risk if it can be avoided, and they do not want an experimental product. They want a standardized product, lower prices, reliability, and, importantly, competing products to choose from.

Because of these differences, visionary early adopters are *unlikely* to be credible sources of word-of-mouth recommendations for the pragmatist early majority. In fact, positive descriptions of a technology product by a visionary early adopter may even alienate and discourage adopters in the early majority, because they are looking for something fundamentally different from the early adopter. As a consequence, the high-tech firms may well experience that it suddenly runs out of positive references to drive further sales. "There is," in Moore's paraphrasing of a Zen proverb, "a market. Then there is no market. Then there is" (p. 27). The market for a new technology may suddenly be saturated, just as it was beginning to grow, because the customer has profoundly changed and because the references that propelled early growth cease to drive expansion into mainstream markets. That is why the Chasm is littered with the broken bodies of failed technologies and entrepreneurial ventures that no one remembers.

Crossing the Chasm is difficult because it requires substantive change to the product. Early majority customers "want *the whole product* to be readily available from the outset" (p. 111, italics added), as opposed to innovators and early adopters who (more) happily figure things out and piece solutions together themselves. The whole product, as Moore defines it, comprises not just the generic, "in-the-box" product. The whole product covers everything that a mainstream customer will need to use the product in a way that lets them realize the benefit they expected to get from the purchase: the tools to integrate the product with existing systems, any additional software they might need, training and support tools, installation and debugging, additional hardware and cables, and so on (p. 113). Importantly, when a company begins to address mainstream markets, "investing in additional R&D at the generic level has a decreasing return," while investments that expand the whole product to meet the needs of early majority customers begin to have increasing returns. When marketing to early adopters, those whole product investments are not really called for.

This introduces a very particular need for *focus*, Moore asserts. A focus that is akin to choosing a *beachhead* in over-the-beach invasions: the firm must commit to a single point of attack and concentrate all of its efforts on that single point, because spreading the invasion force across too wide of an area eliminates the possibility of gaining momentum in any one area. Momentum, Moore asserts, is as necessary for chasm-crossing as for invasions. In the case of transitioning into mainstream markets, firms must commit to a beachhead market of early adopters, precisely because they now have to deliver whole products, as opposed to generic products. Generic products can meaningfully be sold to multiple types of early adopters because early adopters "fill in the gaps" to adapt the solution to their particular needs. By contrast, any particular segment of early majority users will make demands on the firm to tailor the *whole* product to address their specific needs, and trying to deliver whole products to multiple segments will often lead to underfulfilling the needs of all of them. That becomes a problem precisely because early majority adopters, if they are to positively reference the product to others in the early majority, need to get a whole product that fully fulfills their needs. So, committing to a single beachhead is called for. Organizations *need* to find a narrow segment of early majority customers to market to specifically. Without commitment, there will be another body in the chasm.

This, unsurprisingly, is difficult. Not only is commitment to a particular segment uncertain – the choice of which segment to commit to is a moment of true Rosenbergian uncertainty (cf. 2.3) – but also the required change to the product requires extensive organizational change. A company offering whole products to specific markets is different from one offering generic ones to multiple markets (cf. 4.2). R&D transitions from a technology focus to a market focus, and organizational learning transitions toward exploitation. The pioneering salespeople and innovation workers that were essential for early success may be "liabilities" after crossing the chasm (p. 200). The organization not only has to begin hiring a different sort of employee (one content to serve the mass market through incremental developments); it also has to develop procedures to ensure reliability, building itself toward bureaucratic specificity and becoming less agreeable to innovators in the "romantic" mold (cf. 1.3). Concomitantly, the organization adopts performance metrics that push attention toward the bottom line (cf. 7.2). It may also be at this point that the organization's leadership transitions from the entrepreneurial founder toward a professional manager because the founder may also be turning into a liability (Greiner, 1998). A company that crosses the chasm is a changed company.

All of these difficulties raise interesting questions. Why would one even bother taking this route? Why try to cross the chasm? Why not stay with early markets and serve early adopters? The economics of serving early markets play a significant role here. Early markets are by definition small and serving them is expensive, and so it makes "sense" to leave them behind in favor of larger and more easily served markets when possible. Early investors, having accepted substantial risk by investing in the company, will be pushing for a successful company to monetize that success through some "meteoric rate of return" (p. 192) to offset the losses that investors make on the majority of investments (Nicholas, 2019). In this way, accepting money from investors pre-chasm tends to force post-chasm commitments on the organization to grow, and growth means transitioning into the mainstream market. It is, however, not obvious that innovative firms *necessarily* need to make the transition. You might for instance consider Mouritsen et al's SuitTech (Section 7.2) as an organization that successfully operates in a pre-Chasm market and has found a way to do so sustainably. Moreover, it is a myth that technology-based ventures de facto need venture capital (Catalini et al, 2019) and so certainly there are circumstances where technology organizations can avoid the commitments that force upon them the need for crossing the chasm.

8.2 Lieberman and Montgomery: First-Mover Advantages and Risks

Is it important to be the first to bring a product to market? Popular wisdom suggests that it is incredibly important, and some examples might lead you to agree. Amazon, for instance, was first to bring an online bookstore to market in a large-scale way. But there are other examples that would suggest a "no" to the question. Google in a sense was the *last* search engine company.[1] Facebook was neither the first nor the last social network. In a strategic and financial sense, all three companies do well (so well in fact that trying to learn from their example borders on being meaningless – they are incredible outliers). What are we to think, then? Does being first-to-market matter?

What is at stake in this question is "order-of-entry effects," in Lieberman and Montgomery's terms, and how first-mover firms (can) capture enduring benefits from early market entry. Are there *first-mover advantages*? And where do they come from?

Consider first the downsides to bringing a new product to market, the first-mover *dis*advantages. A first mover necessarily undertakes investments that later entrants can free-ride on. Being the first to market a product may well require extensive innovation development effort, and because *ideas* are nonrivalrous and only partially excludable goods (Romer, 1990), late-movers might be able to benefit from the costly learning of early entrants, in some cases at no cost. Consequently, they may be able to offer products more cheaply than the first mover. In addition to investments, first movers undertake considerable market and technological uncertainty and by their action in the market reduce that uncertainty (cf. 9.1). They may pursue opportunities that turn out to not be viable or valuable, and late movers can learn from their example and make more informed decisions than were possible for early entrants, and avoid the failure traps of pioneers. Moreover, when first-movers become incumbents, they begin to suffer all the liabilities that this entails, most notably inertia and inability to adapt to changes in markets and technologies that occur after their entry. Indeed, it is not obvious that being first is necessarily a good thing.

Early entry can, however, confer several different sorts of advantages, and Lieberman and Montgomery group them into three categories: technological leadership, the enduring effects of early buyer choices, and the pre-emption of scarce assets. Not all advantages will apply to all early entrants, and there is, as the authors state in a later paper, no guarantee that any potential advantages associated with early entry are "sufficient to ensure a strong position as the market evolves" (1998b, p. 1113). Moreover, there will certainly be *more* potential sources of competitive advantage than the ones listed here, being more or less relevant across specific cases.

---

[1] Or, rather, the last search engine company of its generation. Generative artificial intelligence (AI) may well turn out to bring the search industry back to an era of ferment (cf. Section 3.2).

Technological leadership comes from two sources. First, being a first mover may allow a firm to capture patents that preclude imitation of their innovations or that bar competitors from entering into the field by barring their access to foundational technologies in it. Patent protection is temporary by definition and not all innovations can be protected under patent laws. Also, to be awarded a patent, an innovation must be disclosed, meaning that others can attempt to copy it. As a consequence, some firms rely on secrecy instead of patenting, but this secrecy (unlike patents) does not preclude others from developing the same technology as the secret-keeping innovator. Second, being first can allow a firm to get a head start on learning, which may translate into that firm being able to offer products cheaply (through "learning curve effects"). There are certain products for which it is the case that production costs decline very sharply as production volume and experience increase. An early entrant that can push costs down very quickly can deter competitive entry through that route, because later entrants will struggle to compete on price (absent competition or, at least, the *threat* of competitive entry, the early entrant might simply charge monopoly prices).

Early buyer choice can similarly confer advantage in two ways. Buyers make choices under uncertainty, and being first to market may lead a firm to attract attention or shape customer perceptions in a way that will be difficult for later entrants to match. It is, for instance, unlikely that any electric carmaker, or any electric car marketed by incumbent automakers, will attract the adulation of commentators or devoted praise from early adopters that Tesla and its vehicles have attracted. Considering Moore's argument (Section 8.1), it also seems likely that being first to break into mainstream markets and offer a "whole product" may reduce the uncertainty of adoption for a nontrivial share of customers (see also Hoffman & Yeh's [2018] suggestion of first-*scaler* advantage). Buyers, having made an investment in the product offered by an early entrant, will also face a switching cost of moving to a competing product. Buyers may not want to spend the time searching for a new solution if that search is effortful ("transaction costs"), they may not want to spend the effort required to learn how to use a new solution (costs of "supplier-specific learning"), or there may be demands of exclusivity associated with the adoption of early entrants' products ("contractual switching costs").

Finally, early entry allows for the preemption of scarce assets: acquiring assets that are necessary, or merely important, before competitors recognize that those assets are in fact central to competing effectively. In some cases, input factors (e.g., raw materials, manufacturing capacity, employees with specific skills) may be available more cheaply than will be the case later on, as the entrants industry evolves and market participants come to understand their "true" value (cf. 9.1). An early entrant may also be able to establish control of scarce resources that to some extent "lock out" future competitors, provided alternative input factors are not available. In other cases, early entrants might engage in "spatial preemption." While empirically rare, an early entrant might be able to capture "spaces" that are necessary to reach consumers, such as physical shelf space, actual geographic spaces, or more cognitive categorical spaces (cf. 8.4). In other empirically rare cases, early entrants can, by preemptive investing in manufacturing capacity and undertaking other sunk costs, signal to potential competitors that they are strongly committed to the industry and willing to engage in intense price competition, denying others potential profits. Such signals could, in principle, deter entry (or simply be interpreted as folly and bad economics).

For Montgomery and Lieberman, first-mover advantages like the above are built up through a combination of proficiency and luck but are contingent on industry circumstances. First movers can proficiently use foresight to make deliberate choices about how to design their products, for instance, those that create switching costs and confer a first-mover advantage, or can seek to strategically secure control of important assets. They might also through sheer luck "stumble upon" advantages simply by doing something under conditions of uncertainty that then turns with hindsight to have conferred considerable advantages. However, whether first-mover advantages can in fact be built up and sustained is also very much beyond the control of the firm. The rate of technological change, the evolution of a market, and the emergence of dominant designs might play central roles (e.g., Suarez & Lanzolla, 2007; Dowell & Swaminathan, 2006), meaning that some industries will be more impacted by order of entry than others. Nonetheless, it is standard fare in strategic management to suggest that early entrants should at the very least attempt to capitalize on making it into an industry early. As Porter (1985) puts it,

successful technological leaders actively pursue first-mover advantages rather than rely solely on their technological edge. They take every opportunity to use their technological leadership to define the competitive rules in ways that benefit them. They invest in marketing to reinforce the reputation benefits of being the leader, and price aggressively to make early sales to buyers with the highest switching costs. (pp. 72–73)

Whether by proficiency, luck, or circumstance, technological leadership, buyer choice under uncertainty, and preemption of scarce assets all seem capable of conferring competitive advantage (Porter, 1980) in the sense that they allow a firm to reap profits that would not otherwise be reapable, at least for a time. However, this interpretation misses that the competitive advantage conferred by early entry comes, in most cases, from *competitive avoidance*, from successfully foreclosing competition by deterring subsequent entry or entirely locking competitors out of the market by erecting insurmountable barriers to entry. First-mover advantages are largely a matter of "building a moat" around the first-mover idea (e.g., Gans et al, 2018), such that later entrants cannot threaten the first-mover, allowing them in effect to act as monopolists and dampen the anxiety of competitive threats (cf. 1.1). It is, in most cases, not the sort of advantage that comes from offering better, cheaper, or more innovative products to consumers, but the advantage that comes from barring others from doing so. It is not winning the race by running fastest (i.e., competitive performance), it is winning the race by keeping competitors off the field (i.e., competitive avoidance), so to say. In that capacity, it is most certainly socially valuable that they are transitory, and that early entrants might overestimate them.

There is one slightly glaring, final thing to say about first-mover advantages: not everyone gets to *choose when to enter*. "Firms," as Lieberman and Montgomery state in a later paper, "may be *forced* to positions of late entry" (1998b, p. 1113, italics added) if they do not have the innovative capabilities required to pioneer. But *somebody has to make the first move*. It is good that someone does it, and it seems that capitalism uniquely encourages it.

8.3   Navis and Glynn: Collaboration, Then Competition

Christensen argued that one of the central organizational causes of disruptive innovation is that *markets that do not exist cannot be analyzed*. To innovate disruptively, he argued, meant (among other things) to find consumers not currently consuming, either because no product was available for them to consume or because available products overshot their needs and budgets. This issue of nonexistence is, however, not only a feature of disruptive innovation. It is a feature of marketing of new technology much more broadly. When a new technology is developed, there may well be no obvious market to address with it, no obviously valuable problem to solve (cf. 2.3). Once a potential application is found and a beachhead market identified (cf. 8.1.), it might also be the case that consumers in that imagined market do not understand what the technology actually is, or what it is meant to do for them, or how to make sense of it. The "product category" might not yet exist.

A *market category* exists "when two or more products or services are perceived to be of the same type or close substitutes for each other in satisfying market demand; the organizations producing or supplying these related products or services are grouped together as members of the same market category" (p. 440). A company is able to claim to produce cars, smartphones, Virtual Reality headsets, organic pet food, or management consulting services and when it does, consumers and other audiences understand because these are distinct market categories. Categories and the labels attached to them "describe the core features or underlying concept of the category, articulating its shared identity and carrying identity codes that set audiences' expectations" (p. 441, references excluded). When people say something to the effect of "An alien looks down on Earth and sees people sitting in metal boxes that go fast and often collide with deadly consequences," what they are describing is a situation absent categories, and therefore absent taken-for-granted meaning that we use to make things intelligible. In turn, categories help *legitimate* companies belonging to the category. Legitimacy is what enables companies to "acquire resources and create wealth" (p. 439). What that alien saw, after all, is not going to sell a lot of SUVs.

Market categories, despite all their taken-for-grantedness, do not come into the world fully formed; they do not simply exist. Rather, they emerge through deliberate efforts. A "nascent market category is characteristically ambiguous or ill-structured" (p. 439). They begin as "unstable, incomplete and disjoined conceptual systems held by market actors" (Rosa et al, 1999, p. 64). They stabilize because particular efforts turn out to be successful: efforts by producers to bring the category into existence and efforts of audiences (customers, investors, commentators, etc.) to make sense of it. Only when a category fully emerges, stabilizes, and becomes legitimate does it begin to assume that taken-for-granted quality. The question for the new-technology marketer, then, is how actors in industries that do not yet exist create legitimacy around those yet-to-be-legitimate categories.

To see how actors try to create such legitimacy, Navis and Glynn's study looks at the development of satellite radio industry from 1990 to 2005. In 1990, a start-up petitions the US Federal Communications Commission to allow satellite radio by allocating satellite radio stations space in the frequency spectrum. In 1997, two "digital audio radio service" licenses were put on auction. The two companies that would ultimately be named Sirius and XM bought a license each. During the period of "emergence" (1997–2001), these two companies launched satellites, created receiver chipsets, and partnered with automakers to get satellite radio reception into automobiles. In 2002 ("commercialization"), "the technology advances, penetration into retail consumer markets [occurs], and increases in radio subscriptions of the earlier period yielded widespread commercialization" (p. 452). Then comes a period of "early growth" (2003–2005) where markets expand considerably, and further technological improvement enables new applications of the technology. The firms also focus increasingly on content development and begin to appeal more strongly to mainstream consumer markets.[2] Across these discernable stages, the ways XM and Sirius legitimacy-building efforts change, and audience perceptions of the companies also change.

During emergence, the two firms work to advance the legitimacy of the category as a whole and downplay their differences and the unique achievements of the individual firm. What they are promoting and normalizing is the collective identity of "satellite radio" as something distinct from other forms of radio and related technologies. Both firms present their own and their competitor's achievements as advancing the industry, not their own interests. The partnerships that they establish are not exclusive but shared so as to create value for the category. The partnerships are also used to signal that the category, as opposed to the individual firm, is viable. In turn, audiences interpret the firms as "undifferentiated actors within a new market category that was becoming increasingly comprehensible, real, and appealing" (p. 452). Like the firms themselves, audiences are making comparisons between satellite radio and terrestrial radio. The achievements of the individual firms are used to suggest that the industry as a whole is viable.

During commercialization, the category first seems to reach a threshold of legitimacy. It is at this point that the two firms begin to claim distinctiveness from one another. They both refer to their membership of the category but also begin to "index[] their claimed gradient of membership" (p. 454). They emphasize their distinct value and their distinct visions for what they will become and what they will offer. Audiences pick up on this distinctiveness, and market analysts begin to describe how the two firms pose competitive threats to each other and the particular challenges that the individual firm will have to contend with, as opposed to their shared challenges.

During early growth, firms begin to position themselves as direct competitors. They describe themselves as differentiated from each other and promote themselves and not the category. It is now meaningful to claim to be the leading provider of satellite radio (because the category now exists) and both try to claim that identity, typically by focusing on specific consumer groups and dominating the delivery of content to that

---

[2] The study stops in 2005, and so does not cover the lead-up to 2008, when the two firms merge. So much for differentiation.

group. Both firms also aggressively pursue partnerships that are deliberately exclusive in order to "shut out" the other (p. 455). The firms' distinctiveness becomes clearer to audiences. Analysts will now analyze their specific advantages and the degree of those advantages, such that one firm may be claimed to be 12 months ahead in technology development, while the other has a modest advantage in content. The two companies also get described as engaged in a "pitched battle" (p. 456).

This demonstrates two very distinct competitive dynamics playing out over time. Before the legitimacy of the category is established, the firms effectively collaborate, jointly competing against *other* categories. They are distinct firms, but their fates are closely tied to the fate of the category and so the creation of the category is their primary and shared goal. Then, once the category achieves legitimacy, this collective effort ceases and firms shift to distinguishing themselves from others *within* the category. They begin to make claims to unique identities, begin to "talk up" their differences, and mobilize affiliations that mark them out as different from other firms in the category. In turn, audiences shift from focusing on the category collective to the identities of the individual firm. It is only at that point that the two firms begin to compete against each other in earnest.

As an example of this, consider the emergence of the "plant-based meat" category. At the time of writing, the revenues generated in this category are almost decimal dust compared to those of what we might call a Meat Industrial Complex and widespread legitimation has yet to occur. It was, therefore, not entirely surprising – given Navis and Glynn's argument – to hear the CEO of Impossible Foods (a company that has invested extensively in basic and applied food science to re-engineer meat and make it from plant-based components) describe increased competition from other plant-based meat producers as positive for the category in an interview with Vergecast (March 24, 2020). Increased competition, he argued, helped Impossible Foods in growing the category and, ultimately, taking down the animal-based meat industry. This suggested, as Navis and Glynn would, that the "real" competition in a pre-legitimate category is not within-category competition but across-category competition and that more within-category competition is actually a benefit for pre-legitimate category actors. What was perhaps more interesting was the caveat presented in that same interview, namely that more within-category competition was *only* beneficial if it came from firms capable of delivering high-quality products, that is, products that would in a post-legitimate category be considered serious competitive threats. Entrants offering low-quality products, the CEO argued, would actually impede the legitimation of the category by reinforcing audience perceptions that plant-based meats typically, in his words, sucked. "I wish that all those other companies would make something equally delicious [i.e., on par with Impossible Foods]. That would actually be better for us" (22.10–22.59). This certainly inverts the usual logic of competitive markets.

What this shows is how the scope of possible positions that a firm might adopt changes over time. It is clear that firms generally need to differentiate themselves, striking a balance between some level of sameness with others in their category with a level of uniqueness from them (Brewer, 1991). Assimilating into a category is important to be considered by audiences in the first place, but being unique is required to be selected from among the options considered, and different audiences and circumstances might well impact what level of distinctiveness is in fact optimal (see, e.g., Zuckerman, 2016b). However, while firms might aspire to a particular position that it would consider optimal, the choice of position is limited by the opportunities afforded by particular categories and, more generally, the maturity of the category in which they operate. Prior to category legitimization, it may not be possible to adopt a position of distinctiveness that audiences will recognize, and so firms may be forced to forego their pursuit of distinctiveness until a category is sufficiently stabilized. What may be optimal once a category is legitimate might well be self-defeating before, and what is optimal prior to category legitimation may be insufficient after.

More broadly, this problematizes the idea that firms should aggressively pursue first-mover advantages. First-mover advantages, often, serve to exclude competitive entry into an industry, such that the first-mover can maintain a strong position in it – they can serve as "isolating mechanisms" that prevent competitive imitation or entry (Suarez & Lanzolla, 2007). However, if first-mover advantages are successfully pursued and competition excluded, the first-mover firm might find itself alone in trying to build up the legitimacy of the category. Were this to be the case, several outcomes are imaginable. The firm might succeed, in which case a brand might become the category. Airbnb seems in some respects to encapsulate this, but this strategy certainly brings with it the risk of incurring large costs of building up this identity. The first-mover firms might also be forced to persistently differentiate themselves relative to established categories, maintaining a perpetual outsider status in the eyes of consumers. In the counterfactual situation where Sirius successfully excluded XM by capturing decisive first-mover advantages, for instance, that firm might have had to forego developing a novel category and simply continuously position itself as a competitor to terrestrial radio, with somewhat uncertain implications for further competition.

Finally, the first-mover firm might simply fail to create legitimacy for the novel category, becoming in turn unable to acquire further resources that it would need to develop (e.g., Navis et al, 2012). In what might perhaps instead be thought of as "joint-mover advantages," "firms' collective efforts that downplay their distinct, competitive advantages can offer entrepreneurial advantages in an emerging market category, even in a potential 'winner takes all' duopoly" (p. 466).

9 What Do Entrepreneurs Do?

> **Texts in This Chapter**
>
> Schumpeter, J. A. 1934 (1911). The theory of economic development: The fundamental phenomenon of economic development. In *The entrepreneur: Classic texts by Joseph A. Schumpeter*, ed. M. Becker, T. Knudsen & R. Swedberg. Stanford University Press.
>
> Baumol, W. J. 1990. Entrepreneurship: Productive, unproductive, and destructive. *Journal of Political Economy*. 98(5), 893–921.
>
> Gans, J. S., Hsu, D. H. & Stern, S. 2002. When does start-up innovation spur the gale of creative destruction. *The RAND Journal of Economics*. 33(4), 571–586.
>
> Nightingale, P. & Coad, A. 2013. Muppets and gazelles: Political and methodological biases in entrepreneurship research. *Industrial and Corporate Change*. 23(1), 113–143.

It would be remiss to have a discussion of innovation without addressing the role that entrepreneurs and entrepreneurship can play in it. To begin that discussion, we turn first to Schumpeter's early work and its enthusiastic (almost theatrical) celebration of the entrepreneur and Baumol's historical analysis of what it is about our current economic system that leads entrepreneurship to take particularly productive forms and not the unproductive and destructive forms that might have dominated earlier epochs. Then, we problematize. With Gans et al, we explore what conditions might contribute to entrepreneurship spurring Schumpeter's gale of Creative Destruction and think about why any rational entrepreneur would even attempt to do so. To close the chapter, Nightingale and Coad lay bare the counterintuitive argument that entrepreneurs, for all the bravado and cultural celebration, typically really don't do that much. Much of what most people believe to be true about entrepreneurs, it turns out, is just a result of survivorship biases and other methodological problems.

9.1 Schumpeter: Enter the Entrepreneur, Resplendent

As mentioned earlier (Section 1.3), there is a stark difference between the young Schumpeter (of "The Theory of Economic Development," from 1911) and the mature Schumpeter (of "Capitalism, Socialism and Democracy," from 1942). While the mature Schumpeter would look to large, incumbent firms as the instigators of economic development, the young Schumpeter located the entrepreneur at the heart of the process of economic development.[1] The entrepreneur "is *the* cause of *economic development*" (p. 111, italics in original) and "[a]ll development happens only through him, only through his energy"[2] (p. 132).

Schumpeter begins his argument with a description of the economy in a state of constancy, "an economy without development" (p. 83). This is what he refers to as an economy in a static state of "circular flow" (not unlike "eras of incremental change," cf. Section 3.2), with well-trodden paths of behavior by well-behaved, rational economic agents. In this economy, "nothing 'new' will ever be created, no *independent* development of each field will take place; there will only be passive adaptation and drawing consequences from data." It is an economy well-analyzed with the theories and tools of the economics of the day and, as well the asserted case of eras of incremental change, this is reasonable enough because this is the modal state of economy and the society more broadly throughout the history of humanity. When this book was published, it was Schumpeter's claim that economics as a discipline generally functioned in describing this state of the economy, but failed in explaining precisely why economies actually developed, why the society of his day was so profoundly different from that of ages past.

Before turning to the dynamism, it is worth understanding why economics worked (and works) well under conditions of stability. In such situations, economic agents are not just well-behaved and rational. They are also both placid and hedonic. These economic agents act in the world primarily with the intention of fulfilling basic ("hedonic") needs, working more or less to make a comfortable living. They may or may not have ideas and develop insights, but they do not act on them, preferring instead stability and predictability. Human psychology predisposes

---

[1] Do note that this chapter relies on Becker's translation of the *first* version of *The Theory of Economic Development* (from 1911) and not the revised second version (from 1934) that was the basis the first English translation. In the revised edition, Schumpeter would soften many of his claims about the entrepreneur and focus more on the "entrepreneurial function." We use this version because it highlights the discontinuity in Schumpeter's thinking and because of its very stark vision of the entrepreneur. It is the high-contrast version of the argument, not necessarily the most reasonable version.

[2] To Schumpeter, being the product of his times, the entrepreneur is always a man.

9.1 Schumpeter: Enter the Entrepreneur, Resplendent

them to this preference, because "[f]ollowing a well-trodden path is infinitely easier than setting out on a new one" (p. 91). Moreover, humans exert social pressure on one another not to stick out and most people very reasonably conform to those pressures. Taken together, these two factors conspire to create in economic agents a "static-hedonic disposition." Much like how the economy is modally in a state of circular flow, so too do people of this disposition make up the broad, broad masses of human society. Such people "do not have the disposition to experiment with something new. Even when it occasionally happens that they have an idea that this or that might be done better or more easily – they lack the moral courage to try ... organization as well as the influence of their colleagues inflicts untearable chains on them" (p. 122).

Enter, then, the Entrepreneur.

The Entrepreneur is a very distinct type, fundamentally different from the typical economic agent and up to something equally different. "Most people do not see the new combinations. They do not exist to them ... [but] A minority of people with sharper intelligence and with a more agile imagination perceive countless new combinations" (p. 122). It is to this minority that entrepreneurs belong and not only do they see new combinations, they also refuse to be cowed by the resistance that weighs others down as they create those new combinations, bringing them into the world and forcing them through to the market. This is the essence of the entrepreneur's *creative construction*. It is driven by an energetic and dynamic impulse that allows these rare leaders and "men of action" to "vigorously rise above the masses" (p. 100). They are "not cowards who incessantly ask themselves anxiously whether any effort they were making would lead to a sufficient excess in pleasure" (p. 104). Instead, they boldly take up insurmountable challenges. To them, "obstacles actually represent more of an incentive than a deterrent" (p. 100) as entrepreneurs "scorn[] the hedonic equilibrium and face[] risks without timidity."

Why? Because they cannot help it. Entrepreneurs are motivated to engage in the kind of audacious behavior by the joy of creating, an inability to *not* be active, and a deep desire simply to *win* and be the best. They "[do] not care about the hedonic fruits of their deeds.... Such men work because they cannot do otherwise" (p. 104). They are so possessed by energy and determination that they are best understood as having "exactly the same foundations as the creative actions of the artist, the thinker, or the statesman ... the only difference is the object of action" (p. 107). The entrepreneur is, in other words, an artist transposed into the economic domain and best understood as such – it is only the mode of expression that differs, such that what artists express in art is what entrepreneurs express in the economic domain. For such entrepreneurs, "the laws of economic behavior that rest on hedonic motives also disappear, as the hedonic motives do not apply.... The measure of what has been achieved never becomes a reason for settling down to rest" (p. 110).

You may have gotten the sense (it certainly gets built up) that *this* entrepreneur has a profoundly transformative effect on the economy. The role Schumpeter affords entrepreneurs is to jolt the economy and its economic agents out of their placidity. They personify and force through discontinuity. They *disequilibrate*, propelling the economy out of the equilibrium that is the "circular flow." Where static-hedonic agents draw inferences from data, the entrepreneurs *shape* the data, changing their form, shifting their context, and moving the world through the Archimedean lever of their will. Where static-hedonic economic actors respond to demand, the entrepreneur "does not just follow given demand, [but] forces his products on the market" (p. 101). The entrepreneur educates the consumer, creating demand that was not there before. In the altogether less floral terminology of microeconomics, this disequilibration takes the form of shifting supply curves, changing demand curves and thereby bringing about a new market equilibrium.[3]

The entrepreneur, to Schumpeter, is a genius and a hero. The entrepreneur is different in kind from other agents (economic agents, in this case) and almost otherworldly. As Hamilton (1957) put it, the entrepreneur "performs miracles of production" (p. 250), has a "color and flair not granted to any of the other characters in the economic drama" (ibid.) and is "gifted with the powers of 'foresight', 'initiative', and 'enterprise'" (ibid.). This figure towers above the drudging masses that comprise the populace by virtue of their superior endowment of skills and their very particular psychology, and effects what is almost superhuman change (Becker et al, 2003).

This account, because of its grandeur and exaggeration, can feel almost farcical, but it becomes more intelligible when we think about the kind of ideas that informed it. The entrepreneurial genius is pure genius in the mold of nineteenth-century German Romanticism. As Reinert and Reinert (2006) argue, the young Schumpeter draws directly

---

[3] For an interesting discussion of how entrepreneurship might *also* contribute to less dramatic developments in the market process, see, for example, Kirzner (1978) and comparisons between the "creative" Schumpeterian entrepreneur and the "alert" Kirznerian one (Kirzner, 1999). Needless to say, not every entrepreneur is of the Schumpeterian kind, and Kirzner gives us an interesting take on what entrepreneurship as a more distributed activity might entail. Schumpeter's entrepreneur clearly plays a key role in economic development but does not for that reason represent a useful description of entrepreneurship generally. By analogy: some inventions change the world, but those inventions are not good examples of the typical invention.

and indirectly on the intellectual legacy of German philosophers such as like Hegel, Schopenhauer, and especially Nietzsche. The focus on the entrepreneur as a *willful* creator borrows heavily from Nietzsche's ideas of the "will to power" and of the "noble man" that is driven to create. The distinction between the entrepreneur and the static-hedonic masses, similarly, draws from Nietzsche's distinction between the Übermensch ("compelled by the inner necessity constantly to overcome himself and eventually even his own humanity," ibid., p. 66) and the Letzte Mensch ("the prelude to the worst of all human specimens, the 'most despicable man', the embodiment of decline," ibid., p. 66). Schumpeter's confrontation with economics as a discipline was precisely to allow for this creative genius and the kind of agency that they could have.

It is, I think, fundamentally interesting to think about the trajectory of this image of the entrepreneur. Schumpeter – who no doubt thought of himself as akin to the Romantic genius of German Romantic philosophy (cf. Reinert & Reinert, 2006; McCraw, 2007) – developed this image in the early 1900s, but then toned down his singular focus on the entrepreneur as he revised the book and developed his ideas, before ultimately abandoning the idea of entrepreneurs as central to economic development. In the 1990s, with the rise of the internet-propelled New Economy, we not only entered the "Age of Schumpeter" (Giersch, 1984) but also saw entrepreneurs rise to prominence in the popular imagination with what some have called a "cult of entrepreneurship" (Gehman & Soubliere, 2017). With this rise, entrepreneurs began to be described (and, increasingly, to self-describe) in ways strikingly similar to those of the early Schumpeter. Consider, for instance, how figures like Steve Jobs and Elon Musk are depicted in popular culture, respectively in messianic and superheroic terms. Or how entrepreneurs describe themselves, their ventures, and what it takes to be a "real" entrepreneur (e.g., Hoffman & Yeh, 2018; Masters & Thiel, 2014). Indeed, we can see this as the pendulum swinging (cf. Section 1.2; see also Bodrozic et al, 2024), but you do have to wonder whether Schumpeter himself would not think that our current infatuation with these entrepreneurial heroics has led us to crash completely through the cabinet wall....

9.2 Baumol: The Allocation of Entrepreneurs to Entrepreneurship

Schumpeter saw the entrepreneurs as creative individuals that commit their creativity (their creative genius, he would surely say) to the business domain. Those individuals could presumably have used their talents in lots of places and been quite successful. An intelligent, hard-working, obsessive, creative genius bent on shaping the world to her vision could, you would think, apply those same talents to become a successful creator or leader in many other domains, such as politics, social movements, military settings, or religious organizations. They could probably also have become wildly successful criminals or terrorist leaders. If they had chosen different fields in which to practice their talents, their efforts might have been more or less productive for society. Conversely, some of the people we recognize as particularly successful politicians, artists, and leaders (whatever the setting) could also conceivably have been successful also in the realm of business. Not all, but surely some.

This is the issue that concerns Baumol. Why is it, he asks, that we see these individuals apply their talents to innovating, starting business, and marketing products, forcing as it were new combinations into the economy and propelling economic development? Why are *these* the activities to which talent is channeled? As he puts it, "entrepreneurs are always with us and always play *some* substantial role. But there are a variety of roles among which the entrepreneur's efforts can be reallocated, and some of those roles do not follow [a] constructive and innovative script" (p. 894). Why, you might ask, do entrepreneurs allocate their efforts to the field of *business*?

To see that this is the case, Baumol looks to historical examples: Ancient Rome, Medieval China, the early and later European Middle Ages, and (briefly) fourteenth-century Europe. If, as Baumol suggests, we can define entrepreneurs as "persons who are ingenious and creative in finding ways that add to their own wealth, power, and prestige" (p. 897), then it stands to reason that there have been entrepreneurs in all of those settings. Who they were differed, and they did something dramatically different[4], and arguably that has something to do with why "The Great Enrichment" that took place in eighteenth-century Europe (cf. Section 1.2) did *not* take place somewhere else, at some other time.

In Ancient Rome, there were strong conventions regarding what constituted acceptable and "honorable" sources of income. Accruing great wealth was a path to social advancement in the thin upper crust of Roman society, but it could come only from landholding, usury, and "political payments" (p. 899). What we would recognize as commercial activity was largely the preserve of freed slaves who, by virtue of having been slaves, were looked down upon by social elites and thus commerce was never seen as a prestigious endeavor. What was prestigious was, in

---

[4] The examples that Baumol mentions are all male entrepreneurs, or activities that would typically be undertaken by men. This is not to say that there has been no "entrepreneuring" by women, of course.

effect, "extractive" (cf. Section 10.1), and this made for a particularly unproductive form of entrepreneurship. The advanced science of the empire was largely devoted to architecture, enabling infrastructure to tie the empire together and grand buildings to attest to its glory, and military engineering in support of imperial expansion. This was the case *in spite of* the Library of Alexandria having descriptions of "virtually every form of machine gearing that is used today, including a working steam engine" (p. 910). That steam engine was used for toys, just as the water mills that Romans also understood were used only for grinding grain. Both of these *potentially* general-purpose technologies were only put to narrow use.

In Medieval China, social advancement largely happened through the Mandarin bureaucracy of the imperial court. A position in the bureaucracy allowed for considerable extraction of wealth (through political payments, much as in Ancient Rome), with higher positions allowing for greater extraction. What was central, then, was accessing and advancing in this bureaucracy, and one did this through a highly formalized and incredibly difficult series of exams. Naturally, because these exams focused on advanced mastery of calligraphy and philosophy, those were the subjects to which the brightest minds of Medieval China were turned. This did not prevent science and invention, but when inventions were made, they tended to be appropriated by the Mandarin elite and applied for the purposes of this elite and the Empire. A whole range of sophisticated technologies were only applied in very limited ways, and never for what we might call "industrial" use. The practice of commerce was looked down upon and often obstructed, and its proceeds at risk of governmental confiscation.

In both Ancient Rome and Medieval China, then, it is safe to say that entrepreneurship took rather unproductive forms. In the Early European Middle ("Dark") Ages, it was altogether more destructive, as bright minds and forceful personalities intent on advancement took to the battlefield. Warfare provided a socially acceptable, even esteemed, way to enhance a noble's landholdings (from which resources could be extracted) and wealth, and prowess in a King's wars was a respectable way to move up the rungs of the feudal ladder. With warfare came demand for military innovation, and this period saw substantial advance in weapons, armor, and war machines. Commerce and trade, as in earlier periods, were beneath the nobility, and certainly played a limited role in the local economies that were centered around agriculture and suffered the brunt of the instability that comes with warfare.

As the Middle Ages came of age, warfare was suppressed somewhat, and this enabled the growth of towns and cities and the freeing up of capital for investment in more advanced architecture. This allowed for the beginnings of more productive forms of entrepreneurship. Water mills spread and were put to a whole range of productive uses and combined with other technologies, such as gears, to enable further uses still. Especially Cistercian monks played decisive roles in implementing labor-saving innovations and invested dramatically in scaling up production to increase efficiency.

Alas, in the fourteenth century, much of this productive entrepreneurship was stunted. The Hundred Years War once again made warfare prime territory for the entrepreneurially minded, either in the form of direct military work or innovations in military technology. Military work, by being organized around mercenary companies, allowed wartime entrepreneurs to escape the shackles of only working for their local lords and instead seek out profitable employment with "the side that could offer the most attractive terms, and in lulls between fighting, when unemployment threatened, wander about thinking up military enterprises of their own at the expense of the general public" (p. 907). A hundred years of war prompted inventive thinking, and "[m]ore imaginative war devices were proposed: a windmill-powered war wagon, a multi-barreled machine gun, and a diving suit to permit underwater attacks on ships" (p. 907). As resources were increasingly drawn into warfare, increasing enforcement of religious orthodoxy also worked to stifle creative thinking in more productive sectors of the economy. It was only with the Italian and Dutch Renaissance in the fifteenth century that this would start to change and set Europe on a path toward the Industrial Revolution.

The explanation for this variation in entrepreneurial behavior lies, according to Baumol, in the *institutional contexts* in which entrepreneurs find themselves. Institutions are those "prevailing rules of the game that govern the payoff of one entrepreneurial activity relative to another" (p. 898). These rules may be both formal and informal. Formal rules might include enforced laws about private property, such that people can confidently expect their wealth to not be confiscated by the state. Informal rules might take the form of social norms about what constitutes appropriate and praiseworthy, or repugnant and deplorable, behavior, such as whether one can extract "political payments" or engage in commercial activity and still be an upstanding member of society. Payoffs could be pecuniary, such as when one amasses economic capital through usury or plunder. They could also be nonpecuniary, and involve accruing prestige, respect, and other forms of social capital from particular activities (e.g., in a system that values chivalrous behavior, displaying courage and prowess in war might carry a payoff even if it brings no plunder and few new lands). What a society allows and the kinds of payoffs associated with particular activities play important roles in what activities ingenious and creative people engage in, and whether enterprising individuals choose to engage in behaviors that are destructive (e.g., warfare), unproductive (e.g., usury), or productive (e.g., innovating).

This is not to say that all ingenious and creative people are equally likely to act entrepreneurially in all institutional contexts. All Baumol puts it,

> if the rules of the game begin to favor B over A, it may not be just the same individuals who switch their activities from entrepreneurship of type A [e.g., warfare] to that of type B [e.g., building more efficient watermills]. Rather, some persons with talents suited for A may simply drop out of the picture [e.g., becoming professional boxers instead of warlords], and individuals with abilities adapted to B may for the first time become entrepreneurs [e.g., becoming makers of watermills instead of stonemasons].

Rather, it is to emphasize that the total supply of *potential* entrepreneurs (i.e., the total number, not a group of specific individuals) may be constant and that institutions shape the ends to which entrepreneurs apply themselves. The institutional context shapes who sees that they have opportunities for advancement, and therefore choose to apply themselves to entrepreneurial action. Because the rules *and* our view of entrepreneurship changed (cf. Section 1.2), it became meaningful and viable for those Schumpeterian superhero-geniuses to begin to apply themselves to productive, positive-externality endeavors that benefit society at large.

It is, however, worth dwelling on what is essentially an empirical question coming out of both Schumpeter and Baumol: to which degree are the skills and traits and resources that enable one to succeed as an entrepreneur transferable, both to other fields (i.e., beyond entrepreneurship) and across entrepreneurial ventures? For Schumpeter, the will to create and, more broadly, the psychology of entrepreneurs is a key part of what allows them to succeed, and for that reason entrepreneurs in the realm of commerce are like entrepreneurs elsewhere. "[T]he only difference is the object of action" (Schumpeter, 1911, p. 107). Baumol, similarly, works from the assumption that the *psychology* of the entrepreneur – the will to further one's station, especially – is what propels a talented individual to cease opportunities. Alas, working from this assumption can easily lead us to the fallacious assumption that psychology *in and of itself* is what drives success, neglecting that even excellent entrepreneurs could fail because of simple "execution errors." Also, closer examination of entrepreneurial success might well reveal that particular circumstances enabled success in the first instance (cf. Section 8.2) and that a particular fit might have existed between entrepreneur and opportunity (cf. Section 5.3). Entrepreneurial success, as we will return to (Section 9.4), is never a given, and neither is the transferability of it.

A final question left only partially examined in Baumol's treatment of institutions relates to the effect of entrepreneurship. As he presents it, institutions shape whether entrepreneurs *overall* pursue productive, unproductive, or destructive endeavors. It is, however, possible that the same set of institutions could enable and drive both productive and unproductive behaviors. We have stock markets, for instance, which are part of the institutional context of contemporary business. Those stock markets afford entrepreneurs and growing companies access to capital that can help enable and support their growth, but they also enable entrepreneurial financiers to engage in behaviors that many people consider unproductive or destructive. We also have a patent system that allows innovators to protect their innovations from imitation, which certainly encourages some forms of innovation, but that same system can be leveraged by enterprising "patent trolls." The question, then, is whether it is possible to "design"[5] rules of the game that do not produce undesirable unintended consequences, or if it is not precisely the nature of entrepreneurs (as Baumol defines them) to look for the opportunities that others do not see and exploit them where others might dither.

9.3 Gans et al: Entrepreneurship without Creative Destruction

If the early Schumpeter is correct, entrepreneurship plays an absolutely key role in economic development, spurring what the later Schumpeter would call Creative Destruction. If Baumol, too, is right, there is nothing natural about entrepreneurship taking the particular productive form that allows it to play that role. Economic development, in other words, is contingent on entrepreneurship as a driver of change in the economy, and entrepreneur is in turn contingent on the presence of institutions that propel what we might call "natural entrepreneurs" into productive forms of entrepreneurship.

We can read the argument that Gans, Hsu, and Stern present as adding further nuance to our thinking about the way that entrepreneurship shapes the economy and its development and further caveating Schumpeter's idea. By asking the question right there in the title ("When does start-up innovation spur the gale of creative destruction"), it is

---

[5] Institutions, because they are a complex combination of formal rules and informal norms, are not really "designed" by anybody. Rather, they *emerge* over time as numerous agents intentionally act and interact to produce outcomes that are beyond the control of any one agent (see, e.g., Harper and Lewis (2012) for an overview or Elias' two-volume *The Civilizing Process* (1982a, 1982b) for one of the classical sociological takes on emergence).

almost immediately implied that the answer is not "all the time." There might very well be institutions that channel people into entrepreneurship, but beyond that you also need a particular set of conditions for that productive entrepreneurship to take the particular forms that might allow it to contribute to creative destruction. Absent those conditions, entrepreneurship might end up entrenching the market power of established firms and not, as we would expect of Schumpeterian entrepreneurs doing about their creative destruction, contesting it.

The intuition of the paper is that there are essentially two broad categories of entrepreneurship. There is a *competitive form*, characterized by challenging the market power of incumbents. This is the entrepreneurial firm that the likes of Foster and Christensen imagine, the start-up that uses new technology or opens up new markets in order to upend established industries, to dislodge established firms from their dominant positions, to conquer that position for itself. Netflix definitely pursued a competitive form of entrepreneurship, competing head-on with Blockbuster. There is, however, also a *collaborative* form of entrepreneurship to consider. This is a form of entrepreneurial firm that does not seek to upend the market, but instead seeks to support those established firms in order for them to better compete and, thereby, defend or expand their market power. This is the kind of startup that relies, for instance, on networked ambidexterity: it might pursue a strategy of being the external-and-explorative partner to an established-and-exploitative firm. It could also be a startup that supplies solutions to incumbents, allowing them to perform better. Netflix *could* have gone that route. It could in principle have based its strategy on developing a streaming solution that Blockbuster could have licensed or acquired, or some other solution that would have allowed Blockbuster to maintain its position.

Given this distinction, the fact to be explained in the paper is *why* we might see entrepreneurs choose to align themselves with a competitive, as opposed to a collaborative, approach. Why might an entrepreneur choose to pursue a competitive commercialization strategy (that might spur the gale of creative destruction) over a collaborative commercialization strategy (that is fundamentally unlikely to do so)? And why is it that some *industries* seem to be so dominated by collaborative approaches, as is the case in biotechnology, while an industry like electronics is so defined by competitive ones.

To study this, they surveyed 118 startups about their commercialization strategies and compared firms that seem similar in key regards. At the highest level, they compare seemingly similar firms that receive venture capital financing as opposed to nondilutive government funding. The operant word in that sentence is *seemingly*. While they compare firms that are similar with respect to their geography, industry, and revenue, there can be *a lot* of variation between two startups, even if they're both working on IT in Silicon Valley and make no money. This is what economists call "unobserved heterogeneity," and it is, by virtue of being unobserved, hard to control for. Moreover, as the authors are quick to point out, the variables that they are working with here are challenging to quantify and interpret in unambiguous ways even once they are quantified. Caution about drawing strong inferences, then, is in order.

Before turning to what they observe about those startups, it is worth just underscoring the authors' key idea here, which is that in principle *any idea could be commercialized in numerous ways* (Agrawal et al, 2021; Gans et al, 2019). Entrepreneurs have *choices* to make about the specific way that they decide to commercialize their ideas and innovations. For that to happen, entrepreneurs need what I would call an "entrepreneurial imagination," borrowing from Mills' (1959) concept of a sociological imagination. To have a sociological imagination, Mills argues, is to be able to think about problems that appear to be individual (e.g., drug use, unemployment, poverty) as being in fact social and very often societal and structural. To have an entrepreneurial imagination is to be able to see any given entrepreneurial strategy as just one of many possible instantiations of how an idea could be commercialized. As Gans, Scott, and Stern argue and illustrate elsewhere (2018), any particular entrepreneurial idea can probably be commercialized in at least *four* distinct ways. Those four strategies might not all be equally viable, nor may they fit the preferences and personalities of the founders in questions, nor may they be equally obvious. But certainly, we could imagine alternatives. In many cases we probably should.

To see why that is the case, consider the entrepreneurs attempting to commercialize 3D-printing technology that Shane (2008) interviewed. Shane's entrepreneurs, as it were, embody a complete absence of entrepreneurial imagination. They recognize only one opportunity, the one that presents itself to them in a flash of insight, drawing on their own personal work experience, and they seem to never question whether that opportunity is a particularly good one, much less think systematically about alternatives that might be better along some dimension of merit (commercial viability, potential upside, risk profile, fit with their aspirations, etc.). As evidenced by the fact that the strategies they pursue vary so greatly in terms of their potential value, it seems plausible that at least one of them might have chosen differently had they had more to choose from. Phrased slightly differently: It does not seem particularly plausible that *every* entrepreneur is *necessarily* best served pursuing the *very first* idea that comes to their mind. In some cases, surely, thinking things through a bit would not be a bad thing. If they did, they could probably imagine both competitive and collaborative strategies for the same underlying idea.

The question, then, is why startups choose the strategies they choose. And according to Gans et al, there are three factors that determine this.

Cost of market entry is one of these. Startups looking to compete with an incumbent face a situation in which the incumbent already possesses a range of complementary assets. To the extent that they are compatible with the innovation, assets like "distribution channels, regulatory or manufacturing expertise, and brand name recognition" (p. 574) can be complementary to any given innovation if they increase the value of that innovation, by making it for instance cheaper to produce or easier to distribute. There will be situations where the startup will *need* to replicate those assets to compete effectively with the incumbent, which may be costly (e.g., the startup may need to invest in building up a large-scale production facility if the returns to scale are considerable) or, if the incumbent has effectively secured control over certain assets, almost impossible (e.g., the incumbent may control the point of sale, such that the startup cannot reach its intended customer). All of this increases the startup's cost of market entry. As the costs of market entry increase, startups become *less* likely to compete and *more* likely to collaborate: collaboration will allow the startup to exploit those assets that the incumbent already controls; competition will force them to develop those assets for itself, and the investment in them may not be recoverable should the startup fail.

To see that this is the case, consider what appears to be an absurd example. Imagine that you had created the world's undisputedly greatest car windshield wiper. It is, for all intents and purposes, an absolutely stand-out, fabulous solution, hands-down the best-in-class way to wipe a windshield. Equally absurdly, you now have only two opportunities to choose between: do you collaborate with an incumbent automobile manufacturer, or do you compete? In the competitive strategy, you would have to build up a lot of assets around your central innovation, including the ability to design and produce automobiles in their entirety at efficient scale and in accordance with prevailing safety standards. That would surely be incredibly and unjustifiably costly. Needless to say, much could also go wrong in that effort and your startup would be relying on what Eisenmann calls a "cascading miracles" strategy with multiple profound challenges, where "each challenge represent[s] a 'do-or-die' proposition: Missing the mark on any of them would *doom the venture*" (2021, p. 13, italics added). Compare that to a collaborative strategy, where you would license your immaculate wiper design to the automaker against whom you would otherwise compete. That licensing process is not without its challenges but pulling it off would surely be much less miraculous. Most founders would choose to collaborate.

To pull off that collaborative strategy, however, you would need to be able to disclose your innovation to the incumbent while being fairly certain that they do not engage in expropriation (in more plain terms, that they do not just rip off your idea). Ideas have the funny quality about them that they can sometimes be replicated at zero cost, such that if I tell you the recipe for the world's greatest cookies, you too can bake them and indeed share them with everyone else who may then do the same. If you tell an automobile manufacturer about your windshield wiper, they may thank you for your time and then turn around and simply copy your invention. That means that you have considerable risk when you disclose the idea. At the same time, there really is no way around not disclosing, because if you do not disclose it, the incumbent does not know what they are buying and so they will not buy. This situation is termed Arrow's Paradox, crystallized in a 1962 book chapter by Kenneth Arrow. You need disclosure without expropriation risk, but because they are *ideas*, disclosure of inventions necessarily comes with the risk of expropriation.

Intellectual property rights (IPR, abbreviated) might solve that problem for you. By making ideas subject to property rights, such that one can own an idea, a startup can secure intellectual property protection of its idea through a mechanism like a patent. If you get a patent on it, you *own* an idea and expropriation of it becomes *de jure* theft. This implies that you can now disclose the existence of your most immaculate windshield wiper to an incumbent, telling them about it and explaining its many glorious functionalities. If they then copy the idea without your consent, you can take legal action. You are, then, protected from Arrow's Paradox by your IPR. Or, to be more precise, *strong* IPR can protect you – the right way to think about intellectual property rights is that they can differ in the kind of protection they offer such that it is not a binary question of whether or not there is a patent system, for instance, but rather a matter of degree, such that certain kinds of ideas may be amenable to strong protection while others are amenable only to weak, or no, protections. If you have strong intellectual property rights, it becomes less risky and less costly to engage in a collaborative strategy. Also, it becomes more valuable to do so, because you do not foreclose the threat of subsequently competing with the incumbent, should your disclosure not result in a collaborative arrangement. This is the benefit of negotiating "in the 'shadow' of potential product market competition" (Gans et al, 2002, p. 573).

Another way out of Arrow's Paradox might be to rely on *intermediaries* in the market for ideas, that is, brokers who connect and "matchmake" startups and incumbents. These intermediaries can reduce the costs of search for incumbents (i.e., contribute to their absorptive capacity) by connecting them to startups that are relevant to their particular interests. They can cultivate "long-term reputations with incumbents and therefore credibly certify the expected value of specific innovations" (p. 573) for those incumbents, just as they can reduce the costs of contracting between startups and incumbents. By reducing the costs of pursuing a collaborative strategy, intermediaries thus contribute to making such a strategy more worthwhile. Moreover, we can imagine that such intermediaries can also to some extent protect startups, because they can help ensure that incumbents suffer reputational damage should they engage in expropriation – intermediaries may be an ecosystem for longer than individual startups, and so they can serve as a memory of "bad behavior" on the part of incumbents, making those incumbents less likely to take advantage of a small and less well-resourced startup.

This has two implications. Consider first the implications of the cost of market entry. Previously, we might have understood the cost of market entry and similar barriers to entry (including those erected by first-mover advantages) as deterring entry into a particular market. We might have understood certain markets, including monopolistic or oligopolistic ones, as simply not worthwhile for entrepreneurs to pursue. If we instead think of those barriers as deterring *competitive* entry, it becomes reasonable to think about these hard-to-access markets as nonetheless relevant for entrepreneurs, if those entrepreneurs would orient themselves toward *collaborative* strategies. It may well be that competing head-on with incumbents in the automobile industry or the pharmaceutical industry was so challenging as to be meaningless, but that does not at all rule out the possibility that startups can succeed in those industries through collaboration with those incumbents, by serving either as "idea factories" or suppliers throughout the value chain (Gans et al, 2019) and in those ways bringing substantive innovation into markets that appear dominated by one, or a few, dominant actors.

The other implication is that we should probably understand the nature of competition in the market for ideas as central to determining the nature of competition in the product market. It may be that competition makes sense only insofar as there *are imperfect conditions* in the market for ideas: it is the *deficiencies* of the market for ideas that get entrepreneurs to compete and spur the gale of creative destruction. If those markets functioned well, few would undertake all the liabilities of newness and the risks and costs of competing. When intellectual property regimes are weak and the market for ideas is poorly mediated, entrepreneurs may have no way to engage in the collaborative strategies that would in many cases be the best (or only viable) option. Competition, Peter Thiel once said, is for suckers. Poorly functioning markets for ideas might make suckers of many a startup.

That these conditions – the cost of acquiring complementary assets, the attributes of prevailing intellectual property regimes, and the existence of intermediaries in the market for ideas – matter for startup strategy is interesting, especially, of course, in understanding the strategic decisions of entrepreneurial ventures and in expanding the entrepreneurial imagination. Beyond that, however, it is worth appreciating that these conditions might in turn shape the *kind* of innovation that startups might engage in. In conditions that lend themselves to collaborative strategies, we would expect startups to engage in different types of innovation than they would in conditions conducive to competitive strategies. To be more precise, we would expect collaboratively oriented startups to adapt their innovation processes to their collaborative strategies, emphasizing for instance compatibility with the technologies used by the incumbents with which they want to collaborate and aligning themselves with the incumbents' technological development trajectories. They might, to borrow Henderson and Clark's terms, focus on modular innovations instead of radical innovations because modular innovations might interface more readily with incumbents' existing products. They might orient themselves toward solutions that will address the markets already served by incumbents instead of exploring underserved ones. They might, in other words, pursue innovation in directions and at rates that are different from those of competitively oriented startups.

The caveat to all of this is that we do not actually know from the study *how* the startups in question arrived at the strategies they did: did they, as Gans et al imply, analyze the strength of their IP, their access to market intermediaries, and the costs of acquiring the complementary assets that they would need to compete? More fundamentally, did they clearly recognize that these factors did indeed matter, did they understand their own situation, and did they have alternatives in mind? Or did they, on the contrary, simply do what seemed to be the right thing, because that was the opportunity that presented itself, because that was the way things seemed to get done in their industry, or because that was what they were advised to do? It may well be that they did not act with anything near the level of rationality or with anything near the "choice set" that this study implies, even if they are both clever and thoughtful founders. While this study does tell us what people do and presents compelling arguments for why they might do it, it does not tell us very much about how the people involved thought about what they were in fact up to as they did it.

9.4 Nightingale and Coad: Gazelles and Mostly Muppets

It may be true that entrepreneurs *can* play an important role in economic growth, but what role do they *typically* play? Schumpeter's early work alerted the discipline of economics and, in turn, management to the importance of entrepreneurs, based on observing entrepreneurs who do seem to interrupt "the circular flow" of the economy and, as we have discussed in Chapters 7 and 8, there are specific circumstances that can contribute to this happening. You need institutions that channel a particular kind of people into a certain kind of commercial practice, and you need a particular set of conditions to exist if those commercial practices are going to contribute to Creative Destruction. But even with those institutions in place and those conditions in existence, do entrepreneurs *generally* play an important role in the economy and in innovation? If entrepreneurship brings about innovation (or another outcome that we might care about), surely it would be a good idea to have more entrepreneurship?

Nightingale and Coad depart from the observation that entrepreneurship is subject to such extensive popular celebration and seek to untangle why that is the case. There exists, they claim, "an almost universally accepted belief outside academia that entrepreneurial firms are beneficial to the economy" (p. 114). Policymakers readily assume that "more entrepreneurial activity is 'a good thing'" (p. 114) and consequently allocate large amounts of public funds to the support of it: looking at the UK, the funds going into entrepreneurship promotion are comparable in scale to the amount of money committed to universities or the police service. I would add that we see a similar universal acceptance about the merits and virtues of entrepreneurship outside of policymaking circles. Many firms accept that success lies in being more entrepreneurial, as evidenced by much of the work previously discussed in this book, which seeks precisely to imbue incumbents with some of the supposed vitality and dynamism of startups, just as many individuals seem to think of entrepreneurship as an attractive and socially desirable career path (Hartmann et al, 2022).

This celebration is worth untangling because it is largely divorced from the reality of entrepreneurship. The reality of entrepreneurship is that the benefits that we associate with the phenomenon – benefits such as innovation, job creation, and economic growth – are incredibly *skewed*, in the sense that these benefits come from a small number of wildly successful firms. "One of the most prominent discoveries in industrial dynamics over the past 20 years has been … [that a] small proportion of high-performing firms drive the majority of innovation, wealth creation, and new job creation, while most firms, including the median small business and the median start-up, have only marginal impact" (p. 114). There is, as we will get to shortly, ample evidence that this is the case and little evidence to support the idea that entrepreneurship in general plays an important role in the economy.

To make this somewhat more tangible, consider the relationship between the number of firms created and the number of firms that ultimately succeed as presented by Aldrich and Ruef (2018). In the US, more than 12 million people have ownership roles in some 7 million startups. Of those 7 million startups, only 1.8 million become profitable within a 6-year time frame, and only half a million hire anyone. In other words, less than 10 percent ever develop to the point where they provide work for more than the owners. Of the 7 million startups, only about 70,000 receive angel investment (which would typically be from friends or family of the founders). Only slightly more than 4,000 (0.05 percent of startups) receive venture capital, and only slightly less than 6,000 become public firms. "Once we get to IPO in general and information technology IPOs in particular – that is, the land of unicorns and gazelles – we have winnowed the range of startup attempts to approximately 1 in 50,000" (p. 468). That is a fifth of a percent of a percent. The odds of becoming a successful entrepreneur, then, do not seem all that different from the odds of becoming a successful professional musician.

Alas, "[pro-entrepreneurship] evidence is not needed for the [pro-entrepreneurship] argument to have force" (p. 119). Rather, since the 1970s, with the rise of what is often termed neoliberalism, what we have seen, Nightingale and Coad argue, is instead demand for arguments and findings that confirm a theoretical,[6] even ideological, prior that indeed entrepreneurship is good and indeed that entrepreneurship in general contributes meaningfully to the economy and to individual careers. We call this confirmation bias. It is, of course, fallacious and bad intellectual practice.

To be fair, there are two defenses to be made here. One is that, as the authors rightly point out at the opening of their introduction, some of the insights that we now have into the role of entrepreneurship in the economy are relatively new ones, having resulted from the scientific studies of

---

[6] This theoretical assumption comes out of especially the Austrian Economics tradition associated with Friedrich von Hayek and, most prominently in American academia, Milton Friedman and other "Chicago School" economists. Pertaining to this book, this is the theoretical tradition that informed Shane's study of entrepreneurial opportunity recognition.

9.4 Nightingale and Coad: Gazelles and Mostly Muppets

the past (by now) thirty years. The other, as they also expand on, owes to the nature of entrepreneurship as a phenomenon and especially to how it appears in the official statistics and the scholarship that informs policymaking. There, in their terms, are challenges on the supply side of the debate in the sense that there is something about entrepreneurship that makes it inherently difficult to supply good and systematic evidence on the phenomena.

What are these inherent difficulties, then? For one, we simply do not (generally) have very good data on entrepreneurial firms. The death rate for entrepreneurial firms is high (much higher than for incumbents), and so they disappear from our data sets at equally high rates; the administrative demands that we place on them are small, and so the data that we have on those that do not disappear is limited; and because so many entrepreneurial firms do not survive, there is a survivorship bias in the data set, such that the limited data that we have comes from a biased sample. That, clearly, is not a good basis for generating good evidence. Moreover, we know that entrepreneurial outcomes are immensely skewed, such that particular forms of quantitative analyses of average firms become sensitive to the inclusion (or exclusion) of outliers. What we define as entrepreneurship is also not particularly fixed, such that what "counts as" a startup is inconsistent between studies.

As if this was not enough, two further difficulties that feel somewhat more technical also pervade studies of entrepreneurship. First, there is regression to the mean. Most centrally, this

> problem arises when growing entities are sorted according to their initial size. If a small firm grows large, it will usually be classified as a fast-growing small firm. However, if it subsequently reverts to its original size, it will be classified as a fast-shrinking large firm (because its size at the beginning of the period was large). As such, growth will tend to be attributed to small firms, while decline will be attributed to large firms.

Second, there are conceptual slides. These might include the mixing up of net and gross measures[7] and the failure to appreciate changes relative to levels.[8] It might also include the propensity to attribute "the

---

[7] If a firm hires ten people and subsequently fires four of them, the gross job creation is ten while the net job creation is six. When the firm goes out of business, its net job creation is zero, even though it has created what is called *churn* in the labor market.

[8] "The importance of taking into account levels is clear when understanding changes. For example, SMEs and new entrants often have high growth rates across a range of metrics (such as the usual 'log-difference' growth rates), but this is only because their starting points are so low" (p. 123). It is, of course, very easy to double your profits when they begin being very close to zero, so we should hardly be impressed that a startup doubles its monthly revenues over its first year of existence.

properties of large, established, successful firms [...] to small new firms because [the large firms] were once young. For example, Microsoft, Apple, and Google are regularly used as examples of entrepreneurial firms.... In music policy, we do not extol the virtues of infants just because Beethoven was once an infant."

If we take these difficulties into consideration and try to account for them in our analyses, we get an impression of entrepreneurship that is quite different from its hyped image. As regards job creation, it becomes quite clear that startups do not necessarily lead to net-positive job creation, and that the jobs they do create might on average be low-quality ones. As regards productivity, it is clear that entrepreneurial firms *on average* tend to be far behind the productivity frontier, often because they tend to fail before reaching the size required to achieve economies of scale (cf. Abernathy, 1978; see Section 2.1). As regards innovation, it is now clear that "[s]o few start-ups are innovative that any innovative start-ups are atypical" (p. 127), and it may well be that startups that are innovative tend to be innovative because their innovations were "ripened in the research organization of a large company (or university)," as claimed by Moore (cited in Nightingale & Coad, 2013, p. 129) and reflected in, for instance, the studies by Christensen (see Section 4.1) and Shane (Section 5.3). As regards economic growth, there is no strong basis for claiming that entrepreneurship actually contributes positively to it. All in all, the impression that we are left with is somewhat dismal. The only real high point is that people appear to like working in startups, and so get some utility out of that. I am not fully convinced that this is true, and indeed more recent research suggests that it is not (see, e.g., Hartmann et al, 2022). If it is true, it probably says more about how alienating certain forms of work can be in modern corporations.

To reconcile this dismalness with the fact that *some* entrepreneurship obviously plays a significant role in economic development, Nightingale and Coad suggest to distinguish much more aggressively between startups of different quality, between what they call muppets and gazelles, because "the analytic value of a single category of 'entrepreneurial firms' is questionable" (p. 130). High-quality startups are what they would term gazelles: the young *and* fast-growing, but also rare, firms that unquestionably contribute to economic dynamism. Muppets, by contrast, are much more common and much lower-quality startups. They (caustically, but very memorably)

refer to these poorer performing firms as 'marginal undersized poor performance enterprises,' or muppets, with the category intended to capture the median small business. The firms are marginal because they lack the ambition or capability to grow or innovate, have high death rates, and are poorly captured in statistics or

9.4 Nightingale and Coad: Gazelles and Mostly Muppets

academic studies. They are undersized because they lack the minimum efficient scale needed to perform on par with incumbents in their sectors and industries. As a result, they are poor performance: they have low productivity and low levels of innovation, and generate churn rather than economic growth. (p. 130)

If we observe this distinction, it has obvious implications for how we think about the promotion of entrepreneurship. It

implies that across the board subsidies or encouragement of more market entry may be dysfunctional (Santarelli & Vivarelli, 2007). Entry is high already and arguably excessive (Shane, 2008). If quality is negatively related to quantity, more may mean worse (Greene et al, 2004) and increasing the number of start-ups might merely increase the number of poor performance enterprises (Branstetter et al, 2014)[9], leading to churn and distortions that constrain the growth of other firms (Santarelli & Vivarelli, 2007) (p. 134).

Rather, the kind of policy that may in fact be "good" would be the kind that specifically seeks to only promote high-quality entrepreneurial entry (i.e., to promote what *could* become a gazelle firm) and to further boost the growth of young, but fast-growing, firms. Alas, this kind of policy is difficult to implement because identifying entrepreneurial quality at (or close to) founding is notoriously difficult, because gazelles are rare by definition, because policymakers inevitably will struggle to pick these "winners," and because support may actually distort their behavior in nonhelpful ways (a topic that we return to with more optimism in Section 10.2). That, certainly, would be Austrian Economics' critique of Nightingale and Coad's critique of Austrian Economics. It is not obvious what to make of this. We may know more facts. What to do about them is *almost* inevitably ideological.

---

[9] Nightingale & Coad were citing this paper when it was published online, but not in print. As such, they reference it as published in 2013 when in fact it was published "properly" in 2014. The text appears in this book's reference list as 2014.

10 How Does the State Shape Innovation? How Should It?

> **Texts in This Chapter**
>
> Acemoglu, D. & Robinson, J. A. 2013. *Why nations fail: The origins of power, prosperity and poverty*. Crown Currency.
>
> Mazzucato, M. 2013 (2018). *The entrepreneurial state: Debunking public and private sector myths*. Penguin Books.
>
> Adler, P. S. 2022. Capitalism, socialism and the climate crisis. *Organization Theory*. 3(1), 1–16.

Just as we would be remiss to skip past a discussion of the role of entrepreneurs in innovation, we would be remiss to skip over the role of the state. In this chapter, we move through three starkly different visions of what role government ought to play in bringing about innovation in the economy. The first paper discussed, by Acemoglu and Robinson, suggests that the state actually plays a key role in creating the institutions that make innovation worthwhile. The second reading, a set of chapters from a book by Mazzucato, argues that this institution-oriented view is too limited, provides evidence of how "entrepreneurial states" can also work to develop innovations, and suggests that this implies a state that is much more active in investing in and directing innovation. The third reading turns up this argument further, arguing that the urgency of the global climate crisis and the vast economic reorganization that it demands means that the state should not just be more active in investing and directing: the crisis, it argues, can *only* be solved by a complete socialization of the economy, by the state actively managing innovation and production.

10.1 Acemoglu and Robinson: Institutions Matter (Again)

You hear a variation of the argument all the time: that government is a roadblock to innovation and that the best role for the state is the one where it gets out of the way and sets free the power of individual (entrepreneurial) initiative. As is so often the case of arguments that you hear all the time, this is not a particularly good argument. It is somewhat like a pampered housecat, blind to its own pamperedness, arguing that it would be great if its human servants would just get out of the way, such that it might unfurl its true animal spirit and throw itself at nature red in tooth and claw. Like the housecat, many of the most ardent devotees of the "get out of the way" narrative benefit tremendously from a state that has emphatically *not* gotten out of the way. The reality of the role of the state in innovation is that government plays all kinds of more or less obvious roles in the innovation process, ranging from the extremely active and interventionist to the much more subdued, but nonetheless essential.

Of the perspectives that this chapter covers – which seek precisely to expose some of this range of perspective – Acemogly and Robinson represent the more subdued end of the spectrum. In their interpretation, the state plays a role in innovation as a creator guarantor of *economic institutions*. Closely reminiscent of Baumol's definition, Acemoglu and Robinson use the term to describe "the rules influencing how the economy works, and the incentives that motivate people" (p. 73). Some of those are of course informal, as was the case for Baumol, such as when certain practices are socially praiseworthy and others are not (e.g., owning slaves, partaking in commerce, raiding and pillaging cities), but many fall squarely within the domain of state activity. Consider, for instance, the possibility of creating companies as legal entities, stable laws regulating the conduct of business, enforcement of property rights, access to courts to settle disputes, trade agreements amongst states, or access to labor markets, to name but a few. The economy is thoroughly political and in many places the state is key to creating the institutional context that citizens operate within. It is also often to the state that we look for institutional change or continuity.

Economic institutions can take two forms: extractive or inclusive. Inclusive economic institutions

are those that allow and encourage participation by the great mass of people in economic activities that make the best use of their talents and skills and that enable individuals to make the choices they wish. To be inclusive, economic institutions must feature secure private property, an unbiased system of law, and a provision of public services that provides a level playing field in which people can exchange and contract; it also must permit the entry of new businesses and allow people to choose their careers (p. 75).

Extractive economic institutions are the polar opposite, being "designed to extract incomes and wealth from one subset of society to benefit a different subset" (p. 76). For an example of inclusive institutions, imagine South Korea. For extractive, imagine North Korea. One is a well-functioning, growth-oriented, innovation-driven market economy. The other less so. For other examples, consider the United States and Mexico.

If you subscribe even in the slightest to the idea that incentives matter, it should be apparent that this difference matters and that it would generate vastly different effects. Everything else being equal, under inclusive economic institutions, "[t]hose who have good ideas will be able to start businesses, workers will tend to go to activities where their productivity is greater, and less efficient firms will be replaced by more efficient ones" (p. 77). Also, under inclusive institutions, it is worthwhile to invest in education for oneself and one's children, because one can reasonably believe that one will be allowed to use and benefit from that innovation to create a good life for oneself. That in turn means that those businesses that inclusive economic institutions allow for will be based on better ideas, that the well-educated workers that go into them will be able to be very productive, and that firms can operate at higher levels of efficiency. And, closely mirroring Baumol's argument, inclusive economic institutions create a context where developing and marketing innovations, and where investing in technology, is worthwhile.

By similar reasoning, it should be clear why these effects are unlikely to materialize under extractive economic institutions. In such a context, valuable ideas, entrepreneurial drive, and the productive capacities of workers are left languid and underutilized. The barriers that one faces to use one's skills productively may be nigh insurmountable and, should someone succeed, there is nothing to protect them from others expropriating the fruits of their labors. In such circumstances, there is no real reason to try to better yourself or educate your children, because they too might be stuck with the same kind of hopelessness and precarity, and there is certainly no incentive to invest in innovation and technology. Under the direst of extractive economic institutions, one would be hard pressed to imagine anything like Smithian, Solovian, or Schumpeterian growth taking off; under the slightly less dire, we would expect a much less productive form of entrepreneurship and commerce than would be the case under even the minimum of inclusive institutions. One example brought up by Acemoglu and Robinson is the difference between the (at the time of writing) richest men in the United States and Mexico. Carlos Slim in Mexico and Bill Gates in the United States clearly contributed very differently to economic development in their respective countries.

In ascribing the level of importance to institutions, Acemoglu and Robinson also dismiss other theories that might attempt to explain differences in economic development in other ways. Such alternative

10.1 Acemoglu and Robinson: Institutions Matter (Again)

theories might emphasize the role of geography (which would include both location and natural resources endowments), culture, or the understanding available to political leaders (what Acemoglu and Robinson call the "ignorance hypothesis"). What makes them confident in dismissing these alternatives is their method of comparing countries, regions, or cities that *ought* according to these theories to be similar. The town of Nogales that opens the book is an instructive example of this. The town is divided in two by the US–Mexico border, and so it has an American side and a Mexican side. Those two sides share the same physical geography, do not have markedly different cultures, and most likely have politicians that *know* about the same set of growth-oriented policies. The main difference is that the border just happens to separate them (and that border, in the greater scheme of things, is in a somewhat random place; it could easily have been a few miles to the North or South), and this creates a *natural experiment* (see Acemoglu et al [2005] for a discussion of the place of this approach within the research on institutions and long-run growth dynamics). If institutions matter a lot *and* differ between countries, we would expect to see marked differences between the American and the Mexican sides of Nogales. When we do in fact see them, it speaks to the impact of living under inclusive American economic institutions as compared to less inclusive Mexican ones.

How, then, do societies come to have those inclusive economic institutions that seem so attractive? The answer lies in another set of institutions, namely *political* institutions, and just like economic institutions, these can be either inclusive or extractive. "All economic institutions are created by society" (p. 79), and "[u]nder absolutist political institutions such as those of North Korea and colonial Latin America, those who wield this power will be able to set up economic institutions to enrich themselves and augment their power at the expense of society" (p. 80). Extractive economic institutions, in other words, tend to emerge under absolutist systems. By contrast, inclusive economic institutions tend to develop under inclusive political institutions, defined as the combination of political pluralism and state centralization. To put that final point slightly differently, to have inclusive political institutions that can secure inclusive economic institutions, you need two things: you need political decision-making power to be shared and you need a state that is sufficiently centralized to be able to execute on collectively made decisions.

This is not to say that the state simply creates institutions in splendid isolation. Rather, Acemoglu and Robinson insist that institutions have deep historical roots. This is the case because institutions emerge out of change processes that are *path dependent* and *contingent*: how things develop in any given society depends on the history of that society; and once small differences emerge, those differences can be amplified over time and create radically different outcomes. As such, when we compare the economic institutions of the United States and those of Latin American countries, we can see current differences reflecting differences in experiences of colonization by, respectively, the British and the Spanish centuries ago. Under the Spanish colonization, native South American populations were forced into the ultimate extractive institutions: slaving in mines to extract precious metals to enrich their Spanish colonizers. Under the British colonization, this extractive strategy fell flat because of the absence both of minable minerals and of geographically concentrated populations that might readily be enslaved by the militarily superior British. Their plans for draconian rule repeatedly failed. They thus had to "make do" with less extractive institutions that would, in time, pave the way for the inclusive political and economic institutions of the modern United States.

It is, however, clear that the state plays a central role in shaping institutional environments. Institutions might well result from path-dependent and contingent processes, but the state can certainly contribute to creating and ensuring both inclusive political institutions and inclusive economic institutions. Indeed, you cannot (by definition) have inclusive political institutions *without* a centralized state and it is very hard to imagine reliable and enduring inclusive economic institutions within a state that guarantees them. As Acemoglu and Robinson make clear, "[t]he state is thus inexorably intertwined with economic institutions, as the enforcer of law and order, private property, and contracts, and often as a key provider of public services. Inclusive economic institutions *need and use* the state" (p. 76, italics added).

So much for the pampered housecats.

PS: If you are skeptical of the implicit proposition here – that current institutions might result from events half a *millennium* in the past – I think you would be right to be so. Everything may well be related to everything else, but surely things that are near to each other are more related than things that are distant (Tobler, 1970), and so century-spanning causal connections should ring all of our methodological alarm bells. There is, however, a sizable literature within economics that explores precisely this kind of persistence and finds repeatedly that events centuries in the past can impact contemporary phenomena, even if they do hinge on some not totally unproblematic methodological conceits (Kelly, 2020). Nunn (2008), for instance, has demonstrated that the number of slaves taken from particular areas of Africa in the period between 1400 and 1913 strongly predicts the economic performance of those areas in modern times. By looking at the records of how many slaves were shipped out of

African ports during the period, then estimating the ethnicities of slaves shipped through those ports using different historical records, and then connecting those ethnicities to the areas that today fall within the political boundaries of specific countries, he constructs an estimate of how many slaves were taken to each current African country. This, then, is what he connects to economic growth, finding very sizable effects that are robust to a lot of statistical interrogation. Those effects, Nunn argues, come from the effect of the slave trade on countries' institutions – the slave trade led to warfare, raiding, and kidnapping, undermined trust between ethnic groups, created political instability, and so negatively impacted indigenous institutions that the effects endure to this day.

10.2 Mazzucato: The Entrepreneurial State

In my reading, Acemoglu and Robinson make a very compelling case that institutions matter to innovation processes and that the state is integral to the creation and maintenance of those institutions. It is obvious that the state plays that kind of role in many advanced economies and that the failure of states to play that role contributes very substantially to some economies failing to advance. However, this is far from the end of the story of state involvement in innovation. If we want to understand the role of the state in innovation, institutions are only the beginning of the story. They are necessary, but not sufficient.

Consider, for instance, the role of the state in the emergence of Silicon Valley and of the ICT (Information and Communication Technology) industry that it so dominates. It is clearly true that the inclusive economic institutions of the United States were key to enabling both that iconic cluster and the ICT industry generally, but to say that those institutions alone are responsible is a gross misinterpretation of the historical facts. In her seminal study of the history of what the world now knows colloquially as *The Valley*, Margaret O'Mara (2020) makes this excruciatingly clear. Looking at Silicon Valley, she argues, we are "right to laud people like Jobs and Gates and Hewlett and Packard as entrepreneurial heroes. Silicon Valley could never have come to be without the presence of visionary, audacious business leaders" (p. 5). She continues, however:

> Yet in celebration of the free market, the individual entrepreneur, and the miracles of a wholly new economy, the Silicon Valley mythos left out some of the most interesting, unprecedented, and quintessentially American things about the modern tech industry. For these entrepreneurs were not lone cowboys, but very talented people whose success was made possible by the work of many other people, networks and institutions. Those included the big-government programs... that many tech leaders viewed with suspicion if not downright hostility. From

the Bomb to the moon shot to the backbone of the Internet and beyond, public spending fueled an exploration of scientific and technical discovery, providing the foundation for generations of start-ups to come.... (p. 5)

What we see in Silicon Valley is not the state getting out of the way of Schumpeterian entrepreneurs who simply benefit from inclusive economic institutions. Rather, it is that state that actively enables those entrepreneurs. It is, to Mazzucato, *an Entrepreneurial State:* a state that undertakes risks, has strategic visions, supports innovating firms, coordinates innovation systems, creates markets, and directs explorative efforts and, in doing so, lays the foundation for innovation and economic growth. It is a state that is in fact *crucial* to the functioning of an innovation economy.

Mazzucato's effort in laying out the argument for the Entrepreneurial State is twofold. First, she seeks to highlight the role played by the state in enabling the innovations that propel the economy. This is a role that tends to be overlooked in many accounts, in part because of how the state is conceptualized in much of innovation economics, and in part because of the indirect and often decidedly "stealthy" (O'Mara, 2020, p. 389) ways that American government contributed to the development of Silicon Valley. Second, by highlighting the role of the state, she seeks to dispel some of the key myths that dominate popular and political thinking about government in the innovation process. Naturally, when certain facts are left out, superstitious learning ensues, and myths can proliferate. As was the case of entrepreneurship, this creates space for ideology to take over and that is rarely a good basis for informed policy.

To understand the role that the state actually plays, Mazzucato highlights technologies, firms, and industries that all benefited from state intervention that is, in hindsight, often forgotten or even actively suppressed. Apple, one of the world's most highly valued companies,[1] and the iPhone, the company's flagship product, are both prime examples of the Entrepreneurial State at work. For background, consider the fact that Apple – a company known for its innovativeness – spends strikingly *less* on R&D than many of its competitors. To spend less, of course, is not unreasonable in itself. Organizations can very reasonably be expected to differ in both their R&D investments and the efficiency of those investments. But Apple does not spend *somewhat* less. It spends radically less, investing only something on the order of a *fifth* of what a company like Microsoft invests in R&D (p. 98).

This is possible, Mazzucato argues, because Apple and its products benefit so extensively from the Entrepreneurial State. The iPhone is built

---

[1] At the time of writing of both Mazzucato's book and this one.

around several key technologies: microprocessors, dynamic random access memory, liquid crystal displays, multi-touch screens, signal compression, lithium-ion batteries, GPS, cellular technology and networks, AI-based voice control (i.e., Siri), and, of course, the Internet and HTTP. Apple developed exactly *zero* of those technologies. They were developed by government-funded agencies like the US Department of Energy, the National Institutes of Health, the Army Research Office, DARPA, the National Science Foundation, and CERN. Apple *recognized* (cf. Section 5.3) that those technologies could be *integrated* to create what we now know as the iPhone (p. 99). As Mazzucato writes, with reference to Steve Jobs' advice to itinerant founders,

finding what you love' and doing it while also being 'foolish' is much easier in a country in which the state plays the pivotal serious role of taking on the development of high-risk technologies, making the early, large and high-risk investments, and then sustaining them until such time that the later-stage private actors can appear to 'play around and have fun'... It is indisputable that most of Apple's best technologies exists because of the prior collective and cumulative efforts by the state (p. 118).

As should be clear from the list of government-sponsored technologies, Apple is not alone in benefiting from the work of the Entrepreneurial State. Many of the technologies that underpin the iPhone underpin substantial parts of the ICT industry, and so the technologies that began life inside intercontinental ballistic missiles, fighter planes, surveillance satellites, and other Cold War military hardware are what today power the most modern parts of our modern economy. In other industries, the image is similar. Large swatches of the pharmaceutical industry, for instance, are directly reliant on government-funded research. As Mazzucato puts it, "since the founding of Genentech as the first biotech company in 1976, the [National Institutes of Health] funded the pharma-biotech sector with $624 billion.... This knowledge base was 'indispensable' and with it, venture capital and private equity funds would not have poured into the [biotech] industry" (p. 76).

Moreover, Apple has not benefited from the Entrepreneurial state only by technologies developed by the government. For Apple, government-funded organizations in the form of schools became an essential early customer in the wake of extensive lobbying of the American legislative branch by Steve Jobs (O'Mara, 2020). By the same token, the military not only funded much of the research that would pave the way for the tech industry but was buying early versions of high-technology products before they became viable in other markets. In other cases, the state has been an early investor in companies that we today hold up as exemplars of successful entrepreneurial innovation. Tesla is but one example, having received very favorable government loans early in its history.

Many of these facts are far from common knowledge, and there are two reasons for this. First, much of the technology development that the entrepreneurial state pushed was, in O'Mara's terms, the "state building by stealth" (p. 389). In part, this might owe to a certain preference for discretion in matters of military importance, but it can just as much owe to the fact that many individuals who might be interested in technology development are not necessarily keen on being deeply entangled with the military-industrial complex. It is one thing to be a physicist fascinated by nuclear energy, and a different thing entirely to be implicated in the creation of nuclear weapons. Second, much of the work of the Entrepreneurial State has deliberately been done in the background of commercial ventures. As one example, when the American state funds a venture like Tesla, it does so by giving a loan and not, as a venture capitalist would usually do, by buying ownership. Its funding is, in industry parlance, "non-dilutive," meaning that the owners' equity is not diluted when they accept government funding. Together, these dynamics conspire to create a situation where we may fail to appreciate just how important the state was to creating Silicon Valley and the ICT industry that emerged out of it. What we see in Silicon Valley is clearly not *just* an institution-creating state. It is, instead, a state that takes an active role in innovation: funding research, supporting firms, coordinating industries and regions, and acting as first customers.[2] When the actual role of the state in innovation remains thusly obscure, Mazzucato rightly argues, myths can proliferate and contribute to ideological biases.

Facts alone, however, do not dictate what courses of action deserve to be pursued. In this case it is not obvious that the fact that the state did play a key role in bringing about many of the technologies and firms that created the ICT revolution *necessarily* means that the state should have done it or that it can do it again. Silicon Valley was never the result of a *deliberate plan* to turn a sleepy agricultural area into *the* global hub of innovation. The primary purpose of the space program, or of intercontinental ballistic missile development for that matter, was not to do things that would drive the ICT revolution. Silicon Valley and the ICT industry are the emergent outcomes of a complex process that might not replicate particularly well. The number of attempts to replicate it and their relatively limited success speak to this complexity. As O'Mara says, "no high tech city built by decree could match the exuberantly capitalist, slightly

---

[2] Notice what Mazzucato's Entrepreneurial State is explicitly *not* doing: promoting entrepreneurial entry.

anarchic tech ecosystem that evolved over several generations" (p. 389) in the area now known as Silicon Valley. And, of course, the state *did not build the iPhone*. Apple did, just as countless entrepreneurs built the other commercial products of the Internet Age. On the other hand, there is a reasonable argument to be made that we might be in an altogether worse place technologically and, by implication, economically if the state had *refrained* from playing an active part.

But does this mean that what the American state did to fight the Cold War through the latter half of the twentieth century necessarily generalizes to twenty-first-century efforts to fight, for instance, climate change? Mazzucato devotes a chapter of her book to the idea that governments ought to play a key role in funding a Green Industrial Revolution, focused on transitioning our economy toward environmental sustainability. "The 'green' industry," she argues, "… will not develop 'naturally' through market forces, in part because of embedded energy infrastructure but also because of a failure of markets to value sustainability or to punish waste and pollution.… Only long-term policy decisions can reduce the uncertainty of transforming core business from legacy into clean technologies" (pp. 127–128). This argument clearly builds on the assumption that the entrepreneurial state can do directly (and without the threat of nuclear war) to green energy and sustainability technology what it did indirectly to ICT. Reasonable people can reasonably disagree about that. Nonetheless, making prudent decisions about what role the state *should* play in innovation obviously requires those decisions to be made without too much in the way of mythical thinking and ideological distortion.

10.3 Adler: Dealing with Crisis

Mazzucato showed how the Entrepreneurial American State, by funding especially Cold War science, paved the way for the emergence of what we know today as the Tech Industry. An altogether hotter war, however, occasioned an even more expansive role for the state in innovation. World War II, during which Schumpeter wrote his impassioned defense of the capitalist economy and its emergent dynamics, saw the countries otherwise most committed to that economic system temporarily abandon it in favor of an altogether different system. As Adler reminds us, during "the economic mobilization for World War II, such as we saw in the USA, UK, and Australia, when the business sector acquiesced, not without hesitation, to government control over production, distribution, prices, and wages … government financed and directed most [national] investment" (Adler, 2022, pp. 3–4). This is not the Entrepreneurial State making big bets on uncertain technologies and getting credit for it to spur long-term economic growth. This is what we might call a Directive State, assuming control of the economy to address urgent and existential problems.

One might be tempted to dismiss that experience as a historical aside, irrelevant to modern peacetime capitalism, but Adler insists that one would be wrong to do so. On the contrary, he argues that climate change represents a crisis on par with that of war:

> if we stay on our current course, we will see increasingly frequent and destructive wildfires, hurricanes, ice-storms, and heatwaves over the coming decades. Lower water tables and rainfall levels will cause crop failures and mass migrations. Rising sea levels will force hundreds of millions to flee coastal areas. Climate scientists tell us that the world must get to net-zero carbon emissions by 2050 *to have a reasonable chance of avoiding a chaotic breakdown of civilization.* (p. 2, italics added)

If you accept that the chaotic breakdown of civilization is an existential issue and that it is the logical outcome of a failure to get to net-zero within a quarter of a century, the burning question to ask is whether the economy as currently organized might be able to make this transition. The prospects of that happening, Adler argues, are dismal. The scope, urgency, and cost of achieving net-zero by 2050 are daunting.

> [W]e need to shut down the coal, oil, and gas companies and build a new primary energy system based on renewables; but we also need to transform radically the working assets of myriad companies whose products are powered by fossil fuels – in the transportation sector, most notably. Moreover, we must radically transform vast swathes of our economy whose products and processes contribute to climate change – not only industries such as chemicals, plastics, cement, and mining, but also agriculture and forest products, as well as homes and buildings that rely on gas and oil for heating and cooking. (p. 2)

We also need to do this on a very short timeline and will consequently need to invest *massively* in re-tooling and re-organizing the economy. Even the most aggressive climate policies are, in this scheme of things, far too unambitious to create the kind of change that is necessary. At the same time,

> capitalist firms can mobilize the creative energy of their members and other stakeholders to reduce their carbon footprint to some extent; but no, businesses and their investors cannot be expected to absorb the financial losses implied by such a rapid transition to net-zero. Nor can workers be expected to volunteer for the resulting job losses; nor should we expect customers to volunteer for higher prices.... Had we started this transition 40 years ago, when the science was already clear, perhaps government could have used relatively modest taxes, regulations, and subsidies to ensure a slow but steady retooling process ... but now we are confronted with the dire economic consequences of delay (p. 3).

10.3 Adler: Dealing with Crisis

The same competitive forces that Adler saw as tending to undermine contextual ambidexterity (see Section 6.1) now, some fifteen years later, he sees as undermining our collective ability to transition to a situation that does not inevitably lead to civilizational collapse.

For Adler, there is one solution and it is, in this argument, *the only solution*. Responding to the climate crisis *necessitates* a socialization of the economy. Only if the state takes command of the economy, as it has historically done during wartime, can we hope for sufficient, and sufficiently rapid, change in the economy. The economy would need to transition away from Schumpeter's organic evolution through Creative Destruction to a system of state ownership of the wealth-producing core of the economy, of central planning of what must be done, and of coordination through hierarchy as opposed to through market dynamics. In that system, competition between privately owned enterprises is replaced with collaboration between a "synergistic network of public enterprises" (p. 2). In that system, the state decides what innovation needs to happen and how it needs to happen. Only by transiting to a socialized economy could we hope to stave off the consequences of having done far too little, far too late.

Adler knows as well as anyone that socialization of the economy has a far from illustrious historical record. Most communist economies have either collapsed under the inefficiencies of a centrally planned economy or produced deeply authoritarian and repressive regimes, and in most cases, economic inefficiencies have gone hand in hand with extensive political repression. Socializing the economy has quite reliably not led to the radiant futures imagined by advocates of the idea but led the way to the worst of both the political and economic worlds. Adler is clear on this: "we need something very different from the authoritarian socialism of the former Soviet bloc and China: such authoritarianism is not only politically repugnant; it is also ... an insurmountable obstacle to an effective mobilization against climate change" (p. 4).

As such, Adler sets out to identify a different precedent for the viability of a socialized *and* democratic economy. Rather than looking at the national level, he makes what many will consider a counterintuitive move: he argues that the *largest corporations* in the economy can be understood as a "small-scale working model of democratic socialism right under our noses" (p. 5). Before dismissing this out of hand, bear in mind that the reverse move – analyzing organizations *as if* they were nations – is a relative commonplace in organizational economics.[3] Also, there is a serious argument, made most poignantly in Anderson's (2017)

---

[3] Recall the discussion in Section 7.4 about the relative merits of hierarchies and markets.

book *Private Government*, that many organizations can be understood as communist dictatorship: people are subject to hierarchical control, authority is unaccountable to those on whom it is exercised, dissenters tend to be exiled (i.e., fired), and so on. Adler's argument is a less caustic and much more optimistic version of this latter argument. As he puts it:

> [M]any of our CEOs behave like closeted democratic socialists. Like *socialists*, because, although in public they defend the superiority of markets and competition over coordination and planning, inside their own corporations, where they could leave their various business units to compete with each other, they instead treat corporate resources as a single pool, and they draw the corporation's various business units into a strategic management process for deciding how to use those resources to achieve the best outcomes for the corporation as a whole... Such coordination of economic activity *across business units* within a big enterprise is much like the nation-wide coordination *across enterprises* that we envisage under democratic socialism (p. 5).

A working model of a socialized economy would need to solve four challenges and it is Adler's claim that the best-run private corporations of our day have developed practices that solve these problems, and the best management science understands those practices sufficiently for us to generalize them. A socialized economy needs to be efficient, and we know that efficiency is best achieved when work is heavily standardized, but also that the standards are developed collaboratively between technical experts and frontline workers. We know, in other words, how to design enabling bureaucracies. A socialized economy – and especially one that needs to transition rapidly to be carbon neutral – also needs innovation, and we know that innovation is best achieved through large centralized R&D units that draw local business unit managers into directing that R&D work. We know, in other words, how to manage innovation in the interest of the corporate goals. Moreover, a socialized economy needs to sustain motivation, and we know from corporate practice and academic research how to design incentive schemes that can do just that. Finally, a socialized economy needs to be democratic. Here, corporate practice seems less well developed than we might ideally want, but nonetheless collaborative and open forms for corporate strategizing seem to hold some promise that there can in fact be broad participation within hierarchical arrangements.

In this explanation, then, the failure of previous (state-level) attempts at socialized economies should be understood as failures of *knowledge*: it was ignorance, the lack of understanding of how to run a socialized economy, that led to the economic collapse of the Soviet Union and to the runaway authoritarianism of China. If Soviet central planners had only had access to the management science that we have and through that known what we know about how to ensure efficiency and innovation, perhaps they might have been able to avoid the economic outcomes that ultimately led to the collapse of the Soviet system. If Chinese leaders had only known what we know about how to design effective systems for political inclusion, China might have avoided becoming the repressive state that it is today.

You can agree or disagree with this assessment of the state of management science and its ability to direct organizational (and national) practice, but *if* you believe that management science is "worth its salt," Adler is challenging you to explain why it is that you would not accept socialization of the economy as a viable solution to the climate crisis. Say that you accept that the climate crisis is indeed a crisis beyond the scope of what private companies will solve in the economy as currently organized; say that you accept that management science does in fact know how corporations can be efficient, innovative, motivating, and democratic; what grounds do you then have for dismissing the last, best hope for solving that crisis? Would you really trust inclusive institutions and the entrepreneurial state to be enough to keep us from a chaotic breakdown of civilization? And if you don't believe that management science can do that, why are you studying management?

11 What Is the Societal Impact of Innovation?

> **Texts in This Chapter**
>
> Perez, C. 2009. The double bubble at the turn of the century: Technological roots and structural implications. *Cambridge Journal of Economics.* 33(4), 779–805.
> Zuboff, S. 2015. Big Other: Surveillance capitalism and the prospects of an information civilization. *Journal of Information Technology.* 30(1), 75–87.
> Autor, D. H. 2015. Why are there still so many jobs? The history and future of workplace automation. *Journal of Economic Perspectives.* 29(3), 3–30.
> Bessen, J. 2014. *Learning by doing: The real connection between innovation, wages, and wealth* (Ch. 5–6). Yale University Press.

Having looked at how firms develop innovations and bring them to market, and the role of entrepreneurs and states in shaping those processes, we turn now to the question of what innovations *do* to society. Innovations, after all, do not just concern the firms that create them. We begin at the most macro of macroscopic levels with Perez's paper on technology bubbles, asking how societies are transformed through successive waves of technological revolution and what happens as those waves flood over society. Staying at the macroscopic perspective with Zuboff's paper on Big Other, we look at how technological change transforms capitalist dynamics and ushers in both new logics of accumulation and new forms of exploitation. Then, we move to the question that the popular press tends to phrase as "Will robots take our jobs?" as we look at the history and future of workplace automation with Autor's paper and Bessen's analysis of the conditions that lead to widespread, as opposed to highly concentrated, societal gains from technology.

11.1 Perez: A Cyclical Model of Technological Revolution

Anderson and Tushman offer a conceptual model to explain how industries evolve because of technological change. Perez offers a model that

11.1 Perez: A Cyclical Model of Technological Revolution

seeks to do the same for societies, drawing inspiration from Schumpeter's work on business cycles. In this work – published in 1939, after his early work on entrepreneurs but slightly before Capitalism, Socialism, and Democracy – Schumpeter tried to demonstrate how long-term economic development and periods of boom, bust, and crisis are dependent on technological change, driven by the simultaneous emergence of clusters of innovations and the uneven adoption of them across industries. Progress, he argued,

> not only proceeds by jerks and rushes but also by one-sided rushes productive of consequences other than those which would ensue in coordinated rushes. In every span of historic time it is easy to locate the ignition of the process and to associate it with certain industries and, within these industries, with certain firms, from which the disturbances then spread over the system (Schumpeter, 1939, p. 102).

Perez follows Schumpeter's lead (her theory is "Neo-Schumpeterian") in understanding economic development as proceeding through successive technological revolutions, each taking on the order of sixty years to transpire and proceeding in a series of recognizable phases. The 1770s saw the first of these, nominally the "Industrial Revolution," take off in England. In the 1830s, the age of steam and iron railways began in the UK and unleashed the second. In the 1870s, the third revolution begins with the dawn of the age of steel and heavy engineering, this time with the USA and Germany playing important roles alongside the UK. In early twentieth-century America, the fourth revolution begins and ushers in the age of the automobile. And in the 1970s, the age of IT and digital communication begins the fifth revolution, again centered in America. Each revolution has begun with an installation period (composed of an irruption phase and a frenzy phase) lasting two to three decades, followed by a major crisis, followed in turn by a two- to three-decade-long deployment period.

Each revolution begins with the irruption of a cluster of general-purpose technologies. Contrary to our prior treatment of general-purpose technologies, the Neo-Schumpeterian observation is that several impactful general-purpose technologies tend to emerge at around the same time and that they tend to become revolutionary precisely because they are complimentary to one another: in the first revolution, you had not just machines, but also water power and canals; in the second, you had not just steam engines, but also advances in coal and iron mining, railroads, and telegraphs; in the third, there was cheap steel, but also worldwide shipping on steel ships with improved engines, telephones, electricity and electrical equipment, bridges and tunnels, and transcontinental railways; in the fourth, there was automobiles and internal combustion engines, but also networks of highways, airports and ports, universal electricity and worldwide telephone and telex networks, petrochemicals and plastics, and new sources of oil; in the fifth, IT was not just computers and the Internet, but also cheap microelectronics, satellites, biotech, and wireless communication. There are, in more theoretical terms (Perez, 2010), advances in the *motive branches* that reduce the cost of inputs with broad applicability, in the *carrier branches* where those inputs are used, in *infrastructure* that expands markets, and – playing mostly an enabling role – in the *induced branches* that enable the other branches. Those advances are mutually reinforcing and that is what creates the potential for revolution.

When these technologies irrupt, they are not universally adopted. They are concentrated in a few leading-edge industries that are wholly based on the possibilities of new technologies and on the changes in relative cost structure that they bring. These leading-edge industries become iconic of a "new economy" where the rules and constraints of the old economy no longer apply, as do the firms that comprise the industry and the entrepreneurs that started those firms. In that new economy, profits tend to vastly outpace the rest of the economy. Financial capital comes pouring in, increasing the price of assets and spurring speculation. "Soon there is more capital wanting a piece of the action than projects looking for funds" (Perez, 2009, p. 781). Consequently, entrepreneurs also pile in, creating new ventures looking to repeat the successes of leading-edge firms. So many that

[a]fter the fact it seems astonishing that people could believe that such extreme acceleration in the number of companies entering the race, counting on equally exaggerated growth in market value could be anything but a process of overinvestment and a bubble destined to collapse. Yet every time the notion of a 'new economy' seems to take hold, to spread and be held by serious people. (p. 783)

This phase of what Perez calls *frenzy* and it inevitably leads to the build-up of a *major technology bubble*.

When the major technology bubble bursts (and it always bursts eventually), the economy is thrown into an economic crisis that soon becomes a social crisis. The most well-known of these is The Great Depression of the 1930s that marked the end of the Roaring Twenties during which the major technology bubble of the fourth revolution was built up, but there were similar spurts of speculative frenzy and similar collapses in asset values also in the first three revolutions. In more recent history, the dot-com crash of 2000 saw technology stocks lose close to 80 percent of their value, falling by almost 10 percent in a single day (April 14, 2000), and a mass of bankruptcies among previously celebrated and much-hyped companies with.com in their name. This kind of value destruction spills over into the rest of the economy. That creates economic hardships throughout society that often turn to social unrest and anger that the "new economy" both did not deliver on its promises and left behind so many.

Historically, the crisis that follows the major technology bubbles leads to extensive political reforms. During the frenzy period, leading-edge firms typically benefit from laissez-faire regulatory regimes, owing to a combination of new economy romanticism, unwillingness to slow down what appears to be successful and beneficial industries, and a lack of understanding of the business processes that underpin them. When crisis hits, much of that romanticism tends to falter and the leading-edge industries lose their luster and mystique. This paves the way for regulation of these industries and the financial sector that propelled the asset inflation of the major technology bubble. This is also the phase where redistributive policies that seek to counter the wealth concentration of the frenzy period tend to be put in place. The New Deal of 1930s America is the classic example here.

The deployment period that tends to follow these reforms sees the diffusion of the revolutionary technologies throughout the economy. During the installation period, revolutionary technologies are used primarily in leading-edge industries and create vast productivity improvements in that narrow sliver of the economy. In the deployment period, many industries across the economy see dramatic productivity improvements as they adopt both the revolutionary technologies and the "techno-economic paradigm" (i.e., the "best practice model for the most effective ways of using the new technologies" (Perez, 2010, p. 189) that they open up. This is the point where, for instance, all companies start using electricity, get telephones, or "go online" and where revolutionary technologies become ingrained in the fabric of society. This is the point where the economy as a whole is truly revolutionized and transformed in the image of the new technologies, and these tend to be remembered as economic "golden ages" of widely shared prosperity. Indeed, the Great British Leap, the boom of the Victorian period, the European Belle Epoque, and American Progressive Era, and the post-World War II boom all tend to be remembered as periods of great social and economic progress.

The deployment period ends with a phase of exhaustion, when the general-purpose technologies that spark the revolution have been fully exploited and offer no further opportunities for improvement within the prevailing techno-economic paradigm. Like individual technologies, the revolution runs out of steam. What was once the "new economy" has become "the old economy," and financial capital on the lookout for higher returns goes adventuring, pouring resources into new firms and emerging industries based on unproven technologies. Thus begins a new technological revolution, once again concentrated in leading-edge new economy industries and once again with the potential to radically transform society. And thus, the cycle repeats itself.

Two things bear underscoring here. First, like Anderson and Tushman's model of punctuated equilibrium, this model presents a picture of *uneven* development. Indeed, it is precisely because of the unevenness with which revolutionary technologies are adopted that we see the emergence of leading-edge firms and such substantive lags between the irruption of new technologies and widespread productivity improvements (cf. Section 4.3). We may well be interested in outcomes of the economy as a whole, but the thing to pay attention to is really sectoral and industrial differences. At any given time, there will be industries that are in the throes of eras of ferment and others that are humming along in the circular flow of eras of incremental change, and assuming that the gale of creative destruction blows equally across all of them at any one time is fundamentally erroneous. Second, this is a model in which crisis is an inherent and important part of economic development. Like the swings between installation and deployment, the crisis that marks the transition from the former to the latter is "in the nature of the market economy" (p. 780). The same forces that enable new leading-edge industries to emerge are the ones that – together with financial innovation – ultimately lead to the speculative asset inflation of the frenzy period. As such, it is not obvious that one could have economic development without the crisis that follows this *particular* kind of bubble.

It is the distinction between different kinds of bubbles that motivates Perez's paper. More specifically, she distinguishes between major technology bubbles and easy liquidity bubbles. Being bubbles, both are driven by speculation and the desire to profit from *changes* in asset prices instead of from dividends. Both can also lead to economic crisis. They are, however, caused by profoundly different things. Major technology bubbles build up during periods of frenzy because of speculation and asset inflation around new technologies. Underlying this is the sense that there are opportunities to be exploited in these new industries and so capital gets *pulled* into the bubble. Easy liquidity bubbles do not result from technological opportunities. They result from cheap credit. When credit is cheap because interest rates are low, investors seek out new things to invest and speculate in, looking for places to "put their money." When they do, and when that money is plentiful, asset prices also increase. But easy liquidity bubbles do not necessarily have anything to do with the dynamics of technological revolution. Easy liquidity may well pour into technology-exploiting ventures but could just as easily pour into any other number of asset classes. Recent bubbles in asset classes like cryptocurrency and nonfungible tokens seem, for all intents and purposes, to exemplify ones driven by easy liquidity.

The Neo-Schumpeterian framework that Perez lays out is alluring, but therein lies a risk of overgeneralizing. The model clearly offers up a very grand narrative of recent centuries of development and the identification of recurrent dynamics can be immensely compelling. However, in attempting to explain almost everything, it also abstracts away important contextual differences between the different revolutions and what produced them. Nontrivial phenomena such as wars, global pandemics, or rapid industrialization of particular countries (e.g., Japan or China) and their effects are, for instance, not treated in the model. Moreover, it has, like Schumpeter's work, something of a tendency toward historical determinism or, as Schumpeter's student Paul Samuelson would put it much less graciously, "Pythagorean moonshine" (McCraw, 2007, p. 253). It becomes very easy to assume, for instance, that just because major technology bubbles have historically produced crises that lead to social and economic reforms, they will do so again. Or that future technological revolutions will take about half a century to transpire in the future because they have done so in the past.

This abstracting away becomes particularly pressing as we use the model to understand recent events, because our current moment is *not* particularly well explained by it. Perez's own paper can, in fact, be read as an attempt to deal with the analytical troubles of the revolution in which we find ourselves: the crisis, this time around, is too darn long, the political interventions that we would expect are not really playing out as predicted, and the golden age is not really materializing. Also, a new batch of general-purpose technologies with AI at the helm seems to irrupting perhaps a bit too early?

11.2 Zuboff: New Logics of Accumulation, or a Different Kind of Exploitation

Google was founded in 1998. Working on a grant from the US National Science Foundation, Sergey Brin and Larry Page had come up with the PageRank algorithm (Mazzucato, 2013, p. 27) and Google was set up as a vehicle for commercializing it. Like many other dotcom companies of that era, there was no clear idea of how the company would make any money on the idea. Also in 1998, Hal Varian published the book Information Rules, together with Carl Shapiro. Varian was an economics professor at the University of California, Berkeley, and his book was an effort to explain the implications of information technology, to "systematically introduce and explain the concepts and strategies you need to successfully navigate the network economy" (Shapiro & Varian, 1998, p. 2). "[A] few basic economic concepts," they argued, "go a long way towards explaining how today's industries are evolving" (ibid, p. 2). Four years and a dotcom crash later, in 2002, Google was under pressure to get a clear idea of how to monetize search and to execute on that idea. It was that year that the company recruited Hal Varian to be its chief economist. To people inside Google, his economics must have looked like it could go a long way toward helping them turn their technology into profit.

It is Varian's efforts to theorize Google's offerings and the possibilities of then-new technologies, that form the basis of Zuboff's analysis in this particular paper – a paper that would serve as an initial step toward Zuboff's later book, *The Age of Surveillance Capitalism*, unsubtly subtitled *A fight for a human future at the new frontier of power* (2018). That book would draw on a range of data sources, but in this early work her analysis is based specifically on two papers that Varian published during his tenure at Google: *Computer Mediated Transactions* from 2010 and *Beyond Big Data* from 2014. These two papers reflect, Zuboff argues, "the substance of Google's business practices, and, to a certain extent, the worldview that underlies those practices" (Zuboff, 2015, pp. 77–78). There is a particular logic to these practices, and "[t]his emerging logic is not only shared by Facebook and many other large Internet-based firms, it also appears to have become the default model for most online startups and applications" (ibid., p. 77).

Zuboff claims that this new default model is based on four key ideas: "'data extraction and analysis,' 'new contractual forms due to better monitoring,' 'personalization and customization,' and 'continuous experiments'" (p. 78). These are, for Varian, positive qualities. As he puts it, "computer mediate transactions have enabled significant improvements in the way transactions are carried out" (Varian, 2010, p. 2) and the digital innovations underlying them will "offer a huge boost to knowledge worker productivity in the future" (ibid. 8). Zuboff is less enthusiastic.

Data extraction and analysis, for Varian, allows for better customer insight, more optimal pricing, and other "exciting applications" (2010, p. 5). Zuboff argues that data – from computer-mediated transactions, but also from ubiquitous sensors, corporate and government databases, and private and public surveillance cameras – is extracted through "incursion into undefended private territory until resistance is encountered" (2015, p. 78), typically "in the absence of dialogue or consent" (p. 79). More and more small bits of information on the behaviors, sentiments, and attributes of individuals are constantly being collected from ever more sources (your online search history, your credit card payments, your heart rate, the photos on your smartphone, your social media likes, your geo-location, etc.), and these get compiled into very large datasets that can then be analyzed "to construct detailed individual profiles" (p. 78). This kind of analytical product constitutes, Zuboff argues, "surveillance assets" that can be traded, enabling things like hyper-targeted advertising, predictions about market developments, identification of particular populations, or simply surveillance on a scale undreamt of by the intelligence organizations of decades past.

The possibility for new contractual forms is similarly interpreted as an invasion of private space. Where Varian sees great promise in the possibility of tracking behavior and writing contracts based on that tracking (e.g., imagine a car insurance that only applies if you never drive too fast, and therefore can be offered at a lower price), Zuboff sees the possibility of annihilating individual freedom by creating an architecture of constant observation "existing somewhere between nature and God" (p. 81) that she labels "Big Other."[1] In that architecture, surveillance capitalists aggressively exploit the public's lack of understanding of just how expansive and extractive surveillance actually is and go to great lengths to obscure it. It is no accident, in her argument, that precise descriptions of what exactly it is that Facebook and TikTok do with your data are so hard to come by and that the terms of service that you accept when you use "free" goods online are so opaque. To put it mildly, many things happen when you click "Accept all."

Some of what happens is that online service providers are able to create a product that is customized specifically to you and, hence, provides greater value to you, the user. For Zuboff, however, this value is based on both the creation of social dependency, such that you need to engage with surveillance capitalist offerings in order to effectively partake in social life, and on the ability of surveillance capitalist firms to operate "with its current freedom from meaningful regulation, sanction, or law" (p. 83). Moreover, those customized and personalized products can be refined through continuous experiments to make them more useful or, in Zuboff's interpretation, more dependence-inducing. Equally, or perhaps more importantly, is the fact that digital technologies allow producers to experiment with not only their product but also with their users. As Zuboff puts it, "Facebook has consistently made inroads here too, as it conducts experiments in modifying users' behavior with a view to

---

[1] With unrepentant reference to the Big Brother of Orwell's novel Nineteen Eighty-Four and its totalitarian dystopia of ubiquitous surveillance, Thought Police, doublethink, and Newspeak.

eventually monetizing its knowledge, predictive capability and *control*.... This is a new business frontier comprised of knowledge about real-time behavior that creates opportunities to intervene in and modify behavior for profit" (p. 84, italics added).

Working together, these four ideas constitute a new *logic of accumulation* that Zuboff describes as *surveillance capitalism*. A logic of accumulation is a framework for taking as raw materials something that was previously *outside* of the economy and bringing it inside the economy as an asset. Land, for instance, may once have been "unowned," but if that land can suddenly be taken and turned into a productive asset that may be used for agriculture, it allows the agriculturalist to get access to an essential resource at zero cost. Oil, similarly, existed in the world for thousands of years before being brought into the economy with the discovery that it could be refined for lubricants and burnt for light and, later, energy, creating a vast surplus for oil companies. The same is the case for behavioral data under surveillance capitalism. As Zuboff puts it in her book, "Page [Google's co-founder] grasped that *human experience* could be Google's virgin wood, that it could be extracted at no extra cost online and at very low costs out in the real world [...] Once extracted, it is rendered as behavioral data, producing a surplus that forms the basis of a wholly new class of market exchange" (Zuboff, 2018, p. 99). Your lived experience, in other words, becomes a thing that Google can take, refine, bundle, modify, and sell.

Thus, we can read Zuboff's argument as an exposition (and extremely trenchant critique) of the workings of surveillance capitalism in itself. In this paper she is beginning that exposition, showing how our private experiences are commoditized and controlled by what we broadly refer to as tech companies that are unaccountable for their business practices but massively powerful in shaping our social reality. In and of itself, this is the paper's agenda and, indeed, the agenda of the later book.

Very close to this exposition, we can also think about how surveillance capitalism represents the discovery and exploitation of opportunities immanent in digital technologies. Thus viewed, we can read Zuboff as offering an explanation of how the technologies of our present moment are poised to impact society precisely because digital technologies have certain "built-in" attributes, affordances, and potential applications,[2] that have been identified by technology firms. This is very analogous to how Shane's entrepreneurs discovered that 3D printing *could* be applied toward a range of different ends that were not immediately obvious or, at

---

[2] See, for example, Gibson (1979) for an extended discussion of these such affordances or, more recently, Felin and Kauffman's concept of "functional excess" (2023).

11.2 Zuboff: New Logics of Accumulation

least, difficult to predict in any practical detail. Understood this way, the tech companies of Zuboff's analysis have simply discovered that the particular technologies that they base their products on also allowed them to record, transmit, and store lots of information about how their products are used. Once they discovered that, they doubled down on these attributes and began to refine their technologies to deepen that potential, much like how 3D printing companies discovering that you could apply the technology to a particular end might deliberately seek out ways to refine the technology to that end. The affordances were there, but it took deliberate exploitation of them to bring us to the state of ubiquitous surveillance in which we currently find ourselves.

Alternatively, we can think of Google's business agenda as disruptive of their "real" market, namely advertising. Thinking back to Christensen's understanding of underserved and unserved markets, you can imagine how the kind of deep insight on current and potential customers that Google offers has always been something that marketers (and, indeed, intelligence agencies) have been desirous of, but unable to assess at meaningful cost. It has simply been too expensive to meet the market demand for real-time, in-depth information on customers' intentions and sentiments, and it has often been prohibitively expensive to make consumers aware of new products using poorly targeted advertising. With the coming of digital technologies, however, companies such as Google and Facebook have been able to massively reduce both the cost of insight into consumer behavior and the cost of shaping consumer needs, thus massively expanding the market for advertising and rising to positions of enormous power in that industry. Indeed, when startups talk about pursuing a "data play," it is precisely because their real product is user data and their real customers are companies that want to shape user behavior in other spheres of life.

We can, however, also read it as an instance of the wider pattern that Perez's work describes. Google, like Facebook and many other tech companies, is a company built on the general-purpose technologies of the fifth technological revolution, and one that rose to become what Perez would describe as a "leading-edge" company of that revolution. In this regard, there is nothing particularly novel about the idea that Google's business model is expressive of a new logic of accumulation. In any technological revolution, leading-edge firms are almost always based on new logics, and that is what allows them to prosper. It is also not particularly novel that the business model is based on new input or that it creates undesirable social problems. That, too, is what tends to happen: steam-powered factories, for instance, exploited cheap coal, covered cities in smog, and produced horrendous and deeply alienating working conditions; oil powered the fourth revolution and created, among other problems, the environmental crisis of our moment. What we see with Zuboff's work is that the social costs of this revolution are beginning to come fully into view. What happens next is, then, the real question.

11.3 Autor: Will Robots Take Our Jobs?

The Spartans were not the first people to be concerned about the negative effects that technologies might have on society, and they certainly were not the last. Supposedly, one of the chest-beating reasons that Sparta had no city walls was that the ruling class of that ancient Greek city believed that it would undermine the martial spirit of its citizens if the city was enclosed by defensive walls (Frye, 2018), that something important would be lost if this particular technology was embraced. In more recent times, anxieties about the effects of especially automating technologies have been a mainstay of popular discourse since at least the onset of the Industrial Revolution (i.e., the *first* industrial revolution, in Perez's parlance). Since then, what Mokyr et al (2015) call *Automation Anxiety* has typically revolved around the question of whether machines will put us all out of work or, in more technical terms, whether automation leads to long-run technological unemployment. History is, as Mokyr and colleagues note, *full* of concerns that it does.

It is this debate that Autor's paper intervenes in and indeed the title betrays his view on whether machines will put us all out of work: if automation does indeed lead to long-term technological unemployment, *why are there still so many jobs?* The brute fact of the matter is that the technologies of the past two and a half centuries have *not* meant the end of work, even as those technologies were often designed precisely to reduce the need for labor in the productive process. As Autor puts it,

> Given that these technologies demonstrably succeed in their labor saving objective and, moreover, that we invent many more labor-saving technologies all the time, should we not be somewhat surprised that technological change hasn't *already* wiped out employment for the vast majority of workers? Why doesn't automation *necessarily* reduce aggregate employment, even as it demonstrably reduces labor requirements per unit of output produced? (p. 6).

Autor's explanation highlights two ways that technology impacts labor, namely substitution and complementarity. Substitution means that technology takes over work that was previously done by human labor. When telephone systems transitioned from manual switchboard operation to mechanical switching, that technology took over from human labor and eliminated jobs (e.g., Feigenbaum & Gross, 2020). If cars ever become *fully* self-driving, taxi drivers might find their jobs completely automated. That is substitution and substitution was the whole point of adopting that technology, to make telephone operations more efficient and cheaper. But substitution is only one side of the story, because technology also complements workers, allowing them to do their work more efficiently *without* putting them out of work. When the automatic hedge trimmer was introduced, it did not put out of work the gardeners who would ordinarily trim hedges manually. By the same token, ATMs did not put bank tellers out of work, forklifts did not obviate warehouse workers, and autopilots did not automate pilots. Behind this lies "an economic reality that is as fundamental as it is overlooked: tasks that cannot be substituted by automation are generally complemented by it" (p. 6).

A key idea in that last sentence is that the thing we should focus on when assessing the effects of technologies on work is tasks, not jobs. Most jobs are comprised of a bundle of tasks, and those tasks are bundled into jobs because that bundling "makes sense" under a particular set of circumstances, including technological circumstances. Long-distance truckers, for instance, do not *only* drive trucks on highways in fair weather and low traffic. They also drive in more challenging conditions (snowstorms and traffic jams) and environments (urban areas and small roads). They also do different work around their vehicle and its cargo, like performing light maintenance on the vehicle and making sure that the cargo is strapped safely to the bed of the truck. Moreover, they handle documents pertaining to the cargo (e.g., customs documents or receipts for cargo changing hands) and in some cases play a role in loading and unloading. Those are all *tasks* and together they comprise the job.

This distinction is important because it is pretty rare that a job can in fact be *fully* automated. Even in the not-so-probable event that we were to get fully self-driving cars that could in fact drive under difficult conditions and in challenging contexts, it is hard to imagine that *all* of a trucker's tasks could be automated. We might be able to automate the highway driving such that trucks can drive continuously without the need for the driver to rest, which will clearly increase efficiency, and maybe even automate the part about driving through a crowded city in a snowstorm, but it is hard to imagine a truck that can do everything that a trucker can do. Gardeners, bank tellers, warehouse workers, airline pilots, management consultants, university professors, farmers, doctors, and mostly everyone else have job wherein *some* tasks can be automated, but almost no one has a job where *everything* can be automated. And when only *some* of the tasks that comprise a job get automated, the people doing that job tend to become *more efficient* at it. In those cases, technology *complements* them. In Autor's words, "when automation or computerization makes some steps in a work process more reliable, cheaper, or faster, this increases the value of the remaining human links in the production chain" (p. 6).

The impact that this has depends chiefly on three factors. First, "workers are more likely to benefit directly from automation if they supply tasks that are complemented by automation, but not if they primarily (or exclusively) supply tasks that are substituted" (p. 7). When technology changes, the way tasks are bundled into jobs may well change, such that the job becomes very different. People who were good at only those tasks that are automated will likely find that they cannot perform well in their new job, because they are unable to perform well on the tasks that it now consists of, while those who are complemented by automation will become more productive and perform better.

"Second, the elasticity of labor supply can mitigate wage gains" (p. 7). When workers become more efficient, demand for those workers might increase, and that will tend to lead to increased wages become the price of labor increases when demand increases. However, whether workers benefit from this depends on whether the increasing price of labor leads to more people supplying that labor. In situations where it is easy to learn to do a particular kind of work, many people will pour into the field and provide it (e.g., writing advertising copy when you have ChatGPT). In that case, expect wages to *not* increase. In situations where it is hard to learn to do a particular kind of work, or where you need a particular professional license to do it, few new people will enter, and wages might increase.

Third, "the output elasticity of demand combined with income elasticity of demand can either dampen or amplify the gains from automation" (p. 7). In other words, whether workers benefit from technology-driven efficiency depends on what consumers do when their incomes change. For some products (e.g., food), increased wages may do little to change the quantity[3] of goods consumed, such that increased efficiency in the sector (agriculture) may lead to reduced employment in the sector. For other sectors, increased efficiency may lead to dramatically increased demand as income increases (e.g., healthcare), especially when reduced demand for the goods of one sector frees up resources to be spent in another. What has historically been the case is that some of this freed-up demand moves into new spaces of consumption that did not previously really exist (e.g., personal training, computer games, etc.) or that arise because of other technological advances (e.g., highway restaurants and gas stations in the case of the automobile, influencer marketing in the case of social media, etc.).

---

[3] It may of course change the *quality* of goods consumed.

Over the past fifty years, from the 1980s onward, these mechanisms have interacted to produce noticeable polarization effects in the labor market. The technologies that have been available and economically meaningful to implement in this time period have primarily targeted *routine* tasks often found in settings like manufacturing or simple clerical work. Computers and computer-supported automation, it turned out, made routine tasks eminently automatable. They did not, however, lend themselves well to automating the nonroutine and abstract tasks that comprise a large share of managerial, professional, and technical jobs. In these jobs, you need "workers with high levels of education and analytical capability, and [these jobs] place a premium on inductive reasoning, communications ability, and expert mastery" (p. 12). Computers, it turned out, were not particularly well suited to those tasks. Moreover, computers were not well-suited to automating nonroutine manual tasks. "Manual tasks are characteristic of food preparation and serving jobs, cleaning and janitorial work, grounds cleaning and maintenance, in-person health assistance by home health aides, and numerous jobs in security and protective services. These jobs tend to employ workers who are physically adept and, in some cases, able to communicate fluently in spoken language" (p. 12).

This has had the consequence of shrinking employment in "middle class" jobs that were comprised of many routine tasks and increasing demand for workers to do abstract and manual tasks. Those tasks tend to cluster at opposite ends of the skills distribution and the wage distribution, such that jobs comprised mostly of manual tasks tend to be "low skill" and poorly paid and those comprised of abstract tasks tend to be "high skill" and well-paid. The result is that employment shifts away from middle-skill jobs toward either end of the distribution. Somewhat polemically put, people whose parents had middle-class jobs in factories and offices will find that those jobs are no longer available, because computers and other machines have taken them over; what is available to them will instead be manual service-sector jobs that tend to be poorly paid, because many people are able to do them, thus exerting downward pressure on wages. Only some subset of people will be able to pursue (for many) more attractive abstract "knowledge work." That latter type of work, however, tends to be hard to learn, requiring a combination of skills and typically extensive tertiary education, meaning that not everyone who would in generations past have worked in factory jobs can do them.

It is not obvious if that trend will necessarily continue. When Autor published this piece in 2015, there was already some evidence to suggest that growth in the high-skill jobs was decelerating and that some high-skill professions were in fact losing employment. He explains this as possibly owing to automation, IT, and technology "encroaching upward in the task domain and beginning to substitute strongly for the work done by professional, technical and managerial occupations" (p. 21), but also notes that this may simply be a passing short-term phenomenon. Long-term, however, it may prove to be more enduring because of two developments: environmental control[4] and machine learning. Especially machine learning – the technology underlying current advances in artificial intelligence – seems to hold the promise of automating work that was previously thought to be "high skill." As will be obvious to anyone, commercially available artificial intelligence has made stupendous progress in recent years and has proven remarkably capable at tasks that were previously un-automatable, implying both immense complementation of knowledge workers and, maybe, extensive substitution (an issue that we return to in Section 12.3).

11.4   Bessen: Technology, Wages, and Engel's Pause

There are lots of dilemmas in capitalism, the fact of creative destruction being an obvious one. Another and closely related one has to do with the gains from technology. *Who* benefits from technological change? Recalling McCloskey's chapter (discussed in this book's Section 1.2), there is no doubt that all the innovation that capitalism contributes to bringing about *dramatically* increases human living standards. We are incredibly wealthier today than we were 200 years ago. And yet, when we look for instance at living standards during the early Industrial Revolution – that great leap forward in human history – they were dismal. When Victor Hugo and Charles Dickens wrote their most famous works, they were describing very real poverty, destitution, and exploitation. When Karl Marx and Friedrich Engels wrote about the workings of capital and the conditions of the working classes and co-authored the Communist Manifesto, their analyses were (probably) mostly right. Workers were producing more and more but gaining almost none of the fruits of their more and more machine-complemented and efficient labor. We see similar patterns today, as productivity grows more rapidly than wages, the middle classes are shrinking, and an increasing share of

---

[4] To engage in environmental control, in this context, refers to making a task more amenable to automation by removing some of those obstacles to automation that come from the environment by reengineering that environment. It may, for instance, be difficult to automate bricklaying on a construction site, because construction sites are a difficult setting for machines to operate in. However, it may be possible to automate bricklaying by having a machine lay bricks in a factory, such that the machine creates a prefabricated wall that can subsequently be taken to a construction site and installed by human operators. That would be one example of environmental control.

wealth seems to be concentrating with "the 1%." How do we make sense of this dilemma? How is capitalism both of these things at once?

There are two questions in play to understand capitalism's two-faced nature, then. Put somewhat simply, they are about the size of the "economic pie" and about how that pie is divided. It is quite clear that capital is complementing labor, increasing efficiency, and allowing new jobs to be invented, as Autor argues (indeed, technologies typically will not be implemented if not to increase efficiency). In the process, the economic pie grows because we become able to produce more with the same resources. It is less clear that all of us benefit from this growth. At least in the current historical moment, the benefits of growth seem to be concentrated in particular parts of the income distribution, in particular demographics, and in particular geographies. As Schumpeter argued, we may on average be made better off *as consumers* of goods and services, but in the simultaneous capacity as *workers* producing goods and services, we experience increased variance in outcomes, as Marx would have expected.

To understand the dynamics of why this happens, Bessen's book is an analysis of the wage developments of textile workers during the Industrial Revolution. To be more precise, he looks at textile workers in Lowell (Massachusetts, USA) and their wages from 1830 to 1890. This may seem offbeat, but at the time Lowell was quite the Silicon Valley. At the time, the textile industry was as powerful a force as "tech" is today and Lowell was at the bleeding edge of the technological dynamism that drove this industry. Also, between 1830 and 1860, textile workers in Lowell experienced a situation that is strikingly similar to what we see today. They saw their productivity rise incredibly but saw little increase in their wages. From 1860 onward, however, their wages began to rise. In this sense, they follow the pattern of what Robert Allen (2009) has called "Engel's Pause" – an extended period of productivity gain without wage increases. Looking in detail at this particular site allows Bessen to observe micro-level patterns that would not be visible at more aggregate levels. He can see, for instance, how productive individual workers were, what they were paid, how much companies invested in new technology, and all kinds of other details. That allows him to offer an explanation of *why* Engel's Pause occurs and *what* it is that brings it to an end.

To understand why wages were stagnant at the beginning of the period, we have to understand what defined technology in the industry at its early stages, during what Anderson and Tushman would call its era of ferment. You have to imagine that the textile industry at this point is relatively new and small, and geographically scattered (Rosenberg & Trajtenberg, 2004). Workers would typically be farm girls, moving from their country homes to a particular factory where they would work and board, much like migrant workers in contemporary Chinese factories. More importantly, there is no dominant design for production machines, as you would expect from an era of ferment. As a result, machines were idiosyncratic to the particular factory. As workers gained experience in a particular factory, they would often become much more productive – if they did not become more productive, they would tend to leave the factory and return to the farms they came from. However, the experience that they gained was *only* valuable in *that* particular factory because another factory would use different machines. In economics jargon, the skills they learned on the job were "firm-specific" (pretty much worthless in another factory) and the labor markets they operated in were "thin" (with few employers). Taken together, this gave factory workers poor alternative employment opportunities. And that weakened their ability to negotiate better wages, irrespective of their productivity. The market for textile labor was a buyer's market.

That started to change around 1860 as the industry reached increasing maturity. The industry grew dramatically due to elastic demand (Autor, 2015) and this led to more employers. It also grew increasingly geographically concentrated. Both of these things, you would think, would make the labor market "thicker," increase workers alternative employment opportunities, strengthen their bargaining position, and ultimately lead to higher wages. The real driver of change, however, was that technological change in the industry *slowed down*. As you would expect following Andersen and Tushman, an era of ferment closes with the emergence of a dominant design. With that emergence comes not only reduced competition between designs, and therefore less intense innovation, but also increased standardization. When machine designs stopped changing rapidly, it made increasing sense for workers to invest more in learning how to use a particular machine, for example, by going to school and learning it or by acquiring more advanced skills on the job. Also, it turned textile work into something that you *could* actually learn in professional schools, because it could actually be taught as a standardized subject. When more factories started using similar machines, skills learned either in school or at a particular factory ceased to be firm-specific and became transferable. That made skills more valuable and made investments in building skills much more attractive. When it started to make sense to invest in acquiring skills, it also began to make sense to do a job for longer. In Lowell, that meant that textile work stopped being done by farm girls, who would typically work for only a few years. Instead, it was something that city dwellers did for a livelihood and thus deeper investments in developing skills that you could use for ten or twenty years became sensible, making workers more productive. It also meant that workers remained in the cities that had many potential employers, making it more lucrative for firms to set up shop there. All in all, this allowed workers to gain a stronger bargaining position and demand higher wages, allowing them to capture a larger share of value created by their increased productivity. The slowing down of technological change in the textile industry made the market for textile labor more of a seller's market.

While interesting in itself, it is an interesting aside to this description that while Engels' work on the conditions of the working class was very true at the time it was published in German (1845), it was remarkably *less* true when it was published in English (1885). Put another way, both Marx and Engels were right about the immiseration of the working class, but only until they were wrong. Like many other theories, they *became* wrong because the world changed. There may be times when they are right again.

If we extrapolate the pattern Bessen describes to today, living as we do amidst dramatic technological change on multiple frontiers, what is in store for us? Bessen's argument would clearly be that we are living in a new Engel's Pause and that we should expect a period where productivity increases much more than wages. We can also reasonably expect this period to be long as we wait for the gale of creative destruction to calm and for the myriad new technologies that surround us to stabilize and standardize. Especially for workers in the lower part of the wage distribution (but probably also at the high end), things may very well get worse for a long time before they get better. They will, however, get better eventually and when that happens, not only will we (if Bessen is right) see that living standards have increased *on average* but also that the variance in outcomes is reduced and the gains from technology become widely shared. Until that happens, we can hope that the social unrest that inevitably follows increased variance in social outcomes will not spawn political agendas that seek to stop technological change, but instead seek to limit its negative impacts on those most adversely affected. As McCloskey made clear, ideologies can change and so can the ideology of innovation.

12 How Does Innovation Shape Organizing?

> **Texts in This Chapter**
>
> Bodrozic, Z. & Adler, P. S. 2018. The evolution of management models: A neo-Schumpeterian theory. *Administrative Science Quarterly*. 63(1), 85–129.
>
> Beane, M. 2019. Shadow learning: Building robotic surgical skill when approved means fail. *Administrative Science Quarterly*. 64(1), 87–123.
>
> Dell'Acqua, F., McFowland, E., Mollick, E. R., Lifshitz-Assaf, H., Kellogg, K., Rajendran, S., Krayer, L., Candelon, F. & Lakhani, K. R. 2023b. Navigating the jagged technological frontier: Field experimental evidence of the effects of AI on knowledge worker productivity and quality (September 15, 2023). Harvard Business School Technology & Operations Mgt. Unit Working Paper No. 24-013. Available at SSRN: https://ssrn.com/abstract=4573321 or https://doi.org/10.2139/ssrn.4573321.

As innovation changes society, so too does it change organizations and work. In some ways, the same questions arise: What kind of work will we be doing, and what work will disappear or be changed? How does technology make it possible to increase worker productivity, possibly through ever more exploitative means? At what timescales should we expect technologies to impact industries, professions, and workers in different ways? But these are, in a way, "just" societal questions writ small. We should not leave them behind when we turn our attention to organizations. They should stay with you, but you also want to be asking additional ones. In this chapter, we raise some of these additional ones and ask how technologies change how we work and organize. The paper by Bodrozic and Adler looks at the longue durée and takes an incredibly broad view, showing how management concepts evolve in response to the possibilities and problematics of (Neo-Schumpeterian) technological revolutions. Beane's paper does almost the opposite. It looks very closely at how a very specific technology influences how people learn in organizations, highlighting all the variation and nuance and complexity that plays out at the micro-level of organizations. To close, we turn to Dell'Acqua et al's very recent working paper and its examination of artificial intelligence (AI) and how that particular technology might influence work and organizing as we know them.

12.1 Bodrozic and Adler: Organizations, Transformed

You cannot really be faulted for thinking that the Digital Transformation is an unprecedented event in the history of business. Media coverage tends to emphasize the epochal nature of this transformation and even serious specialist commentary often conveys a sense that the challenges facing organizations are of such magnitude and such consequence as to be wholly new. Much of that, I believe, is probably hyperbolic. The challenges of the digital transformation are very real, but it is obviously not the case that massive, technologically driven transformations of the economy have not happened before. Think back to David's argument about how production was fundamentally transformed with the advent of the dynamo, or to Bessen's description of the tumultuous experience of automating the textile industry. We have seen radical transformations of business organizations and their environments in the wake of companies adapting to railroads or canals or container shipping, to using plastics or steam engines, to using telegraphs and radio. These changes differ in their content, but not necessarily in their structure.

We can think about these transformations through the lens of Perez's theorization of how successive waves of technological change have shifted society's techno-economic paradigm. Recall how what she described as technological revolutions has recurred over the past two and a half centuries, following the same structural patterns. In it, a cluster of general-purpose technologies emerges and gets adopted by new firms in new, leading-edge industries. Some of these firms succeed, drawing financial capital into the new technologies, bringing about a period of frenzied build-up in asset values, and leading to a major technology bubble. That bubble eventually bursts, and the economy is thrust into (first) economic and (subsequently) social crisis. The crisis persists until progressive policies intervene in the economy, opening up a "golden age" of widespread improvements in productivity and standards of living. Eventually, those productivity improvements are exhausted, setting financial capital off on new adventures that lead to investment in a new cluster of general-purpose technologies. Thus, the cycle begins again.

In their paper, Bodrozic and Adler connect this understanding of technological revolution to the concept of management models. Management models, they posit, "are the organizational analogues of what neo-Schumpeterian scholars of technology call 'generic all-pervasive technologies' (Perez, 2009) or 'general purpose technologies'" (p. 87). Where for general-purpose technologies you might think of steam engines, electricity, or internal combustion engines, for management models you might think of the line-and-staff model of organization and the organization chart, of Scientific Management and process standardization, of the divisionalized corporation, of total quality management, and of lean production. If you go to business school, many of the ideas you are exposed to about how to manage an organization take a particular model of the organization for granted – that model is a management model – and many of the specific tools that you might be introduced to were developed to manage organizations that function according to those models.

To be most precise, a management model is "a distinct body of ideas that offers organizational managers precepts for how best to fulfill their technical and social tasks" (p. 86). That body of ideas is sufficiently pervasive to be applicable in a very wide range of industries and it is sufficiently general to open up new ways of working and organizing.

Technological revolutions, Bodrozic and Adler argue, bring about change in management models. When a new cluster of general-purpose technologies emerges, new industries and organizations emerge to exploit them. These industries and organizations tend to encounter new kinds of management and organizational problems that eventually become so acute that existing management models cease to be sufficient. Consider, here, the railroads. As a technology, rail had very considerable *potential* economies of scale (Rosenberg, 1978). There were, in other words, potentially extremely large economic benefits from operating at larger scales. This was quite clear in principle, as is often the case of general-purpose technologies (cf. Section 4.3.). However, "full utilization of the new technologies was limited by the absence of a management model that would help firms cope with the size and complexity of single-track networks. Lacking such a model, railways experienced *dis*economies of scale and major train accidents" (p. 93).

Railroads are not unique in this regard. Rather, every technological revolution has brought about the need for new ways of organizing to take full advantage of new technologies. Technological innovation, in other words, begets a process of organizational innovation that proceeds in four stages. First, companies in leading-edge industries "run into" the failures of established management models and seek to articulate those failures as a problem. Then, organizational actors begin experimenting with new piecemeal solutions. Of these, some will prove successful, and these may then be bundled with other piecemeal solutions into a management model that offers a theoretically integrative solution to the problems of the prior management concept. Once that theorization has happened, the management model can diffuse, first through leading-edge industries and eventually into the economy at large as a part of a new techno-economic paradigm. With the railways, size and complexity became the problem. The organization chart, salaried managers, divisional superintendents, new accounting techniques, new principles of reporting, and ideas of functional differentiation were some of the solutions to the problem. These ideas were bundled into the "line-and-staff" model and diffused from especially the Erie Railroad throughout the railway industry and beyond.

These four phases constitute what Bodrozic and Adler call the *paradigm-revolutionizing cycle* that begins with the onset of a technological revolution. The resulting new management model successfully solves the problems encountered in exploiting new technologies, but it also creates a new kind of problem. For the railways, the development of the line-and-staff "led also to a degradation of working and living conditions for workers, which provoked conflicts" (p. 107). Railways had successfully figured out how to coordinate and manage at scale, but in doing so had created an adversarial and exploitative system that produced massive labor unrest. Like other revolutionizing cycles, the development of the line-and-staff model had created a set of *dysfunctions* that also obstructed the smooth running of organizations. These dysfunctions kick off a second cycle of problem solving, what Bodrozic and Adler call the *paradigm-balancing cycle*, that again proceeds in four phases as (1) problems created by the paradigm-revolutionizing cycle are articulated, then (2) addressed by piecemeal concepts and solutions, then (3) bundled and theorized as a new management model, and then (4) diffused.

In the case of the railways, companies needed a way to solve the problems of angry and restless workers and unions, incessant and increasingly violent strikes, and disruptions of operations. This gave rise to the organizational function of "welfare secretaries," experiments in improving working conditions, the engagement of companies in various kinds of social work, and the provision of "food, shelter, baths, libraries, athletic facilities, classes, and religious meetings" (p. 94) to workers by railway companies through the Young Men's Christian Association. These kinds of initiatives were eventually bundled into the model of "Industrial Betterment" that could then be diffused through the work of organizations that "educated welfare secretaries, sponsored conferences, published success stories, and gave advice to clients" (p. 95).

Together, the paradigm-revolutionizing cycle and the paradigm-balancing cycle constitute the *wave* of management model change that a technological revolution sparks, the full transformation of management and organizational practice that follows from a technological revolution.

First, the technological revolution brings about a revolutionizing cycle of organizational innovation that makes it possible to realize the potential of new technologies. Second, the dysfunctions of that revolutionizing cycle become apparent and sufficiently problematic to prompt a balancing cycle that corrects for those dysfunctions and makes it possible to both tap the potential of new technologies *and* to do so in organizationally and socially sustainable ways.

Thusly viewed, there is nothing structurally unprecedented in the current digital transformation. The fact that a new bundle of technologies emerges and creates new opportunities for organizations has plenty of precedent, as does the challenge of finding ways to organize that allow organizations to reap the benefits of new technologies. We have seen that since the onset of the Industrial Revolution in Britain in the 1770s, a familiar pattern of revolutionizing and balancing cycles has accompanied every major technological revolution since then. What is unprecedented is the specific challenges brought about by specific technological change. Railways are not automobiles and neither of them are computers, and the problems that they each create for organizations are different ones. However, the fact of them creating problems for organizational innovators to solve is not unprecedented at all. Structurally, few things are truly unprecedented, and suggestions that things are unprecedented *tend* to reflect a lack of historical awareness. That said, given the duration of technological revolutions, many things that feel unprecedented do tend to be unprecedented *within the lifetime* of almost everyone working in contemporary organizations. Little wonder, then, that we tend to forget that there was a time when transitioning to *electricity* was an absolute novelty and where only a few, immensely sophisticated companies were what you might call *electric firms*. Now, there are no companies that have a Chief Electricity Officer.[1] Today, all companies are electric firms, of course. In due course, all firms will be digital firms.

12.2   Beane: Learning, Interrupted

Historical studies like the one discussed in Chapter 11 easily give off the wrong impression. When we read about how something as grand as a technological revolution transpires and see arguments that it even transpires according to a recurrent pattern, it is easy to get the impression that things were bound to happen that way. It might not have been

---

[1] "Businesses rely no less on electricity than on IT. Yet corporations don't need a 'Chief Electricity Officer' and a staff of highly trained professionals to manage and integrate electricity into their businesses" (Brynjolfsson et al, 2010, p. 32).

obvious that radio should be used for broadcasting entertainment, but of course people would have figured that out and of course that would eventually create something like popular music. It is also easy to extrapolate from what happened to what will happen. Of course, you might think we will see the Digital Transformation playing out on a similar timescale to prior revolutions; of course, the crisis that follows a major technology bubble will unleash a golden age of shared prosperity; of course, financial capital will be regulated after a crisis. We might even be tempted to look to the past for validation of ideas. Of course, there is no obvious use case for cryptocurrency beyond speculation and illegality, but many general-purpose technologies did not have a great use case when they emerged; of course, there was a huge bursting of the crypto bubble, but there was a great bursting of the dotcom bubble as well, and just look at what subsequently happened to the internet.

I say that this is the wrong impression, both because all these inferences are obviously wrong and because the people doing historical studies certainly do not want you to draw such inferences[2]. There is always an immense amount of contingency to historical outcomes, but that contingency tends to fade into the background. Macro-level narratives by definition cannot take into account all the contingencies that are in play. If you are trying to tell the story of how successive waves of technological revolution transformed ideas about how organizations are to be managed, you cannot reasonably take into account all the details of individual workplaces.

On the contrary, when we zoom in on organizational practices in the encounter with new technology, contingency can tend to leap off the page. In a now classic study of the introduction of CT scanners in two radiology departments, Barley (1986) demonstrated that identical technologies through seemingly identical processes lead to very different organizational outcomes. It turned out that the contingencies around how technologists (i.e., the technicians operating the scanners) interacted with radiologists (i.e., medical specialists who interpret the medical images) shaped how this technology would ultimately be used in ways that no one expected, much less intended. More recently, Lebovitz et al (2022) studied how radiologists use AI in diagnosing cancers. For all the promises of increased accuracy and efficiency that AI might bring, the radiologists they studied were reluctant to trust AI solutions for critical decisions because of the systems' opacity and so did not incorporate the technology. A subset of radiologists, however, *did* incorporate

---

[2] In relation to the text in Chapter 11, the authors wrote a follow-up piece that specifically looked at *alternative* futures for the digital transformation.

it because, it turned out, they had developed routines about how they might interrogate AI-driven diagnoses. In both Barley and Lebovitz et al's work, one is hard-pressed to retain the vaguest of senses that what happened had to happen. There is very little inevitability to be had at the micro level.

Beane's study is a particularly illuminating example of that. As a starting point, we should appreciate that the technologies that an organization uses shape what you might call its "teaching-learning ecology[3]," that is, the established social context of systems and routines for learning from and teaching others that allow people to develop and evolve their competence in the organization. By implication, you could reasonably expect technological change to impact how people learn and that substantive technological change would be very disruptive to especially newcomers to the organization. Beane's question is what those newcomers then do: How do newcomers adapt to technological change disrupting the ways that they would ordinarily develop competence? Through a combination of ethnographic observation and interviews, he finds that some newcomers are simply unsuccessful in developing competence in the use of new technologies. Indeed, their experience is "just" more evidence in support of the widely accepted theoretical proposition that technological change can disrupt teaching-learning ecologies in pretty deep ways. The truly interesting finding in the paper is that a minority of newcomers *are* successful and that they are successful because they engage in "an interconnected set of norm- and policy-challenging practices enacted extensively, opportunistically, and in relative isolation" (p. 87). More pithily, successful learning required *shadow learning*.

To see why this might be the case, envision the situation in which trainee-doctors learn surgical skills before and after the introduction of surgical robots, the technological change under study. In "open" (i.e., pre-robotic) surgery, trainees learn by being in the operating room as surgeries are performed. There, they "watch a procedure a number of times, participate in it a number of times, and then teach others how to do the procedure a number of times" (p. 96). Trainees are right in the thick of the surgical action, working next to the experts, very much in the role of apprentices. Very junior people primarily watch, less junior ones are given increasingly complex tasks to do, and senior ones take on whole procedures and instruct junior ones, all with experts on hand to take over in case of unforeseen complications. This is a fully legitimate way to learn and "the structure of medical residency was tailored to this learning pathway" (p. 96).

---

[3] I am borrowing and somewhat distorting the term from Bailey and Barley (2011).

In robotic surgery, the kind of handing-off of tasks to trainees is much harder. The attending physician (i.e., the expert doctor in charge of the operation) sits at a console where they use their hands and feet to control the four arms of the surgical robot, doing almost all the work of the surgical procedure themselves. If they want to hand control of a task over to a trainee, they have to disengage from the procedure completely and the trainee has to take over all of the control. It is a binary choice to hand over control, much like how handing over control of a car is a binary choice in the sense that you are either in the driver's seat or not in the driver's seat. You cannot hand over a little bit of control the way you would do in open surgery, and so attending physicians hand over control much less and trainees get much less practice doing and teaching. The implication is that you cannot rely on the "see one, do one, teach one" approach in robotic surgery and so the learning pathway that medical residency is structured around ceases to be effective. "The barriers to progression from the periphery [i.e., watching a surgical procedure] to the core [i.e., doing important and complex parts of it] of the work were few, discrete, high and were infrequently crossed as work could proceed without residents' help, and it was exceptionally difficult to recover from residents' errors.... Well-intended surgeons [...] ended up micro-managing apprentices" (p. 101). Predictably, trainees fail to develop surgical skills.

A small subset of trainees, however, do learn and they do so through shadow learning. Unlike their counterparts who rely on a legitimate and ineffective learning pathway, they specialize *very early* in their training and forego the development of broad knowledge within their field. They also rely heavily on developing the skills required to control the surgical robot in computer simulations and use videos of surgical procedures in very analytical ways to develop understandings of the procedures. Finally, they do much of their learning in isolation and with little or no supervision, very much unlike the very social situation that learning usually happens within. Doing all of this was successful in that it allowed them to develop relevant skills, but it was also in violation of norms and policies about how learning ought to happen. To be clear, shadow learning was *not* what people were meant to be doing. They were meant to stick to the "see one, do one, teach one" process.

When you look at the second-order consequences of shadow learning, it becomes very clear why you would not want people to engage in it. Yes, shadow learning did allow them to become proficient at using the new technology, but it also brought about three undesirable effects. *Hyperspecialization* happens because, by foregoing the development of broad knowledge in their field, trainees essentially develop a much narrower set of skills than they are expected to possess, meaning that they are underequipped for the diversity of tasks they will encounter post-training. *The Matthew Effect for skills* – the idea that those who have shall be given in abundance (accumulated advantage, in technical terms) – happens because the conditions of shadow learning imply that only those who already have some expertise become able to build more of it, while those who do not get shut out of developing it. *Limited collective learning* occurs because, by virtue of shadow learning being both counternormative and in violation of formal procedure and therefore happening covertly, whatever people learn tends to not get shared with their community of practice. If the organization learns primarily through shadow learning, it is not really the organization that is learning.

At a slightly more abstract level, the pattern here is that technological change can leave learners to rely on informal learning practices that may be functional locally and in the short run, but dysfunctional in aggregate and over the long run. To add insult to injury, those practices may well be deliberately hidden, meaning that the contingencies involved in determining whether people *actually* learn to work with a new technology can be practically invisible to the organization. One issue that this presents is that, in this kind of situation, it becomes very difficult to understand what problems new technologies introduce (cf. Tucker et al, 2002; Nicolini et al, 2015) and, as a consequence, to adapt the organization's teaching-learning ecology to the practical realities of a new technology. If, for instance, normative expectations are that trainees make limited use of simulations and develop most of their skills in the operating room, it becomes very difficult for successful trainees to publicly voice that their skills largely developed precisely in simulation. How, then, should the organization know to lean into expanding access to better simulation tools, or otherwise providing viable learning pathways for newcomers? Absent a clear diagnosis, it is far from obvious what treatments to apply, and far from evitable what new technologies will do to organizations.

Another issue worth considering is how shadow learning represents an agentic solution to a structural problem. The problem – in this case the destruction of learning pathways by technological change – is structural in the sense that none of the people dealing with it are part of creating it, that it comes about because of changes that are beyond their control and influence. To "blame" the trainees who fail to develop surgical skill is to misunderstand the structural cause of that problem and an expression of a failure of sociological imagination (Mills, 1959). The solution – shadow learning – is agentic in the sense that it is an expression of individual initiative and ingenuity and agency, that it involves working around or against the structures that the trainees find themselves in. In this capacity, it is both interesting and instructive that shadow learning happens, but also somewhat troubling. It is troubling because one cannot really trust that agentic solutions are sufficient to solve structural problems at scale and over the long term. Shadow learning works to solve a problem here, but the fact that what "works" is agentic just reveals a further complexity to the problem. Structural problems need structural solutions.

12.3 Dell'Acqua et al: Fast, Asleep

We know that technology can complement workers, automating certain tasks and increasing the efficiency of others and thus improving worker productivity. This was Autor's central claim and indeed it is a well-documented fact in the history of technology. We would, however, be remiss to think complementarity and its positive effects just happen. Technologies create problems that need to be solved if they are to be beneficial, and what people *do* with technologies matters for the kinds of effects they have for organizations and individual workers. Lu et al (2018), for instance, showed how an automation technology led organizations offering high-quality services to reduce their staff, while organizations offering low-quality services increased their staffing after using automation to make workers more efficient. Low-end organizations recognized a different set of opportunities in the new technology and applied it to different ends, increasing quality instead of maintaining it with fewer resources. Averaging across organizations, there was no real effect to be observed, but looking more closely revealed a range of heterogenous effects manifesting.

The potentially complementary technology on everybody's mind in our current moment, of course, is generative AI. What is so interesting about this technology is that it obviously could hugely impact organizations and work. Equally obviously, the precise effects that this rapidly evolving technology will have on work and organizations are immensely hard to appreciate, especially over the long term. We are, however, beginning to see some contours of those effects. Very recently, Brynjolfsson et al (2023) demonstrated how AI improved worker productivity, but most dramatically increased the productivity of novice workers. In the customer support center they studied, they saw that using AI served to close the productivity gap between the most and least experienced workers. This provides early evidence of a reverse Matthew Effect of AI, suggesting that this particular technology could counter some of the polarizing effects of technologies on labor observed over recent decades (cf. Agrawal et al, 2023). Moreover, customers were measured to be happier, and workers became less likely to quit. All good effects for sure.

Dell'Acqua et al's study is an effort to understand in greater detail the nature of the effects that AI might have and it relies on a large experiment in the management consulting firm Boston Consulting Group. Besides providing background information, 758 strategy consultants were asked to do one of two tasks. One group was asked to do tasks involving creative, analytical, and communication work involving the generation of product ideas, market segmentation, and writing of a press release and a company memo pertaining to those ideas. The other group was asked to do "business problem-solving tasks using quantitative data, customer and company interviews, and including a persuasive writing component." The trick to this task was that the qualitative data would reveal crucial details that would prompt a different conclusion than would the seemingly comprehensive quantitative data. In that sense, this second group had to come up with the "correct" answer to the analytical challenge and then to offer recommendations based on their analysis. Within each group, subjects were then further split up, such that participants solved the task *without AI*, *with AI*, or *with AI and a "prompt engineering overview."*

It is worth dwelling a bit on this setup. Given that the study was interested in the effect of AI, the *without AI* condition is there as a control group. The *with AI and a "prompt engineering overview" condition* is there to take account of the possibility that the quality of prompts that one feeds into the AI interface might be important. It is not obvious that they would be important, given that one of generative AI's most striking features seems to be that they can "do real work with virtually no technical skill required of the user" (p. 4). More interestingly, the two groups had tasks that were specifically designed to be, respectively, within the scope of tasks that the present generation of generative AI tools are good at solving (i.e., generating ideas and prose) and outside of it (i.e., executing analysis and doing basic math). This difference speaks to what Dell'Acqua et al describe as the surprising abilities and the opacity of AI. The Large Language Models (LLMs) underpinning current AI "have surprising capabilities that they were not specifically created to have, and ones that are growing rapidly over time as model size and quality improve. Trained as general models, LLMs nonetheless demonstrate specialist knowledge and abilities ... the effective capabilities of AIs are novel and unexpected, widely applicable, and are increasing greatly" (pp. 2–3). All the while, there is "their relative opacity. This extends to the failure points of AI models, which include a tendency to produce incorrect, but plausible, results (hallucinations or confabulations).... The advantages of AI, while substantial, are similarly unclear to users. It performs well at some jobs and fails in other circumstances in ways that are difficult to predict in advance" (p. 3). The tasks, then, should be understood as being designed precisely to reflect what current AI has turned out to be good at and bad at, and for this to not be transparent to the experimental subjects. Those subjects will not know whether their tasks are, in fact, inside or outside the "frontier" of AI performance.

When we look at what happens when people use AI for tasks that are *inside* the frontier, AI turns out to offer a significant boost to both productivity and quality, but with a heterogenous effect across individuals. On the scales used to measure the quality of ideas developed, having access to AI lead people to produce ideas that were 38 percent better than those of the control group working without AI. For the group with access to both AI and a prompt engineering overview, that number was 42.5 percent. Much of this improvement, somewhat strikingly, comes from straight-up copy-pasting AI-generated text into one's answer, such that efforts to edit actually decrease performance. As regards productivity, having access to AI (with or without the prompt engineering overview) makes individuals work faster, such that they complete more tasks in the same timeframe, and there seems to be no trade-off between quality and productivity. Finally, "the most significant beneficiaries of using AI are the bottom-half-skill subjects … the bottom-half-skill performers exhibited the most substantial surge in performance, 43%, compared to the top-half-skill subjects, 17%. Note that the top-half-skill performers also receive a significant boost, although not as much as the bottom-half-skill performers" (p. 11).

For tasks outside the frontier, the availability of AI had less beneficial results. Predictably, people worked considerably faster with AI, such that relative to the control group access to AI reduced the time spent on a task with 18 percent while access to AI and the prompt engineering overview lead to a 30 percent reduction. Alas, they also made more mistakes that they did not notice. The group with AI experienced a decrease in correctness of 13 percent, while having AI and the overview lead to a 24 percent drop. People, in other words, were going faster, but falling asleep at the metaphorical wheel. This reflects a related study (Dell'Acqua, 2022) that showed that having access to better AI support made less accurate assessments than those with worse support, an effect driven largely by the tendency of users of lower-quality AI spending more effort and more time on their tasks. With AI's tendency to be "confidently incorrect," people simply cease to pay attention, suspend their critical thinking, and stop reflecting. This happens all the time in organizations and tends to have quite negative consequences (Alvesson & Spicer, 2012), but it is certainly not encouraging to see that AI makes it *more* common.

This is doubly concerning when you consider the results of the follow-up task. After having completed their analysis, this group of subjects was asked to generate recommendations based on their analysis, as is typical in consulting work. Those recommendations were then assessed in terms of their quality by a group of graders not otherwise involved in the experiment. Relative to the control group, subjects with access to AI-produced recommendations that were rated as being of higher quality. Those with only AI made recommendations that scored 18 percent better and those with AI and the overview scored 25 percent better. And, as the authors put it, "This result holds true regardless of the correctness of the subjects' answers.... That is, the quality of the recommendation about a business problem-solving case increased, regardless of whether the underlying recommendation was correct or not" (p. 15). AI created what Hannigan et al (2023) call *botshit*.

These findings highlight that AI – for all its obvious potential and all of its immediate benefits – also introduces problems. The kind of productivity increases that AI enables probably makes it inevitable that they will be used very widely and that people will continuously push to put them to use in ever more situations. The problem is that there are some tasks that AI *looks* capable of solving but is in fact not well suited to. In those situations, errors and hallucinations and fabulations will happen, but they might be presented in such very impressive and convincing packaging and users may be so adapted to not thinking critically that they do not get caught. That matters, of course, if they are used in situations that are not fault-tolerant, where the costs and consequences of mistakes are high. What we need in those situations is not better prompt engineering or more skilled use of AIs, but one of two other things. We could try to understand very precisely in which tasks and workflows we should simply refrain from using AI, knowing full well that this will increase their cost relative to AI-augmentable ones. Alternatively, we could think about building up the competence to interrogate AI-generated outputs and build up the competence to be good, critical reviewers of AI-generated output.

The interesting question that this raises is how people will build this reviewer competence and whether the nature of AI would actually make building it harder. AI is evolving incredibly rapidly and the frontier of AI performance is both jagged and constantly moving. This makes it troublesome to understand what domains it makes sense to develop the competence in. Also, one might reasonably think that the readiest pathway to building reviewer competence would be to become expert in whatever domain one wants to apply that competence. In most communities of practice, one becomes expert by practicing, doing ever more complex work under the supervision of a more expert practitioner (cf. 11.2). But what happens if less complex work gets completely automated and that

12.3 Dell'Acqua et al: Fast, Asleep

learning pathway disappears? Then, it seems, we will have to grapple with a "training deficit" (p. 18) that, for many, might lead to uncritical use of AI in tasks that really do call for a critical stance. It is not far-fetched to imagine an even greater speeding up of organizational life and a proliferation of poorly thought-through and poorly contextualized ideas (Kärreman et al, 2021).

This, however, is just the beginning of the adverse consequences. Notice that the subjects of Dell'Acqua et al's study (and Brynjolfsson et al's study) worked in splendid isolation. This is not how most people work. People work in teams, and we are just beginning to understand some of the consequences that AI can have in team-based work. In marked contrast to individuals, evidence from laboratory experiments (Dell'Acqua et al, 2023a) suggests that teams that incorporate AI for tasks where AI outperforms humans see their team performance *decrease* and that this effect is *stronger* for low- and medium-skill teams, such that the Matthew Effect actually shows up again when work is not individualized. Moreover, teams working with AI seem to have more failures of coordination and reduced trust between team members in the team. Clearly, there is a lot for us yet to understand about what AI will mean for work and organizations. These are not good times to be fast asleep.

13 Will Innovation Change Innovation?

> **Texts in This Chapter**
>
> Baldwin, C. & von Hippel, E. 2011. Modeling a paradigm shift: From producer innovation to user and open collaborative innovation. *Organization Science.* 22(6), 1369–1683.
>
> Altman, E. J., Nagle, F. & Tushman, M. L. 2015. Innovating without information constraints: Organizations, communities, and innovation when information costs approach zero. In *The Oxford handbook of creativity, innovation, and entrepreneurship*, ed. C. E. Shalley, M. A. Hitt & J. Zhou. Oxford University Press.
>
> Cockburn, I. M., Henderson, R. & Stern, S. 2019. The impact of artificial intelligence on innovation: An exploratory analysis. In *The economics of artificial intelligence: An agenda*, ed. A. Agrawal, J. Gans & A. Goldfarb. University of Chicago Press.

In the book's Chapter 1, we looked at how technological change created conditions for the emergence and dominance of a specific form of innovation management. Coming full circle, this chapter asks how *further* technological change might challenge that form. We begin with technological change that is already here and that has begun to impact how innovation is managed. In Baldwin and von Hippel's analysis, innovations in communication technologies and design tools are given credit for the expanding role of nonfirms in innovation, effecting shifts in the locus of innovation in society away from producer-firms toward users and peer-to-peer collaborations. In that view, firms might be poised to play a much smaller role in the innovation process of the future. Examining some of the same technologies, Altman et al do not see the imminent end of firm-centric innovation. Instead, they propose that innovation management will evolve, that firms will take on new forms of collaboration and more porous boundaries to fully benefit from the possibilities of technological change. To close, we turn again to the question of how artificial intelligence might play into the further transformation of organizations. Cockburn et al's analysis asks whether artificial intelligence might be a method in the method of invention and what that might mean for the future of innovation and economic development.

13.1 Baldwin and von Hippel: Innovation without Organizations

Up to this point in the book, we have been living in a world of organizations. We have thought of innovation as something that companies do (and often struggle with) and that they do to bring innovative products to market, to remain competitive, and to ward off the threat of creative destruction. We have imagined innovation to be more or less coherently tied to company strategies, understood it as something that is organized within the context of some corporate structure that may be more or less conducive or hospitable to it. Innovation is not always, but often, something that happens within corporate R&D units. Innovation, as we have described it, is in some way targeted at customers who the firm imagines will eventually pay for it or in some alternative way be monetized. We have looked at the challenges of subjecting innovation to planning and hierarchical management but mostly assumed that managers do make efforts to manage innovation. All of this is unsurprising. It is the understanding of innovation that we inherit from Schumpeter and Chandler. It is, in Bodrozic and Adler's conceptualization, the management concept underpinning much of innovation management scholarship and innovation management practice. When we have deviated from this model, it has been to consider entrepreneurial startups, but that is hardly a deviation: startups are companies, too.

If you accept this as a reasonable description of how the world works, the following observations should give you pause.[1] Think of open-source software. It is largely developed by unpaid developers and given away for free. Or think about recurrent findings that in many industries, individual *users* – not companies – are responsible for a very substantial share of all innovations (often between 20 and 30 percent). Users have been found to be dramatically more efficient at innovating than firms and they are more likely to develop innovations that originate new industries or introduce functional novelty into existing ones. Nationally representative surveys find that 3 and 6 percent of *all consumers* innovate. In the UK, consumer expenditures in innovation development were found to exceed company investment in consumer product innovation by 50 percent.

---

[1] As summarized in von Hippel (2017), De Jong (2016), and von Hippel and Von Krogh (2015).

Entrepreneurial firms founded by user innovators were also more likely to survive and grow than those founded by nonusers. One very recent study (Preißner et al, 2024) found that more than 40 percent of innovations described as disruptive innovations in the disruptive innovation literature were developed by users. Clearly, there is more to the innovation process than just firms developing solutions for profit.

As Baldwin and von Hippel put it, "the producer's model is only one mode of innovation. Two increasingly important additional models are innovations by single-user firms or individuals and open collaborative innovation. Each of these three forms represents a different way to organization human effort and investments aimed at generating valuable new innovations" (p. 1399). For single-user innovation, imagine someone developing an innovation that they themselves need in isolation, such as when an individual with a rare disease develops a new way to treat their own illness (e.g., Oliveira et al, 2015). For open collaborative innovation, imagine a collective of people working together to create an innovation, such as when a group of people collaborates in an open-source software project or, as described in, for example, Kesavadev et al (2020), when patients with diabetes collaboratively developed a do-it-yourself artificial pancreas. We know that both kinds of innovation have been practiced for centuries. Nuvolari (2004), for instance, documented open collaborative innovation during the early industrialization, and Hienerth (2016) describes users originating new techniques in the mid-1800s. What is central in Baldwin and von Hippel's paper is that they try to understand why these two additional models have become *increasingly* important and why, by implication, they might become even more so in the future.

We know certain things about the phenomenon of user innovation, as summarized in von Hippel's 2005 book "Democratizing Innovation." As mentioned, user innovation is a phenomenon observed across a range of industries, both in the form of individual consumer-users developing product innovations for themselves and in the form of firms or firm employees developing process innovations for use in their production processes. When users innovate, they tend to do so because they have idiosyncratic needs that are not well addressed by market offerings. Many users have idiosyncratic needs, but what we term "lead users" experience those needs at much greater rates and with much greater intensity than nonlead users. Because of the urgency of their needs and the ensuing high expected benefit of developing a solution, lead users tend to innovate *before* commercial products exist (i.e., you should imagine them as a group of users that precede "innovators" in Rogers' diffusion model, who are using self-developed versions of products before the diffusion of commercial products begins). User innovators tend not to want to commercialize their innovations. Instead, they tend to give their innovations away for free to users who partake in their user communities.

Similarly, we have theories to summarize how collaborative open innovation works. The participants in these kinds of processes, like single-user innovators, will often be motivated by the expected benefits of using the innovations that their collaboration targets, but the collaborative organization also offers other benefits of participants. It may, for instance, be an occasion to signal one's skills or to learn new ones. Open-source projects have that quality, allowing people to hone their software-development skills in ways that might not otherwise be possible or to signal to prospective employers just how skilled they are. We also know that work on this kind of collaborative project tends to be done primarily by a small core of very engaged individuals and that there is a very long tail of people who make only very small contributions, but that these small contributions matter a lot in aggregate. Also, this very long tail also means that people innovate primarily when they are particularly well positioned to do so (i.e., in "low-cost niches"). Collaborative open innovation projects are, effectively, a kind of organization, but one that operates without formal managers and with authority being allocated depending on contributions and their quality.

To explain the ascendancy of these nonproducer-centric, non-Schumpeterian models of innovation, Baldwin and von Hippel develop a model of the conditions that make particular modes of innovation viable. The conditions they consider are design costs, communication costs, production costs, and transaction costs. Design cost is the cost of "creating the design for an innovation – the instructions that when implemented will bring the innovation into reality" (pp. 1403–1404). Communication cost is the cost "of transferring design-related information among participants in different organizations during the design process" (p. 1404). Production cost is the cost of "carrying out the design instructions to produce the good or service" (p. 1404). Transaction cost is the cost of "establishing property rights and engaging in compensated exchanges of property [pertaining to the innovation]" (p. 1404).

In order for a particular mode of innovation to be viable, the expected *value* of having developed a design needs to exceed the anticipated sum of the costs that developing that design might incur under that mode of innovation. For any given innovation opportunity, in other words, the model assumes that all three modes of innovation – producer innovation, single-user innovation, and open collaborative innovation – are in principle viable for *all* innovation opportunities. The design of a car, a blender, a piece of software, a medical device, the instruction for a Lego kit, or a recipe for translucent potato chips could all be developed according to all three modes. In practice, whether an innovation opportunity can viably be addressed depends on the relative total costs and the resultant value that might be associated with it. If costs exceed value, the mode is unviable for that particular innovation opportunity. If value exceeds cost, the mode is viable. To claim that the non-Schumpeterian modes of innovation will become increasingly important, the model needs to show that *more innovation opportunities* will be viable for single-user innovation, open collaborative innovation, or both.

To simplify the analysis, Baldwin and von Hippel then strip out production costs and transaction costs, such that the model depicts an innovation opportunity as being viably addressed by a particular mode of innovation if the value of an innovation exceeds the sum of design and communication costs. That can seem sort of baffling, but the argument for doing so is that production costs and transaction costs are unlikely to massively change in the foreseeable future. Single users and collaborative open innovation will continue to "have a transaction cost advantage over producer innovators" (p. 1010) and producer innovators can reasonably be expected to continue to have a production cost advantage in markets "where economies in production significantly depend on careful and subtle codesign of products and product-specific production systems" (p. 1409), that is, highly routinized and specific mass production. These conditions are so stable as to not radically affect the viability of different models, is the argument.

Thus simplified, they proceed to conceptualize the zones of viability for each mode of innovation as dependent on design cost and communication cost. In this analysis, there are certain innovation opportunities that no one pursues. There may be demand for certain innovations, but the costs of creating them may be prohibitively high relative to the value of doing so, and so demand will go unmet. In the illustration they provide (reproduced later in Figure 13.1), this is the white area where none of the three innovation modes are viable. Other innovation opportunities will only be pursued by producer innovators. Those are the ones where both communication costs and design costs fall below a minimum threshold. The really interesting observation, however, is that there are zones where single-user and open collaborative modes of innovation are *also* viable and where those modes are viable *even when producer innovation is not*. Below a certain threshold of communication costs, Baldwin and von Hippel argue, open collaborative innovation becomes viable, and below a certain threshold of design costs, single-user innovation becomes viable. Sometimes to co-exist with producer innovation and sometimes as the only viable way of addressing an innovation opportunity.

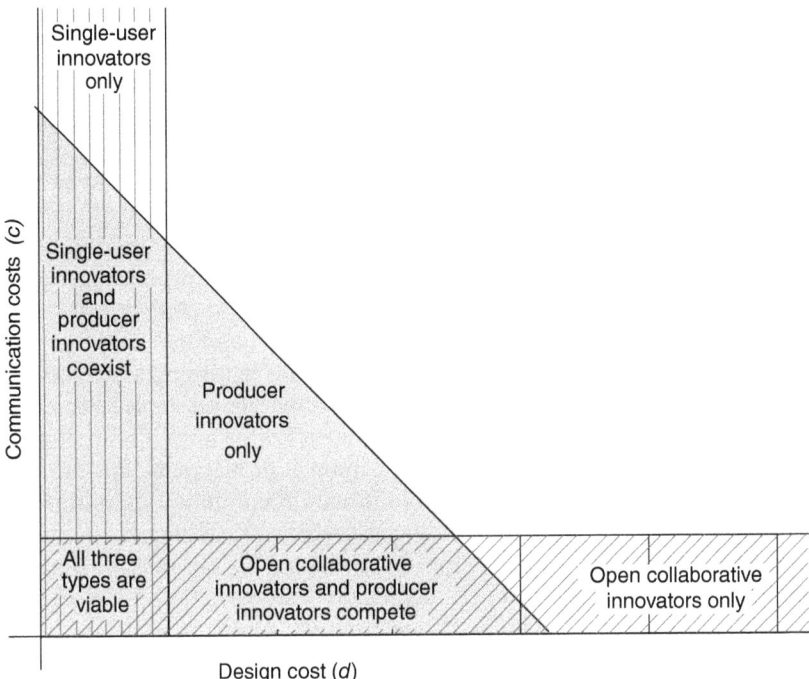

Figure 13.1 Bounds of viability for different modes of innovation
Source: Baldwin and von Hippel, 2011, p. 1406.

This matters hugely, because both communication costs and design costs have been falling significantly since the emergence of especially computers and the internet. With computers, design tools that were previously so expensive as to be available only to companies can now become cheap. This means that for an increasing number of innovation opportunities, design costs will fall below the threshold that limits the viability of single-user innovation. More and more innovations, in other words, can viably be pursued by those single users. With the internet, communication that was formerly slow and costly can now happen quickly and almost costlessly, bringing an increasing number of innovation opportunities into the zone of viability for open and collaborative innovators. We might, then, expect further innovations in communication and design technologies to not only make more producer innovation viable but for nonproducer innovation to also become much more empirically prevalent. Innovation and technological change, in other words, are driving a shift in the locus of innovation in the economy.

This should make you think slightly differently about Schumpeter and Chandler's understanding of the firm as the centerpiece of the innovation process. The reason they, and we with them, have the producer-centric view of innovation that they have is that this was the innovation *practice* that was predominantly viable at the time they were making their observations. Chandler especially is clear about how the modern corporation is the result of several interacting forces, but especially a set of technological changes that made it possible and desirable for that kind of organization to exist. Prior to those changes, the modern corporation would not have been viable. However, further technological change can result in further organizational change (cf. Section 11.1) and make the corporation less relevant, leading some to speak of the "vanishing corporation" (Davis, 2016). In this light, it is almost certainly unreasonable to think of the corporation and corporate R&D as the end of history. Technological change has historically influenced how innovation happens, and it most certainly will continue to do so in the future. If continued innovation in communication and design technologies makes sufficiently many innovation opportunities viable for nonproducers, it is quite possible, as Benkler argues, that "firms will remain significant only where physical capital costs of production are high and concentrated" (2017, p. 270).

13.2 Altman et al: In an Age of Costless Communication

The International Space Station (ISS) is powered by solar energy. Large solar panels are suspended on what are called longerons and how they are positioned relative to the sun determines how much power the space station has available. More power is better, making optimal positioning of the solar panels a matter of some interest to NASA. Herein lies the challenge:

> [w]hile pointing the solar arrays directly at the Sun is fairly straight forward, the ISS must also consider the loads and stresses on the longerons which support the arrays which can be caused by shadowing due to the ISS modules and structure. If these support structure materials are exposed to extreme heat from the Sun on one section and the cold of deep space on an adjacent section, this can cause expansion and contraction of the materials thus causing a stress that damage the structure (Gustetic et al, 2015, p. 15).

To ensure good positioning and stress avoidance, NASA has an algorithm. NASA being NASA, you can confidently expect that algorithm to have been developed by very skilled and motivated people over several years and at some nontrivial cost. It is not a bad algorithm.

Then, NASA ran a crowdsourcing contest. As part of a wider effort to experiment with crowdsourcing, they actually ran many, but this particular contest ran for three weeks and paid out US$40,000 in prizes. In the context of space exploration, developing a technical solution over three weeks is insanely fast and the prize money amount is so small that it could easily be a rounding error. The contest, however, attracted over 400 external solvers generating over 2,000 ideas. The results? They were "*as good* as the ISS current tools for core operations and *a significant improvement* for many edge cases" (Gustetic et al, 2015, p. 15, italics added). It was a better solution, developed more quickly and at lower cost. And this was not even the "home run" example of successful crowdsourcing (Lebovitz et al, 2022): the really spectacular result was the development of an algorithm for predicting solar flares. Solar flares are incredibly dangerous for people and equipment in space and knowing when they will happen lets people take precautions. Knowing well in advance that they will happen is important, as is the accuracy of the prediction. Again, NASA had a state-of-the-art solution. Relative to that state-of-the-art solution previously used, the crowdsourced solution predicted solar flares with 85 percent accuracy (as opposed to 50 percent) eight hours in advance (as opposed to two hours). That crowdsourcing contest ran for three months, with prizes worth US$30,000.

What we are seeing here is that technological change matters not just to the viability of innovation happening without the involvement of formal organizations and their R&D lab. Rather, we can see that technological change also matters for innovation processes inside such organizations. The challenge to the Schumpeterian paradigm that technologically driven cost reductions represent is one that challenges both whether companies should innovate and *how* they do it. Indeed, in the event that Benkler is not right that firms will be insignificant in the future, how they do what they do is likely to be very different.

For Altman et al, the starting point for thinking about the future of innovation management as it happens *inside* organizations is information costs. Information costs, as they conceptualize it, are comprised of three things, namely the costs of information *processing*, of information *storage*, and of information *communication*. Since the emergence of what Perez would describe as the fifth technological revolution – the Digital Revolution – all three types of costs have plummeted to the point where they now approach zero. Because of the compounding effects of Moore's Law, it took less than ten years for "the processing power of a multimillion dollar military supercomputer in 1997 [to] be found in the Sony PlayStation 3 gaming console, released in 2006 for $500" (p. 355). Because of similar effects in storage, "[a] 500 GB disk drive cost $150 five years ago and $50 today, but the same storage space can now be obtained through the cloud for free"[2] (p. 357). And for communication, similar developments: "in 1984, the fastest speed modem available to a home user was 300 bits per second ... in 2010 it was 31mbps, an increase of 100,000 times in just 25 years ... the price per mbps for internet transit has dropped from $1200 in 1998 down to $5 in 2010" (p. 357).

These costs matter. Having read Baldwin and von Hippel's analysis, you would not be surprised by that at all, of course, but they matter *to organizations* because "costs for these three components represent important constraints on how information can be used to drive innovation" (p. 354). With this kind of revolutionary change, these constraints are lifted, and a potential emerges for organizing in new ways so as to take advantage of them (cf. Section 11.1). The corporate R&D model, in this light, can be understood as the least inefficient way for organizations to innovate under the technological constraints of the predigital world. When communication costs approach zero, a whole range of new answers to the question of how best to manage innovation emerge. Specifically, as Altman et al argue, it becomes possible for the organization to engage with ever more external sources of innovation in ever more intense ways.

To be clear, organizations have worked with external sources of innovation for a long time. Independent inventors have long licensed their innovations to organizations (Nicholas, 2010), for instance. The typical way that organizations have sourced external innovation, however, has been through collaboration with a relatively small number of external partners. Large and sophisticated organizations might have had custom-negotiated, strategic partnerships with ten to twenty other firms, and less than ten times that number of more tactical relationships around something like licenses for specific technologies. In this sense of "open innovation," open innovation is a well-known organizational phenomenon and strategic opportunity. Given its nature, it is also not one that is massively impacted by the declining information costs that Altman et al describe.

The impact of declining information costs comes from that new suite of opportunities that become plausible and perhaps even attractive when costs decline. One of these opportunities is for firms to engage with *labor marketplaces*. These tend to be platforms where organizations can find workers for specific tasks. This can be in the form of platforms such as Amazon MTurk, Fiverr, or other "gig work" sites that offer piece rate work, typically on micro-tasks that tend to be quite rote, to a distributed contingent labor workforce (e.g., Gray & Suri, 2019). More interestingly

---

[2] That was, of course, in 2014; in 2024, a quick online search suggests that $150 could buy me sixteen times the storage it could in 2009.

for innovation, platforms such as InnoCentive and TopCoder organize crowdsourcing, often through competitions that in a similar way try to tap into a distributed set of potential solvers. NASA's efforts, described at the top of this chapter, are examples of that. In both instances, relying on labor marketplaces allows the organization to engage with a much more diverse set of workers than most R&D organizations rely on. In the case of NASA's solar flare prediction algorithm, a particular kind of scientists with a particular kind of expertise (i.e., heliophysicists) had been working on the problem. The winner of the crowdsourcing competition, however, was radio engineer and "[h]is solution challenged the boundaries of the knowledge work in this field, using an approach that was completely outside the heliophysics discipline and tradition," namely "[u]sing ground radio-based equipment instead of the traditional satellite-based data" (Lebovitz et al, 2022, p. 756). This is precisely the value of labor marketplaces in innovation. They reduce the barriers to entry into problem-solving, allowing people at the social and technical margin to bring novel perspectives to internal problems (Jeppesen & Lakhani, 2010).

Another opportunity comes from treating external solvers not as contributors to problems framed and broadcast by the firm, but as independently operating complementors. This is the option that Altman et al describe as *developer ecosystems*. In this situation, "firms enable external parties (developers) to create complementary products (apps or accessories) that customers acquire either directly from the external parties or through a marketplace" (p. 360). We can see this phenomenon in many industries, but Google Play and Apple's App Store will be examples of this that are familiar to many: a focal firm develops and sells a product but then also creates a marketplace where users of that product can purchase third-party-developed apps for use with that product. In a world of low information costs, those third-party developers can create a range of complementary products that vastly exceeds what Apple or Google might be able to create. That universe of complementary products can increase the value of Apple and Google's products to customer groups that those companies might not otherwise (be able or willing to) target, and the marketplaces that Apple and Google offer might be markets much larger than what those third-party developers might be able to reach through alternative means.

Finally, declining information costs make it possible for firms to benefit from *user-generated contributions*. Users, as previously discussed (cf. Section 13.1), can both compete and coexist with firms when design costs are reduced, but when information costs decline, it also becomes possible for firms to engage with them and treat them as complementors. In a small way, asking users to rate and review products in the way that you see on, for example, Amazon is an immensely simple way that firms can engage with users once information costs fall. At a larger scale, however, reduced information costs also make it possible for firms to observe their users much more readily. Online forums where users of particular products interact and share their innovations, for instance, can be much more readily observed. Sites such as IKEAHackers and Rebrickable are examples of users of respectively Ikea and Lego products sharing insights with other users about how to repurpose products developed by those firms to different ends, and observing those kinds of user behaviors is radically more viable when information costs are low. Some companies, taking this approach as much more central to their operations, are based almost entirely on user contributions. Reddit is one example of this. Also, in an environment where information costs approach zero, it can be much more viable to seek to shift innovation to users through "toolkits" such that users can develop custom products that fit their own idiosyncratic needs.

As costs decline, it makes increasing sense to have ever more porous boundaries around organizations and to think of the organization not as an isolated unit producing innovations but as a part of an ecosystem that it can try to strategically manage. Firms, Altman et al argue, "outgrow the strategies, business models, and organizational processes theorists have been studying for decades…. While previously, they managed based on a Chandlerian logic emphasizing hierarchy and control …, successful firms today balance multiple logics that incorporate peer production, information sharing, data access, common and free goods, etc." (p. 362). With such porous boundaries, organizations are not operating simply as the "visible hand" that Chandler described (cf. Section 1.3), but rather through a hybrid form of hierarchy and market that they in later work describe as a "translucent hand" (Altman et al, 2021).

The new mode of organizational governance raises a wealth of new challenges for organizations. With more porous boundaries, firms no longer have the same kind of control over innovators who might now no longer be employees. Innovators working through labor marketplaces or as third-party developers might be highly mobile and not necessarily well-aligned with the organization. Reddit, based as it is on user contributions, is exemplary of these challenges precisely because the company's product is based so heavily on unpaid contributors and the work of "redditors." When redditors object to the policies of the company, Reddit clearly faces a challenge very different from those of Chandlerian organizations. The general point is that users and "[c]omplementors act and innovate independently" (p. 367) in a way that is very novel relative to what was the case in a closed Chandlerian model of the innovation process. Beyond the challenges that this might introduce in managing customers' experiences and expectations, this independence can also mean that innovation-related capabilities and knowledge can be less durable sources of advantage. What kinds of capabilities that knowledge that do matter are less clear. Does an organization, for instance, need the same kinds of technical and market-based knowledge that have previously been necessary to compete effectively, or can it rely on ad hoc sourcing of essential knowledge inputs? "Perhaps the knowledge and strategies for utilizing [] free and open assets become the most important assets of, and perhaps the only assets truly owned by, an organization" (p. 365).

In that world of porous organizational boundaries, the work and identity of innovators inside organizations, as well as the challenges of leading them, are set to change. In a world where external solvers can develop solutions that are as good as, or better than, those of internal solvers, we can imagine that valuable skills for internal innovation workers will be the ability to effectively identify which problems are worth shifting to external solvers, the conceptual understanding to frame problems in ways that make them open to diverse contributions, and insights into how to manage communities. For sure, "the roles of team members who create and nurture [external] communities might also increase in importance" (p. 368). With such changes, professional identities are likely to be under substantial threat. In NASA, the run of successful crowdsourcing contests challenged identities based on scientific and engineering problem-solving, leading to opposing movements within the organization (Lebovitz et al, 2022): some employees embraced the opportunities by dismantling knowledge boundaries, while others protected them, either through feigned openness or outright rejection. This provides a challenge to leaders who need not only to influence "staff members but also those in the community who contribute" (Altman et al, 2015, p. 367).

We can understand these organizational challenges in the Neo-Schumpeterian terms of Bodrozic and Adler. Declining information costs are making practices of engaging external innovators viable, in much the same way that other radical forms of technological change have exposed the potential for new ways of managing. However, these new practices do not come into the world fully worked out or coherently integrated. Rather, as some organizations recognize the organizational opportunities afforded by new technologies, piecemeal experimentation begins. Different organizations see that some tasks can be broadcast to labor marketplaces but might find that this requires them to work out ways of picking problems that are "broadcastable" and of managing a crowd of external solvers. Some experiments work out and others do not. The same will be the case for platforms and user communities, and that will reveal a different set of challenges and a different set of boundary conditions for the implementation of this model of involvement. As these practices stabilize, they might diffuse and become normalized in business practice, but this will also reveal their dysfunctions and set off further cycles of management and organizational innovation. Indeed, prevailing management practices are always artifacts of their technological circumstances.

13.3 Cockburn, Henderson, and Stern: Inventions in the Methods of Invention and the Shape of the Future

Think back to the Hockey Stick of Economic Growth. In the discussion of McCloskey's argument, Chapter 1 of this book described how most of human history is a history of nongrowth. Like the handle of a hockey stick, human development is essentially a flat line, thousands upon thousands of years of sameness as we move down the handle. Then, suddenly, we reach the blade. As the handle turns to the blade, we reach the inflection point and suddenly *everything* changes. That inflection point is the run-up to the birth of the Industrial Revolution and the emergence of the modern world. In that modern world, progress is an integral part of the human experience. Before modernity, you would expect your children to grow up in a world fundamentally similar to the one you grew up in and that your ancestors grew up in. Your life would be recognizable to your great-great-grandparents. In modernity, after the inflection point, we expect the world to change and understand that the world our children grow up in will be different, even unrecognizable, from the one we grew up in. In modernity, we got used to what Delong (2022, p. 4) calls "a revolutionized economy every generation." Such is life on the Schumpeterian blade of the hockey stick.

As you think about that image, you get a clear impression of stasis and change. The handle, as it were, comes off as a long period of stasis. With modernity, suddenly there is change. Having you think that way is the whole point of the metaphor. That image, however, is quite inaccurate because what looks like stasis is not static. Just as our modern economy seems to be hyper-accelerated relative to the premodern agricultural economy, that agricultural economy would itself have been hyper-accelerated relative to the preagricultural hunter-gatherer economy. The agricultural economy would have been as unimaginable to a hunter-gatherer as the modern industrial economy is to a premodern agriculturalist. The rate of change *during* the agricultural epoch vastly outpaces the rate of change during the hunter-gatherer epoch, just as the rate of change during the industrial epoch vastly outpaces the rate of change in the agricultural one. What happened with the dawn of modernity was not that change *began*. It began to happen on a human timescale, to happen so fast that it is observable within a single human lifetime.

Hanson's (2008) provides a nice entry point to this argument, the canonical theorization of which is Kurzweil's (2005) book *The Singularity is Near* (which has, to be fair, a strong vibe of science fiction and is not taken very seriously by serious people[3]). In the modern period, Hanson argues, growth rates are such that the economy doubles in size every ca. fifteen years. In the premodern agricultural economy, the economy doubled every ca. 9,000 years. In the preagricultural hunter-gatherer economy, it doubled every ca. 250,000 years. Put slightly differently, the Neolithic revolution that occasioned the transition from hunter-gathering to agriculture meant that growth rates increased 250-fold, and with the Industrial Revolution that marked the transition from agriculture to industrial modernity, they increased again, this time 60-fold. Each of these transitions is what people describe as *a singularity*: a sudden and rapid increase in growth rates.

Another key aspect of this argument is that these singularities are happening in more and more rapid succession. The hunter-gatherer phase of human history, beginning before the emergence of Homo sapiens several hundred thousand years ago, lasted close to two million years. The agricultural phase – that is, the time between the Neolithic Revolution and the Industrial Revolution – lasted some 10,000 years. The industrial phase has so far lasted several centuries. The argument, then, is not just that we have singularities, but also that singularities are happening at shorter and shorter time intervals. Put coarsely, at intervals that get two orders of magnitude smaller, growth rates increase by an order of magnitude.

If you extrapolate that trend out, it becomes apparent that we might be overdue for a singularity. Depending on how you look at the numbers, sometime between now and 2075, we ought to see an order-of-magnitude increase in growth rates. After that, further order-of-magnitude growth rates ought to happen literally all the time and what you would have would be *infinite growth*, centuries of progress achieved every hour. In that situation, the world would, in Bostrom's (2024) terms, be "solved" – there would really be nothing left to figure out, or it would simply be trivial to solve any new problem that might arise. The shape of such a

---

[3] As Nordhaus (2020) put it in his empirical assessment of the idea in the context of economic growth theory, "the Singularity is not near." But 2020 is of course not 2024, and science-fictional ideas are not to be dismissed simply because they are fictional (e.g., Hartmann, 2024).

solved world is inherently hard to understand and think about. To begin to think about it, imagine how different our world is from the world of hunter-gatherers. And imagine, then, that the magnitude of that difference is only the beginning of the difference between our world and a solved one.

It is, of course, not at all obvious that you *can* extrapolate the historic trend forward in time, but it does beg the question that Hanson raises: "What innovation could possibly induce so fabulous a speedup in economic growth?" (Hanson, 2008, p. 47). The specifics of Hanson's answer (involving what I think of as tiny robot brains in giant skyscrapers) can feel somewhat quixotic, but the in-principle answer is that the only kind of innovation that could induce a speedup like that is *innovation of innovation* itself, a technology that creates entirely new ways of bringing about innovation. A new general-purpose technology, or even a Neo-Schumpeterian cluster of them, would simply not do.

In a classic paper titled *The Changing Technology of Technological Change,* Arora and Gambardella described computers as one such technology. Computers, they argued, marked a change in how innovation happened in the economy. Before computers, innovation was based on what they call empiricist, trial-and-error procedures.

> In aeronautics, for instance, engineers have long used wind tunnels to simulate the flying conditions of aircraft. Wind tunnels have enabled them not only to test whether a particular design "works" but also aided in the search for a better design ... such long and costly experiments have been the only reliable way to design aircraft.... Similarly, drug discovery has required the laboratory syntheses of a great many molecules and systematic trials before finding one that showed potential therapeutic effect.... Process innovation has relied heavily on trial-and-error. For instance, in the design of large scale, continuous chemical processes, it has been no simple matter to go from the lab or bench scale process to producing tonnage levels. (p. 524)

With computers, complemented by stronger scientific theories and advances in measurement instruments, it has become possible to move from such *in vivo* experimentation to *in silico* simulations. Alas, for all the change that computers did bring to the innovation process, they did not bring the singularity. We are still chugging along with modernity-level growth rates.

Artificial intelligence, however, could also represent a new technology that changes technological change. As Cockburn et al put it,

> while some applications of artificial intelligence will surely substitute lower-cost or higher-quality inputs into many existing production processes ... others, such as deep learning, hold out the prospect of not only productivity gains across a wide variety of sectors, but also changes in the very nature of the innovation process

with those domains.... [B]y enabling innovation across many applications, the "invention of a method of invention" has the potential to have much larger economic impact than development of any single new product (2019, p. 116).

Deep learning, to be clear, is a kind of machine learning based on what are called neural networks, and it is the technology underlying the Large Language Models that underlie a product like ChatGPT, and Cockburn et al.'s chapter is an attempt – made in 2018 – to assess the plausibility of deep learning realizing that potential and to think through what might happen if it did.

As research tools, deep learning holds out the promise of having two types of impact on the innovation process. One impact could be to "automate discovery" (p. 120). Innovation and discovery have been some of the activities that have historically eluded automation (cf. Section 11.3) and so it has taken evermore resources to sustain current rates of innovation (Bloom et al, 2020). Deep learning clearly has the potential to substitute a lot of the tasks that scientists, whether in academia or industrial R&D, typically do as part of their work, thus making it cheaper and therefore more economically viable to do certain kinds of scientific work and increasing the value of those tasks that cannot be automated. When DeepMind used the AI AlphaFold to predict the structure about almost all the 200 million proteins known to science (Service, 2020), this was what happened. The structure of proteins was something that had historically been discovered experimentally, with some 170,000 proteins having been solved over decades. AlphaFold was trained on the database of known proteins and could, on that basis, predict the structure of all the unknown ones with remarkable accuracy. The emerging evidence suggests that deep learning is being applied in many other domains of science with similarly dramatic effects.

Another impact could be to "'expand the playbook' [in] the sense of opening up the set of problems that can be feasibly addressed, and radically altering scientific and technical communities' conceptual approaches and framing of problems" (pp. 120–121). They provide the example of optical lenses as exemplary of this kind of impact. When applied to the development of microscopes and telescopes, optical lenses made it possible to do entirely new kinds of science. "[B]y making very small and very distant objects visible for the first time, lenses opened up entirely new domains of inquiry and technological opportunity" (p. 121). In much the same way, deep learning systems promise "to generate predictions for physical and logical event that have previously resisted systematic empirical scrutiny" (p. 139), possibly allowing us to not only do what we already do faster (cf. Section 11.3) but also making it possible to do things that were hitherto impossible. If that happens across a range of sectors, then certainly we can imagine that AI can have very far-reaching effects on the rate of scientific discovery and inventive activity and, downstream of that, economic growth.

A crucial fact to be aware of in thinking through these potentials is the availability of data sets that AI can be trained on, or more specifically, "large unstructured databases that provide information about physical and logical events" (p. 127). While the algorithms that underpin deep learning models may well be very sophisticated, the performance of those models depends very much more on the data that those models are trained on. AlphaFold is able to achieve its impressive results because it can be trained on an existing database of protein structures, while conversational AIs such as ChatGPT can create text because they have been trained on enormous amounts of human-generated text available on the internet. "While the underlying algorithms for deep learning are in the public domain, [...] the data pools that are essential to generate predictions may be public or private" (p. 127). As such, the kind of impact that AI could have may depend both on there actually existing relevant training data and on that data being accessible. The natural implication is that fields that already have large datasets to train on might reap enormous benefits from AI, and that the returns from creating large datasets will increase dramatically in those that do not. Whether they will be generated is, however, not obvious.

If it turns out that deep learning does turn out to be an invention that changes the method of invention across domains, what impacts do Cockburn et al imagine? One likely and immediate effect is that invention can become cheaper and that a substantial share of scientific and inventive work will be done by machines. Moreover, it is easy to imagine that the barriers to entry into invention are radically reduced in those areas where large and accessible datasets exist, making it possible for both organizations and individual inventors equipped with deep learning technology to compete effectively against incumbents. Fields where large datasets exist, but are kept proprietary, may observe the opposite effect, such that only organizations and individuals with access to data can hope to compete. Fields without large datasets might not be severely impacted but see their productivity levels relative to other fields decrease dramatically.

The knock-on effects of these impacts are at least as interesting. They might, for instance, make it both harder and less worthwhile to build up deep scientific competence. As Cockburn et al argue, "it is possible that the democratization of innovation [by deep learning] will also be accompanied by a lack of investment by individual researchers in specialized research skills and specialized expertise in a given areas, reducing the level of theoretical and technical depth in the workforce" (p. 140). In Section 5.4, we discussed the burden of knowledge required to contribute to leading-edge science and the substantial investments it requires, and it is easy to imagine that making that investment becomes much less attractive when one can use deep learning technologies to produce findings, even in the absence of substantive understanding. Leaving aside the questions of how scientists will be able to review and assess algorithmically generated findings and whether the introduction of deep learning will undermine the learning pathways that science has come to depend on (cf. Section 11.2), this also raises the problem that "deep learning may undermine the long-term incentives for breakthrough research that can only be done by people who are the research frontier" (p. 140). Indeed, there is a real possibility that deep learning may well turn out to severely "break science" (p. 140) as we know it.

Whether this troubles you should depend on how you understand the possibility that deep learning could lead to a change in how we understand the nature of scientific advances. Since the advent of modern science, *theory* has been an essential part of the scientific process. Scientists have made empirical observations and from those observations tried to derive parsimonious theoretical explanations. Theories have, in turn, driven further empirical inquiry. "[D]eep learning offers an alternative paradigm based on the ability to predict complex multicausal phenomena using a 'black box' approach that abstracts away from underlying causes, but does allow for a singular prediction index that can yield sharp insight" (p. 141). Put differently, deep learning offers a way to think about science that does not need theories. Indeed, with deep learning, prediction can happen *without understanding*. As Cockburn et al put it, "it is easy to imagine a deep learning system trained on a large amount of x-ray diffraction data quickly 'discovering' the double helix structure of DNA at very low marginal cost" (p. 140) without being able to turn that discovery into a theory *and* without noticing "that the proposed structure suggests a direct mechanism for heredity" (p. 140). We could know much more and understand so much less.

In the future, perhaps one of the many things they will find strange about our time is that we even bothered trying to understand things with, you know, our minds.

14 Theories and Some Implications

One of the more interesting developments in management science over the past years has been the development of the "theory-based view" of economic actors. According to this view, we should think of economic actors such as entrepreneurs, innovators, and managers as akin to scientists, as people who hold particular *theories* (Felin & Zenger, 2017). These theories can be about markets, technologies, consumers, organizations, or any number of other things and they matter because the actions that economic actors take depend on, or at least are informed by, the theories they hold. A theory makes opportunities to create and capture value in the environment that economic actors find themselves "light up" and shapes how economic actors might attempt to pursue and elaborate them (Felin & Kauffman, 2023). The environment exists out there in a sort of objective way, but the theories we hold are what allow us to engage with it in meaningful ways. Paraphrasing historian Arnold Toynbee, we might say that without a theory, the environment is just one damn thing after another.

Equally interestingly, it seems that economic actors *benefit* from thinking of *themselves* as scientists and working in scientific ways (e.g., Yang et al, n.d.; Camuffo et al, 2024). When economic actors systematically formulate hypotheses, collect data to challenge their hypotheses, base their actions on systematic theorizing, and test competing theories against each other, they do better. They abandon false beliefs more quickly, their learning is less biased and more accurate, their actions are focused and more coordinated, and they become better able to create value out of uncertainty. This is not to say that these benefits come from holding theories. All economic actors hold theories, but they tend to come up with them in floppy, opportunistic, unsystematic, and tenuously grounded ways that organization theory tends to describe as *sensemaking*[1] and we are all engaged in sensemaking all

---

[1] There is a very strong case to be made that the sensemaking theory itself is a result of a pretty floppy, opportunistic, unsystematic, and tenuously grounded engagement with the

the time. We cannot really help that, but often the theories that result from sensemaking can be very problematic along a range of dimensions. The benefits of working scientifically come from being systematic about theories and the data underpinning them from being rigorous in one's theorizing.

This raises something of an interesting challenge for academic management scientists and students of management science. To put things in somewhat stark terms, the purpose of academic management science was for a long time thought of as creating valuable *insights* about management. The real value of management science was its discoveries and what they revealed about how managers could manage to realize whatever goals they and their organizations might have. Management scientists, by this reasoning, should endeavor to generate more of those research insights, and the insights ought to be both scientifically rigorous (i.e., true descriptions of the world) *and* managerially and societally relevant. By the same reasoning, management education would be about students absorbing those discoveries and insights, such that they could have a state-of-the-art management practice. Indeed, that might be the spirit in which you picked up this book or signed up for the course in which it is assigned: you conceivably wanted to know something about how to do innovation management well and imagined that a textbook on the subject might have some good theories about how to do that. The theory-based view challenges that. What you might get out of management education should not so much be the insights about management, but the *craft* of working like a scientist in doing managerial work.

Why, then, a textbook on theories of innovation management? If theories are not important, why bother reading, much less writing, about them?

Consider the manager's situation. The problems that managers need to solve rarely look like textbook problems. Much of what they do is of course relatively mundane and quotidian, but a lot of the difficult things that managers do is managing messes, not solving problems. And when they try to manage those messes, it becomes very clear that they are also working in very *specific* organizations, not in the abstraction of organizations. They deal with specific people, markets, and technologies. They are mired – sometimes even "quagmired" (Spicer, 2023) – in contingencies, circumstance, and context. It may be all good and fine that an academic theory tells them that things tend to be a certain way for most people, most of the time, but managers are dealing with things

empirical world (Basbøll & Graham, 2006; Basbøll, 2010a, 2010b; Gelman & Basbøll, 2014). There are surely pithy jokes to be made about that.

being a certain way for this particular group of people at this particular time. Add to this that the situation they are dealing with may well be a rare one, one that does not present itself repeatedly, and that it may well be beset by a whole host of knowledge problems (March et al, 1991; Townsend et al, 2018). In that situation, you cannot really expect things to level out over time and you cannot necessarily draw on your prior experience for guidance.

To make sense of that kind of situation in a scientific way, you need to appreciate that what goes on in organizations is often complex and ambiguous. In those situations, you need to *deepen* your understanding of the situation, not just experiment and test more or less formalized hypotheses (March et al, 1991). One way to do this is to generate *more interpretations* of the situation. This is one of the key uses for theory in managerial work: having a broad "interpretive repertoire" (Alvesson & Kärreman, 2007) allows you to generate more ideas about what might be going on and what it means, about the processes that lead to particular situations, and about what dynamics particular interventions in that situation might set in motion. Theory, in that sense, can substitute for experience. Another way to deepen your understanding is to experience a situation more *richly* and to experience more *aspects* of it. In some cases, collecting more data about what is going on might be helpful, but you need ideas to know what kinds of data might be relevant and where to look for it. The experiments that are explicitly suggested as, or implied to be, central to the theory-based practice of management may in that situation do more harm than good. You may need to mobilize a more qualitative set of methods. Theories about how things work in general can help generate those ideas about how things work in the particular and thus help empirical features of the environment "light up" as particularly relevant to explore with particular methods. Theory can help you learn by guiding what it makes sense to learn about and how.

Consider a situation where a specific company repeatedly fails to launch successful products in the marketplace. The solution apparent is to get the company's innovation project management straightened out. You could implement something like Cooper's Stage-Gate System. But your organization might not be quite like the organizations where that system originated, and it is not obvious that your organization has the kind of underlying problems that this system would seek to solve. You are, in a sense, jumping to conclusions, like a doctor prescribing a treatment before making a diagnosis. The manager following a scientific approach might instead want to develop a deeper understanding of why failure is so persistent and to problematize the obviousness of "getting things under control" by implementing the Stage-Gate System (or some other solution).

At first blush, you might think about whether the run of failures has something to do with the kind of projects you undertake. They may be very explorative and disruption-oriented, and so we should in fact expect failure to be the norm and success to be quite rare. They may be based on uncertain technologies, so, again, failure is hardly unreasonable. Perhaps you need to be more tolerant of failure. Alternatively, perhaps you should pursue less ambitious, more incremental innovations with a higher likelihood of success? Contrary to the idea that you should make your innovation project management more efficient, you might also think about whether you are in fact spending too few resources on innovation. Perhaps the reason your projects fail is that you are not giving the innovation projects the resources that they need to succeed, and failure is a result of them running too much on shoestring budgets. Maybe the lack of resources is leading the genuinely great ideas to go unfunded or underfunded, or driving your best people to bootleg their ideas or leave your company. Instead of spending money on consultants to teach your company to work with work more efficiently, perhaps the money should be given to innovation project managers for them to spend at their discretion?

But it could also be that your project managers are more interested in doing projects that look impressive than ones that will succeed in the marketplace, that is, that benefit their CVs and professional standing more than the company's performance. They might be planning to move on to new jobs soon, and having a project fail once they leave will not necessarily bother them – it might even cast them as brave pioneers and the people who take over as incompetent. Or perhaps your workers do not have the necessary skills, and so giving them more resources and having a greater tolerance for failure might exacerbate your problems, because they will simply keep failing and use more resources in the process. Alternatively, maybe the failure is not with the projects themselves, but with how decisions happen around the projects. Top management might lack the knowledge to pick good projects, or they may fail to ensure the integration of new products with existing capabilities. If that is the case, resources, people, or project management may not be the problem at all, and doing something about those things will ultimately do very little and at worst be a distraction. Maybe the products are in fact excellent, but mistimed, relative to industry conditions and the current state of competition. Perhaps they are even ahead of their time. It could also be that it is not even a real problem that projects fail. The fact that you are running those projects may function as a perk to attract good employees, as a way to generate learning or retain knowledge that will be valuable in the future, or as a way to signal that your company is staying relevant. Perhaps you should think of a certain number of failed projects as a "tax" that you have to pay to make other things possible?

I hope this convinces you that there is good reason to deepen your understanding of what is actually going on through some in-depth exploration. Theory, then, will not necessarily be valuable for you as a manager in the sense of providing what you might call actionable insights. None of the theories that you have met in this book will tell you what the problem is *in your situation* and what kind of knock-on, unintended consequences it will have to try to solve the problem in any one particular way. But they will, individually and collectively, give you a sense of the dynamics that might be at work, to entertain multiple hypotheses at the same time, and to begin to pay attention to, and explore more deeply, empirical material that might help you rule out some ideas, generate new ones, and grow more confident in others. The real value of academic theory is that it should enable managers to work better at formulating *their own theories* about the specific messes in which they find themselves and at using data of different types to think those theories through in a disciplined way. It should make managers better management scientists. Thinking is the cheapest form of trial and error,[2] and theory lets you think better.

Notice that I use the notion of good management science and good management scientists in a very specific way here. I invite you to not think of management science in the narrow sense of experimentalist, highly quantitatively oriented science. Good management science appreciates that some problems are amenable to that kind of methods but also appreciates that there are many questions that cannot be resolved in that way and call for a different kind of empirical inquiry and altogether much more open-ended kinds of answers. Good management science would also appreciate that there are questions that cannot be answered by science alone. There are many such questions in management and both management scientists and scientist-managers would do well to appreciate that. If you think of a theory-informed management practice in the very narrow sense of experimentalism along a natural science model, there will be many questions where you will probably just confuse yourself (Hunt et al, 2024).

This conception of theory and of the limits of a narrow understanding of science as experimentalism does not mean that "any old theory will do," that one theory is as good as the next and that the quality of any particular theory does not matter, because its purpose is only to inspire theorizing. As managers engage in theorizing, academic theories

---

[2] Thank you to Thor Hauberg for this adroit phrasing.

of the kind that you find in this book do not just provide scaffolding and repertoires for managerial thinking. How "good" the academic theory is also matters. The strength of the academic theory that scaffolds managerial theories should give the scientist-manager a sense of how strong their own theory is, even before engaging with the data. To see why this is the case, notice how some phenomena described in this book replicate again and again, in the sense that we see this repeatedly in the data. Technological discontinuities change industry structure. Dominant designs shift industries toward incremental innovation. Large firms tend to become bureaucratic. Bureaucracy is a precondition for, but does not guarantee, efficiency. Managers struggle to manage innovation processes. Entrepreneurial companies tend to fail. Technology does not substitute labor in the long run but complements it. We can have some confidence in ideas like these. Other ideas are empirically less well grounded, and we should place less confidence in them.

To see how this matters, imagine a manager with a theory. Let us, for the sake of example, think about a manager in a large logistics firm with a theory that the digital transformation will *not* impact the structure of the logistics industry. There may be good reasons to hold that theory. Our imagined managers might think, for instance, that competition in the industry is primarily about price and that new entrants – even if they are "born digital" – will struggle so much to gain the scale necessary to compete on price that they will be unable to significantly impact the industry. To be sure, this might even be a very valuable theory to hold *if it is true*. If all your incumbent competitors hold a different theory and believe (erroneously, according to your theory) that the digital transformation will matter, they may be tempted to invest massively in new technologies like artificial intelligence (AI), blockchain, and automation and even if they succeed (which they might not), those innovations might not matter very much. They will need to recoup some of that investment, so they will be forced to charge slightly higher prices. If our imagined manager and their company do not make those investments, they have nothing to recoup and may be able to charge lower prices, giving them an advantage over more paranoid competitors on the razor-thin margins that define this industry. Our theorizing manager would be holding a very idiosyncratic theory and if that theory turns out to be true, they stand to benefit.

The strength of theories like the ones in this book ought to matter here, because it should give our imagined manager a sense of how reasonable their theory is. They should appreciate that the theory they hold very much challenges a pattern that we have observed repeatedly, across multiple industries, across multiple technological transitions, and across multiple centuries. This is not to say that they cannot be right, but they should appreciate that they probably *are not*. They should feel that the burden of justifying their theory, in other words, is *on them*. Thus, they would want to have a very strong and well-supported set of ideas about why the commonplace theory that the digital transformation will matter does not hold in their specific situation, and indeed they might find that some of the ideas in this book could scaffold those ideas. They would also want to be very attuned to incoming empirical evidence to suggest that their ideas are, in fact, wrong and worth abandoning. When we have unreasonable ideas, in other words, we should know that they are unreasonable and that we cannot be complacent and intellectually lazy about them. Any old theory will not do. That applies in scholarship and in management practice.

It seems to me that the practice of management that all this calls for is one that is much slower, much more focused, sustained, and undistracted than is typically the case in managerial work (Kärreman et al, 2021) and than might be possible with future technological developments. This in turn calls for organizations hospitable to that kind of slow and scientifically oriented management practice (Hartmann et al, 2022). From studies of managerial work (e.g., Mintzberg, 1973; Korica et al, 2017), we know that management tends to be a hurried affair that leaves little room for reflexivity and thoughtfulness and we can fully expect that problem to be even more acute when it comes to the management of innovation, that most hyped and ideology-infused activity. Managers have to decelerate a bit to work scientifically. At the same time, we might expect that working scientifically will itself force some deceleration – you simply cannot do as much management if you have to invest more thoughtfulness in the management that you do. That is, I imagine, a good thing. Fast management is likely not what leads to what we might think of as good management of innovation or sound thinking on what innovations might mean for the organizations and societies that they touch.

Innovation, I hope to have convinced you, is both much too difficult and much too important for that.

References

Aarts, A. A. et al. 2015. Estimating the reproducibility of psychological science. *Science*. 349(6251), 943–950.

Abbott, A. 1981. Status and status strain in the professions. *American Journal of Sociology*. 86(4), 819–835.

Abernathy, W. J. 1978. *The productivity dilemma: Roadblock to innovation in the automobile industry* (Chapter 4). John Hopkins University Press.

Abrahamson, E. & Fairchild, G. 1999. Management fashion: Lifecycles, triggers and collective learning processes. *Administrative Science Quarterly*. 44(4), 708–740.

Acemoglu, D. & Robinson, J. A. 2013. *Why nations fail: The origins of power, prosperity and poverty*. Crown Currency.

Acemoglu, D., Johnson, S. & Robinson, J. A. 2005. Institutions as a fundamental cause of development. In *Handbook of economic growth*, ed. P. Aghion & S. Durlauf. North-Holland.

Adler, P. S. 2022. Capitalism, socialism and the climate crisis. *Organization Theory*. 3(1), 1–16.

Adler, P. S. & Borys, B. 1996. Two types of bureaucracy: Enabling and coercive. *Administrative Science Quarterly*. 41(1), 61–89.

Adler, P. S. et al. 2009. Perspectives on the productivity dilemma. *Journal of Operations Management*. 27(2), 99–113.

Adner, R. & Kapoor, R. 2016a. Innovation eco-systems and the pace of substitution: Re-examining technology S-curves. *Strategic Management Journal*. 37(4), 625–648.

Adner, R. & Kapoor, R. 2016b. Right tech, wrong time. *Harvard Business Review*. November 2016, 2–9.

Agrawal, A., Gans, J. S. & Goldfarb, A. 2023. Do we want less automation? *Science*. 381, 155–158.

Agrawal, A., Gans, J. S. & Stern, S. 2021. Enabling entrepreneurial choice. *Management Science*. 67(9), 5510–5524.

Aldrich, H. E. & Ruef, M. 2018. Unicorns, gazelles, and other distractions on the way to understanding real entrepreneurship in the United States. *Academy of Management Perspectives*. 32(4), 458–472. https://doi.org/10.5465/amp.2017.0123.

Aldrich, H. E., Hodgson, G. M., Hull, D. L., Knudsen, T., Mokyr, J. & Vanberg, V. J. 2008. In defense of generalized Darwinism. *Journal of Evolutionary Economics*. 18(5), 577–596.

Allen, R. C. 2009. Engels' Pause: Technical change, capital accumulation and inequality in the British industrial revolution. *Explorations in Economic History.* 46(4), 418–435.

Altman, E. J., Nagle, F. & Tushman, M. L. 2015. Innovating without information constraints: Organizations, communities, and innovation when information costs approach zero. In *The Oxford handbook of creativity, innovation, and entrepreneurship*, ed. C. E. Shalley, M. A. Hitt & J. Zhou. Oxford University Press.

Altman, E. J., Nagle, F. & Tushman, M. L. 2021. The translucent hand of managed ecosystems: Engaging communities for value creation and capture. *Academy of Management Annals.* 16, 70–101. https://doi.org/10.5465/annals.2020.0244.

Alvesson, M. & Kärreman, D. 2007. Constructing mystery: Empirical matters in theory development. *Academy of Management Review.* 32(4), 1265–1281.

Alvesson, M. & Spicer, A. 2012. A stupidity-based theory of organizations. *Journal of Management Studies.* 49(7), 1194–1220.

Anderson, E. 2017. *Private government: How employers rule our lives (and why we don't talk about it).* Princeton University Press.

Anderson, P. & Tushman, M. L. 1990. Technological discontinuities and dominant designs: A cyclical model of technological change. *Administrative Science Quarterly.* 35(4), 604–633.

Annosi, M. C., Foss, N. & Martini, A. 2020. When Agile harms learning and innovation (and what can be done about it). *California Management Review.* 63(1), 61–80.

Arora, A. & Gambardella, A. 1994. The changing technology of technological change: General and abstract knowledge and the division of innovative labor. *Research Policy.* 23(5), 523–532.

Augsdorfer, P. 2005. Bootlegging and path dependency. *Research Policy.* 34(1), 1–11.

Autor, D. H. 2015. Why are there still so many jobs? The history and future of workplace automation. *Journal of Economic Perspectives.* 29(3), 3–30.

Azoulay, P., Graff Zivin, J. S. & Manso, G. 2011. Incentives and creativity: Evidence from the academic life sciences. *The RAND Journal of Economics.* 42, 527–554. https://doi.org/10.1111/j.1756-2171.2011.00140.x.

Azoulay, P., Jones, B. F., Kim, J. D. & Miranda, J. 2020. Age and high-growth entrepreneurship. *American Economic Review: Insights.* 2(1), 65–82.

Bailey, D. E. & Barley, S. R. 2011. Teaching-learning ecologies: Mapping the environment to structure through action. *Organization Science.* 22(1), 262–285.

Baldwin, C. & von Hippel, E. 2011. Modeling a paradigm shift: From producer innovation to user and open collaborative innovation. *Organization Science.* 22(6), 1369–1683.

Barley, S. R. 1986. Technology as an occasion for structuring: Evidence from observations of CT scanners and the social order of radiology departments. *Administrative Science Quarterly.* 31(1), 78–108.

Basalla, G. 1988. *The evolution of technology.* Cambridge University Press.

Basbøll, T. 2010a. Softly constrained imagination: Plagiarism and misprision in the theory of organizational sensemaking. *Culture and Organization.* 16(2), 163–178.

Basbøll, T. 2010b. Multiple failures of scholarship: Karl Weick and the Mann Gulch disaster. In *The leading journal in the field: Destabilizing authority in the social sciences of management*, ed. P. Armstong & S. Lilley. Mayfly Books.

Basbøll, T. & Graham, H. 2006. Substitutes for strategy research: Notes on the source of Karl Weick's anecdote for the young lieutenant and the map. *Ephemera*. 6(2), 194–205.

Baumol, W. J. 1990. Entrepreneurship: Productive, unproductive, and destructive. *Journal of Political Economy*. 98(5), 893–921.

Beane, M. 2019. Shadow learning: Building robotic surgical skill when approved means fail. *Administrative Science Quarterly*. 64(1), 87–123.

Becker, M. C., Knudsen, T. & Swedberg, R. 2003. *The entrepreneur. Classic texts by Joseph A. Schumpeter*. Stanford Business Books.

Becker, M. C., Knudsen, T. & Swedberg, R. (eds.) 2011. *The entrepreneur – classic texts by Joseph A. Schumpeter*. Stanford University Press.

Beer, J. J. 1959. *The emergence of the German dye industry*. University of Illinois Press.

Benkler, Y. 2017. Peer production, the commons, and the future of the firm. *Strategic Organization*. 15(2), 264–274.

Benner, M. J. & Tushman, M. 2002. Process management and technological innovation: A longitudinal study of the photography and paint industries. *Administrative Science Quarterly*. 47(4), 676–707. https://doi.org/10.2307/3094913.

Bentzen, E., Christiansen, J. K. & Varnes, C. J. 2011. What attracts decision makers' attention? Managerial allocation of time at product development portfolio meetings. *Management Decision*. 49(3), 330–349.

Bernstein, E. 2012. The transparency paradox: A role for privacy in organizational learning and operational control. *Administrative Science Quarterly*. 57(2), 181–216.

Bernstein, E. 2017. Making transparency transparent: The evolution of observation in management theory. *Academy of Management Annals*. 11(1), 217–266.

Bernstein, E., Bunch, J., Canner, N. & Lee, M. 2016. Beyond the Holacracy Hype. *Harvard Business Review*. July–August 2016.

Bessen, J. 2014. *Learning by doing: The real connection between innovation, wages, and wealth* (Ch. 5–6). Yale University Press.

Bloom, N., Jones, C. I., Van Reenen, J. & Webb, M. 2020. Are ideas getting harder to find? *American Economic Review*. 110(4), 1104–1144.

Bodrozic, Z. & Adler, P. S. 2018. The evolution of management models: A neo-Schumpeterian theory. *Administrative Science Quarterly*. 63(1), 85–129.

Bodrozic, Z. & Adler, P. S. 2022. Alternative futures for the digital transformation: A macro-level Schumpeterian perspective. *Organization Science*. 33(1), 105–125.

Bodrozic, Z., Hartmann, R. K. & Krabbe, A. D. 2024. The ascendance and decline of entrepreneurialism: A neo-Schumpeterian perspective. Paper presented at EGOS Colloquium 2024.

Bostrom, N. 2024. *Deep utopia: Life and meaning in a solved world*. Ideapress Publishing.

Branstetter, L., Lima, F., Taylor, L. J., & Venâncio, A. 2014. Do entry regulations deter entrepreneurship and job creation? Evidence from recent reforms in Portugal. *The Economic Journal*. 124(577), 805–832.

Bresnahan, T. F. & Trajtenberg, M. 1995. General purpose technologies: "Engines of growth"? *Journal of Econometrics.* 65(1), 8–108.

Brewer, M. B. 1991. The social self: On being the same and different at the same time. *Personality and Social Psychology Bulletin.* 17(5), 475–482.

Brown, J. S. & Duguid, P. 1991. Organizational learning and communities-of-practice: Toward a unified view of working, learning, and innovation. *Organization Science.* 2(1), 40–57.

Brunsson, N. 1989. *The organization of hypocrisy: Talk, decisions and actions in organizations.* Wiley.

Brunsson, N. 1993. Ideas and action: Justification and hypocrisy as alternatives to control. *Accounting, Organizations and Society.* 18(6), 489–506.

Brynjolfsson, E. & McAfee, A. 2014. *The second machine age: Work, progress and prosperity in an age of brilliant technologies.* W. W. Norton & Company.

Brynjolffson, E., Hofmann, P. & Jordan, J. 2010. Cloud computing and electricity: Beyond the utility model. *Communications of the ACM.* 53(6), 32–34.

Brynjolfsson, E., Li, D. & Raymond, L. R. 2023. Generative AI at work. National Bureau of Economics Research (NBER) Working Paper 31161 (updated November 2023).

Burns, T. & Stalker, G. M. 1961. *The management of innovation.* Tavistock.

Burt, R. S. 2004. Structural holes and good ideas. *American Journal of Sociology.* 110(2), 349–399.

Camuffo, A., Gambardella, A., Messinese, D., Novelli, E., Paolucci, E. & Spina, C. 2024. A scientific approach to entrepreneurial decision-making: A large-scale replication and extension. *Strategic Management Journal.* 45(6), 1209–1237.

Catalini, C., Guzman, J. & Stern, S. 2019. Hidden in plain sight: Venture growth with or without venture capital. NBER Working Paper.

Chandler, A. D. 1977. *The visible hand: The managerial revolution in American business* (Introduction). Harvard University Press.

Chavda, A., Gans, J. S. & Stern, S. 2024. *Theory-Driven Entrepreneurial Search* (January 25, 2024). Available at SSRN: https://ssrn.com/abstract=4706860 or https://doi.org/10.2139/ssrn.4706860.

Christensen, C. 1997. *The innovator's dilemma: When new technologies cause great firms to fail* (Introduction). Harvard Business Review Press.

Christiansen, J. K. & Varnes, C. J. 2007. Making decisions on innovation: Meetings or networks? *Creativity and Innovation Management.* 16(3), 282–298.

Cockburn, I. M., Henderson, R. & Stern, S. 2019. The impact of artificial intelligence on innovation: An exploratory analysis. In *The economics of artificial intelligence: An agenda*, ed. A. Agrawal, J. Gans & A. Goldfarb. University of Chicago Press.

Cohen, W. M. & Levinthal, D. A. 1990. Absorptive capacity: A new perspective on learning and innovation. *Administrative Science Quarterly.* 35(1), 128–152.

Colaizzi, P. 1978. Psychological research as a phenomenologist views it. In *Existential-phenomenological alternatives for psychology*, ed. R. Valle & S. King, Oxford University Press.

Cooper, R. G. 1990. Stage-gate systems: A new tool for managing new products. *Business Horizons.* 33(3), 44–54.

Criscuolo, P., Salter, A. & Ter Wal, A. L. J. 2014. Going underground: Bootlegging and individual innovative performance. *Organization Science*. 25(5), 1287–1571.

Cusumano, M. A., Mylonadis, Y. & Rosenbloom, R. S. 1992. Strategic maneuvering and mass market dynamics: The triumph of VHS over Betamax. *Business History Review*. 66(1), 51–94.

David, P. A. 1985. Clio and the economics of QWERTY. *The American Economic Review*. 75(2), 332–337.

David, P. A. 1990. The dynamo and the computer: An historical perspective on the modern productivity dilemma. *The American Economic Review*. 80(2), 355–361.

Davis, G. F. 2016. *The vanishing American corporation: Navigating the hazards of a new economy*. Berrett-Koehler.

De Cruz, H. & De Smedt, J. 2010. Science as structured imagination. *The Journal of Creative Behavior*. 44, 37–52. https://doi.org/10.1002/j.2162-6057.2010.tb01324.x.

De Jong, J. P. J. 2016. The empirical scope of user innovation. In *Revolutionizing innovation: Users, communities, and open innovation*, ed. D. Harhoff & K. R. Lakhani. MIT Press.

Dell'Acqua, F. 2022. Falling asleep at the wheel: Human/AI collaboration in a field experiment on HR recruiters. Unpublished Working Paper.

Dell'Acqua, F., Kogut, B. & Perkowski, P. 2023a. Super Mario Meets AI: Experimental effects of automation and skills on team performance and coordination. *The Review of Economics and Statistics*. 1–47.

Dell'Acqua, F., McFowland, E., Mollick, E. R., Lifshitz-Assaf, H., Kellogg, K., Rajendran, S., Krayer, L., Candelon, F. & Lakhani, K. R. 2023b. Navigating the jagged technological frontier: Field experimental evidence of the effects of AI on knowledge worker productivity and quality (September 15, 2023). Harvard Business School Technology & Operations Mgt. Unit Working Paper No. 24-013. Available at SSRN: https://ssrn.com/abstract=4573321 or https://doi.org/10.2139/ssrn.4573321.

Delong, J. B. 2022. *Slouching towards utopia: An economic history of the twentieth century*. Basic Books.

Dennis, M. A. 1987. Accounting for research: New histories of corporate laboratories and the social history of American science. *Social Studies of Science*. 17(3), 479–518.

Dosi, G. 1982. Technological paradigms and technological trajectories: A suggested interpretation of the determinants and directions of technical change. *Research Policy*. 11(3), 147–162.

Dowell, G. & Swaminathan, A. 2006. Entry timing, exploitation and firm survival in the early U.S. bicycle industry. *Strategic Management Journal*. 27(12), 1159–1182.

Duggan, W. 2013. *Strategic intuition: The creative spark in human achievement*. Columbia University Press.

Duhigg, C. 2018. The case against Google. *The New York Times Magazine*. February 20, 2018.

Duncan, R. B. 1976. The ambidextrous organization: Designing dual structures for innovation. In *The management of organization design: Strategies and implementation*, ed. R. H. Kilmann, L. R. Pondy, & D. P. Slevin. North-Holland.

Dunne, J. 1993. *Back to the rough ground: Practical judgment and the lure of technique.* University of Notre Dame Press.
Elias, N. 1982a. *The civilizing process: The history of manners.* Pantheon.
Elias, N. 1982b. *The civilizing process: Power and civility.* Pantheon.
Feigenbaum, J. & Gross, D. P. 2020. Answering the call of automation: How the labor market adjusted to the mechanization of telephone operation. NBER Working Paper 28061.
Felin, T. 2016. When strategy walks out the door. *MIT Sloan Management Review.* August 31, 2016.
Felin, T. 2018. The fallacy of obviousness. *Aeon.* July 2018.
Felin, T. & Kauffman, S. 2023. Disruptive evolution: Harnessing functional excess, experimentation and science as tool. *Industrial and Corporate Change.* 32(6), 1372–1392.
Felin, T. & Zenger, T. R. 2017. The theory-based view: Economic actors as theorists. *Strategy Science.* 2(4), 258–271.
Fiol, C. M. 1996. Squeezing harder doesn't always work: Continuing the search for consistency in innovation research. *Academy of Management Review.* 21(4), 1012–1021.
Flyvbjerg, B. 2001. *Making social science matter: Why social inquiry fails and how it can succeed again.* Cambridge University Press.
Foss, N. J. 2003. Selective intervention and internal hybrids: Interpreting and learning from the rise and decline of the Oticon Spaghetti Organization. *Organization Science.* 14(3), 331–349.
Foster, R. 1986. *Innovation: The attacker's advantage.* Summit Books.
Frye, D. 2018. *Walls: A history of civilization in blood and brick.* Scribner An Imprint of Simon and Schuster, Inc.
Galenson, D. W. 2009. Old masters and young geniuses: The two life cycles of human creativity. *Journal of Applied Economics.* XII(1), 1–9.
Gans, J. S. 2017. *The disruption dilemma.* MIT Press.
Gans, J. S., Hsu, D. H. & Stern, S. 2002. When does start-up innovation spur the gale of creative destruction. *The RAND Journal of Economics.* 33(4), 571–586.
Gans, J. S., Scott, E. L. & Stern, S. 2018. Do entrepreneurs need a strategy? *Harvard Business Review.* May–June 2018.
Gans, J. S., Scott, E. L. & Stern, S. 2020. Entrepreneurial strategy. Available for download from www.entrepreneurial-strategy.net.
Gans, J. S., Stern, S. & Wu, J. 2019. Foundations of entrepreneurial strategy. *Strategic Management Journal.* 40(5), 736–756.
Gans, J. S., Kearney, M., Scott, E. L. & Stern, S. 2020. Choosing Technology: An entrepreneurial strategy approach. National Bureau of Economic Research. Working Paper #27489.
Gehman, J. & Soublière, J. F. 2017. Cultural entrepreneurship: From making culture to cultural making. *Innovation.* 19(1), 61–73. https://doi.org/10.1080/14479338.2016.1268521.
Gelman, A. & Basbøll, T. 2014. When do stories work? Evidence and illustration in the social sciences. *Sociological Methods and Research.* 43(4), 547–570.
Gibson, J. J. 1979. *The ecological approach to visual perception.* Houghton Mifflin.

Giersch, H. 1984. The age of Schumpeter. *The American Economic Review.* 74(2), 103–109. www.jstor.org/stable/1816338. Accessed January 13, 2025.

Gordon, R. J. 2016. *The rise and fall of American growth: The U.S. standard of living since the civil war.* Princeton University Press.

Granovetter, M. S. 1973. The strength of weak ties. Social networks. *American Journal of Sociology.* 78(6), 1360–1380.

Gray, M. & Suri, S. 2019. *Ghost work: How to stop Silicon Valley from building a new global underclass.* Houghton Mifflin Harcourt.

Greene, F. J., Mole, K. & Storey, D. J. 2004. Does more mean worse?: Three decades of enterprise policy in the Tees Valley. *Urban Studies.* 41, 1207–1228.

Greiner, L. E. 1998. Evolution and revolution as organizations grow. *Harvard Business Review.* May/June, 55–68.

Gustetic, J. L., Crusan, J., Rader, S. & Ortega, S. 2015. Outcome-driven open innovation at NASA. *Space Policy.* 34, 11–17. https://doi.org/10.1016/j.spacepol.2015.06.002.

Hamilton, D. 1957. The entrepreneur as cultural hero. *The Southwestern Social Science Quarterly.* 38(3), 248–256.

Hannigan, T., McCarthy, I. P. & Spicer, A. 2023. Beware of Botshit: How to manage the epistemic risks of generative chatbots. *Business Horizons.* Available at SSRN: https://ssrn.com/abstract=4678265 or https://doi.org/10.2139/ssrn.4678265.

Hanson, R. 2008. Economics of the singularity. *IEEE Spectrum.* June, 37–42.

Hargadon, A. & Sutton, R. I. 1997. Technology brokering and innovation in a product development firm. *Administrative Science Quarterly.* 42(2), 716–749.

Harper, D. A. & Lewis, P. 2012. New perspectives on emergence in economics. *Journal of Economic Behavior and Organization.* 82(2–3), 329–337.

Hartmann, M. R. K. & Hartmann, R. K. 2023. Hiding practices in employee-user innovation. *Research Policy.* 52(4), 104728.

Hartmann, R. K. 2024. Hieroglyphs, or science fiction icons and the rate and direction of innovation. *Innovation,* 1–17. https://doi.org/10.1080/14479338.2024.2442303.

Hartmann, R. K., Krabbe, A. D. & Spicer, A. 2022. Towards an untrepreneurial economy? The entrepreneurship industry and the rise of the Veblenian entrepreneur. In *Entrepreurialism and society: Consequences and meanings,* ed. R. N. Eberhart, M. Lounsbury & H. E. Aldrich. Research in the Sociology of Organizations.

Hartmann, R. K., Kärreman, D., Meier, N., Ingerslev, K. & Hauberg, T. M. 2022. Craft, reflexivity and the clinical practice of management. Available at SSRN: https://ssrn.com/abstract=4071584 or https://doi.org/10.2139/ssrn.4071584.

Hayek, F. A. 1945. The use of knowledge in society. *American Economic Review.* 35(4), 519–530.

Henderson, R. M. & Clark, K. B. 1990. Architectural innovation: The reconfiguration of existing product technologies and the failure of established firms. *Administrative Science Quarterly.* 35(1), 9–30.

Hienerth, C. 2016. Technique innovation. In *Revolutionizing innovation: Users, communities, and open innovation,* ed. D. Harhoff & K. R. Lakhani. MIT Press.

Hoffman, R. & Yeh, C. 2018. *Blitzscaling: The lightning-fast path to building massively valuable companies*. Currency.

Hughes, T. P. 1983. *Networks of power: Electrification of Western society, 1880–1930*. John Hopkins University Press.

Hunt, R. A., Townsend, D. M., Lerner, D. A. & Browneel, K. M. 2024. Pivot, Perish or Persist? Knowledge problems and the extraordinarily tight boundary conditions of entrepreneurs as scientists. *Journal of Business Venturing Insights*. 21, e00459.

Iansiti, M. & Lakhani, K. R. 2017. The truth about Blockchain. *Harvard Business Review*. 95(1) (January–February 2017), 118–127.

Jeppesen, L. B. & Lakhani, K. R. 2010. Marginality and problem-solving effectiveness in broadcast search. *Organization Science*. 21(5), 1016–1033.

Jones, B. F. 2009. The burden of knowledge and the "death of the Renaissance man"? Is innovation getting harder? *The Review of Economic Studies*. 76(1), 283–317.

Jones, B. F. 2010. Age and great invention. *The Review of Economics and Statistics*. XCII(1), 1–14.

Jovanovic, B. & Rousseau, P. L. 2005. General purpose technologies. In *Handbook of economic growth*, ed. P. Aghion & S. N. Durlauf. Elsevier.

Kärreman, D., Spicer, A. & Hartmann, R. K. 2021. Slow management. *Scandinavian Journal of Management*. 37(2), 101152.

Keating, G. 2012. *Netflixed: The epic battle for America's eyeballs*. Portfolio.

Kellogg, K. C., Orlikowski, W. J. & Yates, J. 2006. Life in the trading zone: Structuring coordination across boundaries in postbureaucratic organizations. *Organization Science*. 17(1), 22–44.

Kelly, M. 2020. Understanding persistence. UCD Centre for Economic Research Working Paper Series, No. WP20/23, University College Dublin, UCD Centre for Economic Research, Dublin.

Kesavadev, J., Srinivasan, S., Saboo, B. et al. 2020. The do-it-yourself artificial pancreas: A comprehensive review. *Diabetes Therapy*. 11, 1217–1235. https://doi.org/10.1007/s13300-020-00823-z.

Keynes, J. M. 1939. The general theory of employment. *Quarterly Journal of Economics*. 51(2), 209–223.

King, A. A. & Baatartogtokh, B. 2015. How useful is the theory of disruptive innovation. *MIT Sloan Management Review*. September 15, 2015.

Kirzner, I. M. 1978. *Competition and entrepreneurship*. University of Chicago Press.

Kirzner, I. M. 1999. Creativity and/or alertness: A reconsideration of the Schumpeterian entrepreneur. *Review of Austrian Economics*. 11(1–2), 5–17.

Korica, M., Nicolini, D. & Johnson, B. 2017. In search of "managerial work": Past, present and future of an analytical category. *International Journal of Management Reviews*. 19(2), 151–174.

Kuhn, T. S. 1962. *The structure of scientific revolutions*. University of Chicago Press.

Kunda, G. 2006. *Engineering culture: Control and commitment in a high-tech corporation* (revised edition). Temple University Press.

Kurzweil, R. 2005. *The Singularity is near: When humans transcend biology*. Viking Penguin.

Lave, J. & Wenger, E. 1990. *Situated learning: Legitimate peripheral participation*. Cambridge University Press.

Lebovitz, S., Lifsitz-Assaf, H. & Levina, N. 2022. To engage or not to engage with AI for critical judgments: How professionals deal with opacity when using AI for medical diagnosis. *Organization Science*. 33(1), 126–148.

Lepore, J. 2014. The disruption machine: What the gospel of innovation gets wrong. *The New Yorker*. June 23, 2014.

Levinthal, D. 1997. Adaptation on rugged landscapes. *Management Science*. 43(7), 934–950.

Lewinson, M. 2008. *The box: How the shipping container made the world smaller and the world economy bigger*. Princeton University Press.

Lieberman, M. B. & Montgomery, D. B. 1988a. First-mover advantages. *Strategic Management Journal*. 9(S1), 41–58.

Lieberman, M. B. & Montgomery, D. B. 1998b. First-mover (dis)advantages: Retrospective and link with the resource-based view. *Strategic Management Journal*. 19(12), 1111–1125.

Lifshitz-Assaf, H. 2018. Dismantling knowledge boundaries at NASA: The critical role of professional identity in open innovation. *Administrative Science Quarterly*. 63(4), 746–782. https://doi.org/10.1177/0001839217747876.

Lu, S. F., Rui, H. & Seidman, A. 2018. Does technology substitute for nurses? Staffing decisions in nursing homes. *Management Science*. 64(4), 1842–1859.

Lundvall, B. Å. 2010. *National systems of innovation: Towards a theory of innovation and interactive learning*. Anthem Press.

MacKenzie, D. 2008. *An engine, not a camera: How financial models shape markets*. MIT Press.

Mann, C. 2019. *The wizard and the prophet: Two remarkable scientists and their dueling visions to shape tomorrow's world*. Knopf.

March, J. G. 1991. Exploration and exploitation in organizational learning. *Organization Science*. 2(1), 71–87.

March, J. G., Sproul, L. S. & Tamuz, M. 1991. Learning from samples of one or fewer. *Organization Science*. 2(1), 1–13.

Masters, B. & Thiel, P. 2014. *Zero to one: Notes on start ups, or how to build the future*. Random House.

Mazzucato, M. 2013 (2018). *The entrepreneurial state: Debunking public and private sector myths*. Penguin Books.

McCloskey, D. N. 2010. *Bourgeois dignity: Why economics can't explain the modern world* (Chapter 1). University of Chicago Press.

McCraw, T. K. 1995. *Creating modern capitalism: How entrepreneurs, companies and countries triumphed in three industrial revolutions*. Harvard University Press.

McCraw, T. K. 2007. *Prophet of innovation: Joseph Schumpeter and creative destruction*. The Belknap Press of Harvard University Press.

Meisenzahl, R. R. & Mokyr, J. 2012. The rate and direction of inventive activity in the British Industrial Revolution: Incentives and institutions. In *The rate and direction of inventive activity revisited*, ed. J. Lerner & S. Stern. University of Chicago Press.

Melero, E. & Palomeras, N. 2015. The *Renaissance Man* is not dead! The role of generalists in teams of inventors. *Research Policy*. 44(1), 154–167.

Mills, C. W. 1959. *The sociological imagination*. Oxford University Press.

Mintzberg, H. 1971. Managerial work: Analysis from observation. *Management Science*. 18(2), B97–B110.

Mintzberg, H. 1973. *The nature of managerial work.* Harper & Row.

Mokyr, J. 1990. *The lever of riches: Technological creativity and economic progress.* Oxford University Press.

Mokyr, J., Vickers, C. & Ziebarth, N. L. 2015. The history of technological anxiety and the future of economic growth: Is this time different? *Journal of Economic Perspectives.* 29(3), 31–50.

Moore, G. A. 1991 (2006). *Crossing the Chasm: Marketing and selling disruptive products to mainstream customers.* Collins Business Essentials.

Moreira, S., Markus, A. & Laursen, K. 2018. Knowledge diversity and coordination: The effect of intrafirm inventor task networks on absorption speed. *Strategic Management Journal.* 39(9), 2517–2546.

Morison, E. 1966. *Men, machines, and modern times.* MIT Press.

Mouritsen, J., Hansen, A. & Hansen, C. Ø. 2009. Long and short translations: Management accounting calculations and innovation management. *Accounting, Organizations and Society.* 34(6–7), 738–754.

Navis, C. & Glynn, M. A. 2010. How new market categories emerge: Temporal dynamics of legitimacy, identity and entrepreneurship in satellite radio, 1990–2005. *Administrative Science Quarterly.* 55(3), 439–471.

Navis, C., Fisher, G., Raffaelli, R. & Glynn, M. A. 2012. The market that wasn't: The non-emergence of the online grocery category. Proceedings of the Frontiers in Managerial and Organizational Cognition Conference (September 2012).

Nelson, R. R. & Winter, S. G. 1982. *An evolutionary theory of economic change.* Harvard University Press.

Nicholas, T. 2010. The role of independent invention in US technological development, 1880–1930. *The Journal of Economic History.* 70(1), 57–82.

Nicholas, T. 2019. *VC: An American history.* Harvard University Press.

Nicolini, D., Korica, M. & Ruddle, K. 2015. Staying in the know. *MIT Sloan Management Review.* 56(4), 57–65.

Nightingale, P. & Coad, A. 2013. Muppets and gazelles: Political and methodological biases in entrepreneurship research. *Industrial and Corporate Change.* 23(1), 113–143.

Nordhaus, W. D. 2020. Are we approaching an economic singularity? Information technology and the future of economic growth. *American Economic Journal: Macro-economics.* 13(1), 299–332.

Nunn, N. 2008. The long-term effects of Africa's slave trades. *The Quarterly Journal of Economics.* 123(1), 139–176.

Nuvolari, A. 2004. Collective invention during the British Industrial Revolution: The case of the Cornish pumping engine. *Cambridge Journal of Economics.* 28(3), 347–363. https://doi.org/10.1093/cje/28.3.347.

Oliveira, P., Zejnilovic, L., Canhão, H. et al. 2015. Innovation by patients with rare diseases and chronic needs. *Orphanet Journal of Rare Diseases.* 10, 41. https://doi.org/10.1186/s13023-015-0257-2.

Orr, J. E. 1996. *Talking about machines: An ethnography of a modern job.* ILR Press.

O'Mara, M. 2020. *The code. Silicon Valley and the remaking of America.* Penguin Books.

Perez, C. 2009. The double bubble at the turn of the century: Technological roots and structural implications. *Cambridge Journal of Economics.* 33(4), 779–805.

Perez, C. 2010. Technological revolutions and techno-economic paradigms. *Cambridge Journal of Economics*. 34(1), 185–202. https://doi.org/10.1093/cje/bep051.

Polanyi, M. 1966. *The tacit dimension*. University of Chicago Press.

Pollan, M. 2021. *This is your mind on plants*. Penguin.

Porter, M. 1980. *Competitive strategy: Techniques for analyzing industries and competitors*. Free Press.

Porter, M. 1985. *Competitive advantage: Creating and sustaining superior performance*. Free Press.

Powell, W. W., Koput, K. W. & Smith-Doerr, L. 1996. Interorganizational collaboration and the locus of innovation: Networks of learning in biotechnology. *Administrative Science Quarterly*. 41(1), 116–145.

Preißner, S., Raasch, C. & Schweisfurth, T. 2024. When necessity is the mother of disruption: Users versus producers as sources of disruptive innovation. *Journal of Product Innovation Management*. 41(1), 62–85. https://doi.org/10.1111/jpim.12709.

Raffaeli, R. 2019. Technology reemergence: Creating new value for old technologies in Swiss Mechanical Watchmaking, 1970–2008. *Administrative Science Quarterly*. 64(3), 576–618. https://doi.org/10.1177/0001839218778505.

Raisch, S., Birkinshaw, J., Probst, G. & Tushman, M. 2009. Organizational ambidexterity: Balancing exploitation and exploration for sustained performance. *Organization Science*. 20(4), 685–695.

Reich, L. S. 1985. *The making of American industrial research: Science and business at GE and Bell, 1876–1926*. Cambridge University Press.

Reinert, H. & Reinert, E. S. 2006. Creative destruction in economics: Nietzsche, Sombart, Schumpeter. In *Friedrich Nietzsche (1844–1900): Economy and society*, ed. J. G. Backhaus & W. Drechsler. Springer.

Rennstam, J. & Kärreman, D. 2020. Understanding control in communities of practice: Constructive disobedience in a high-tech firm. *Human Relations*. 73(6), 864–890.

Repenning, N. P. 2000. Drive out fear (unless you can drive it in): The role of agency and job security in process improvement. *Management Science*. 46(11), 1385–1396.

Roach, M. & Sauermann, H. 2010. A taste for science? PhD scientists' academic orientation and self-selection into research careers in industry. *Research Policy*. 39(3), 422–434.

Rogers, E. M. 2003 (1962). *Diffusion of innovations*, 5th ed. Simon & Schuster.

Romer, P. 1990. Endogenous technological change. *Journal of Political Economy*. 98(5, part 2), 71–102.

Rosa, J. A., Porac, J. F., Runser-Spanjol, J. & Saxon, M.S. 1999. Sociocognitive dynamics in a product market. *Journal of Marketing*. 63(4), 64–77.

Rosenberg, N. 1976. On technological expectations. *The Economic Journal*. 86(343), 523–535.

Rosenberg, N. 1978. Pressures toward Bigness. *Science*. 200(4342), 640–642.

Rosenberg, N. 1982. *Inside the black box: Technology and economics*. Cambridge University Press.

Rosenberg, N. 1996. Uncertainty and technological change. In *The mosaic of economic growth*, ed. R. Landau, R. Taylor & G. Wright. Stanford University Press.

Rosenberg, N. & Birdzell, L. E. 1986. *How the West grew rich: The economic transformation of the industrial world*. I.B. Tauris.

Rosenberg, N. & Trajtenberg, M. 2004. A general-purpose technology at work: The Corliss steam engine in the late nineteenth-century United States. *The Journal of Economic History*. 64(1), 61–99.

Salter, A. & Alexy, O. 2014. The nature of innovation. In *The Oxford Handbook of innovation management*, ed. M. Dogdson, D. M. Gann & N. Philips, Oxford University Press.

Santarelli, E. & Vivarelli, M. 2007. Entrepreneurship and the process of firms' entry, survival and growth. *Industrial and Corporate Change*. 16(3), 455–488. https://doi.org/10.1093/icc/dtm010.

Schumpeter, J. A. 1934 (1911). The theory of economic development: The fundamental phenomenon of economic development. In *The entrepreneur: Classic texts by Joseph A. Schumpeter*, ed. M. Becker, T. Knudsen & R. Swedberg. Stanford University Press.

Schumpeter, J. A. 1939. *Business cycles: A theoretical, historical, and statistical analysis of the capitalist process*, Vol. I. McGraw-Hill.

Schumpeter, J. A. 1942/2008. *Capitalism, socialism and democracy* (Chapter 7). Harper Perennial Modern Thought Edition.

Schweisfurth, T. G. & Raasch, C. 2018. Absorptive capacity for need knowledge: Antecedents and effects for employee innovativeness. *Research Policy*. 47(4), 687–699.

Service, R. F. 2020. "The game has changed." AI triumphs at protein folding. *Science*. 370(6521), 1144–1145.

Shane, S. 2008. *The illusions of Entrepreneurship: The costly myths that entrepreneurs, investors, and policy makers live by*. Yale University Press.

Shane, S. 2010. Prior knowledge and the discovery of entrepreneurial opportunities. *Organization Science*. 11(4), 448–469.

Shapiro, C. & Varian, H. 1998. *Information rules: A strategic guide to the network economy*. Harvard Business Review Press.

Shih, W. 2016. The real lessons from Kodak's decline. *MIT Sloan Management Review*. May 20, 2016.

Simmons, J. P., Nelson, L. D. & Simonsohn, U. 2011. False-positive psychology: Undisclosed flexibility in data collection and analysis allows presenting anything as significant. *Psychological Science*. 22(11), 1359–1366.

Solow, R. M. 1987. We'd better watch out. *New York Times Book Review*. July 12, 1987, p. 36.

Spicer, A. 2023. Quagmires. *Organization Studies*. 44(2), 340–343. https://doi.org/10.1177/01708406221131940.

Stern, S. 2004. Do scientists pay to be scientists?. *Management Science*. 50(6), 835–853.

Stoller, M. 2017. Citizens against monopoly. *Huffington Post*. Posted August 30, 2017; updated August 31, 2017.

Suarez, F. F. & Lanzolla, G. 2007. The role of environmental dynamics in building a first mover advantage theory. *Academy of Management Review*. 32(2), 377–392.

Tambe, P., Ye, X. & Cappelli, P. 2020. Paying to program? Engineering brand and high-tech wages. *Management Science*. 66(7), 3010–3028.

References

Taylor, F. W. 1911. *The principles of scientific management*. Harper & Brothers Publishers.

Teece, D. J. 1986. Profiting from technological innovation: Implications for integration, collaboration, licensing and public policy. *Research Policy*. 15(6), 285–305.

Ten Bos, R. 2000. *Fashion and utopia in management thinking*. John Benjamins Publishing Company.

Thiel, P. 2014. *From zero to one: Notes on start-ups, or how to build the future*. Virgin Books.

Tobler, W. R. (1970). A computer movie simulating urban growth in the Detroit region. *Economic geography*. 46(sup1), 234–240.

Townsend, D. M., Hunt, R. A., McMullen, J. S. & Sarasvathy, S. D. 2018. Uncertainty, knowledge problems and entrepreneurial action. *Academy of Management Annals*. 12(2), 659–687.

Tsai, W. 2001. Knowledge transfer in intraorganizational networks: Effects of network position and absorptive capacity on business unit innovation and performance. *Academy of Management Journal*. 44(5), 996–1004.

Tucker, A. L., Edmondson, A. C. & Spear, S. 2002. When problem solving prevents organizational learning. *Journal of Organizational Change Management*. 15(2), 122–137.

Tushman, M. L. & O'Reilly, C. A. 1996. Ambidextrous organizations: Managing evolutionary and revolutionary change. *California Management Review*. 38(4), 8–30.

Varian, H. R. 2010. Computer mediated transactions. *American Economic Review*. 100(2), 1–10.

Vincenti, W. G. 1994. The retractable airplane landing gear and the Northrop "anomaly": Variation, selection and the shaping of technology. *Technology and Culture*. 35(1), 1–33.

Von Hippel, E. 2017. *Free innovation*. MIT Press.

Von Hippel, E. & Von Krogh, G. 2015. Crossroads – identifying viable "Need-solution pairs": Problem solving without problem formulation. *Organization Science*. 27(1), 207–221.

Ward, T. B. 1994. Structured imagination: The role of category structure in exemplar generation. *Cognitive Psychology*. 27(1), 1–40.

Weber, M. 1930. *The protestant ethic and the spirit of capitalism*. Routledge.

Weinberg, B. A. & Galenson, D. W. 2019. Creative careers: The life cycles of nobel laureates in economics. *De Economist*. 167, 221–239.

Williamson, O. E. 1996. *The mechanisms of governance*. Oxford University Press.

Wu, L., Wang, D. & Evans, J. A. 2019. Large teams develop and small teams disrupt science and technology. *Nature*. 566, 378–382.

Yang, M.-J., Christensen, M., Bloom, N., Sadun, R. & Rivkin, J. 2023. A scientific approach to business strategy. Unpublished Working Paper.

Yang, M.-J., Christensen, M., Bloom, N., Sadun, R. & Rivkin, J. n.d. How do CEO's make strategy? *Management Science*. In press.

Zuboff, S. 2015. Big Other: Surveillance capitalism and the prospects of an information civilization. *Journal of Information Technology*. 30(1), 75–87.

Zuboff, S. 2018. *The age of surveillance capitalism: The fight for a human future at the new frontier of power*. Public Affairs.

Zuckerman, E. W. 2016a. Crossing the Chasm to disruptive innovation. *MIT Sloan Management Review*. March 15, 2016.

Zuckerman, E. W. 2016b. Optimal distinctiveness revisited: An integrative framework for understanding the balance between differentiation and conformity in individual and organizational identities. In *The Oxford handbook of organizational identity*, ed. M. G. Pratt, M. Schultz, B. E. Ashforth & D. Ravasi. Oxford University Press.

Index

3D printing, 64, 136

absorptive capacity, 48, 85–90, 139
accounting, 91, 96
activity based costing, 98
aerodynamics, 35
agricultural economy, 204–205
AI, 206
   machine learning, 174, 207
aircraft, 206
airplane, 23, 35, 37
   jet, 29
   propeller, 29
airplane landing gear 34
   fixed, 34–36
   retractable, 34
aliens, 59
all hell breaks loose, 25
Alphabet, 45
AlphaFold, 207–208
AlphaGo, 21, 23
Amazon, 115, 200, 202
ambidexterity, 72–76, 78, 80, 83–85, 88, 96, 108, 135, 157
   contextual, 75, 77
   sequential, 74, 77
   structural, 74, 76, 80, 85
American Navy, 110
ancient Greek, 170
Ancient Rome, 130–131
anxiety, 3, 9, 18, 41, 44, 119
Apple, 144, 152–153, 155, 201
apprenticeship, 82
architectural change, 44
architectural innovation, 46–49, 62
Arrow's Paradox, 138–139
art history, 55–56
artificial intelligence, 21, 50, 153, 165, 174, 178–179, 183–184, 187–192, 206–208, 215
artificial pancreas, 194
AT&T, 12, 22

attacker's advantage, 5, 29
Austrian Economics, 63, 142, 145
authoritarian socialism, 157
Automation Anxiety, 170
automobiles, 120, 137, 161, 182
autonomous car, 28

beachhead market, 114, 119
Bell Labs, 22
Belle Epoque, 163
Betamax, 32
Bezos, Jeff, 51
Bill Gates, 151
Bill Hewlett, 151
Blockbuster, 32, 44, 135
blockchain, 50, 52, 215
Blu-ray, 32
bootlegging, 91, 99–100, 102
Boston Consulting Group, 188
brakes, 23
Brin, Sergey, 165
burden of knowledge, 68
bureaucracy, 13, 75, 115, 215

canals, 161, 179
cancer diagnosis, 183
capital-E Exploration, 80
capitalism, 1–2, 7–10, 126, 146, 160–161, 166
Capitalism, Socialism and Democracy, 1–2, 10, 126, 161
car, 23, 28, 37, 120, 170–171
carriage, 23
cash registers, 25
category structure, 59
CD, 23, 29
cement, 31, 156
CERN, 153
Cézanne, Paul, 56
charging infrastructure, 38
Charles Dickens, 174
chasm, 110, 113–115

231

Index

ChatGPT, 43, 172, 207–208
choosing an S-curve, 28
Cinema, 32
circular flow, 126–128, 141, 164
climate change, 155–157
clothes, 25
Coca-Cola, 31
coffee, 7
Cold Wars, 31, 153, 155
colonization, 150
communication costs, 12
Communist Manifesto, 174
communities of practice, 82, 84, 190
competition, 2–3, 14–16, 29–32, 38, 60, 79–80, 99, 117–119, 122–123, 137–139, 157–158, 176, 201, 213, 215
  anti-competitive behavior, 4
competitive advantage, 116, 118
competitive avoidance, 119
competitive dynamics, 18–19, 24, 30, 99, 122
complementary technologies, ix, 37–39, 171, 215
components, 37, 39, 46–48, 60, 62, 74, 97–98, 122, 200
computer game, 104
computers, 20, 22, 29, 31–32, 39, 46–48, 50–51, 60, 62, 74, 97–98, 122, 162, 173, 182, 197, 200, 206
  based on vacuum tubes, 32
conceptual innovations, 57–58
constructive disobedience, 103
container shipping, 179
continuous chemical processes, 206
continuous-aim firing, 110
contribution margin, 97–98
conventional wisdom, 29
core design concepts, 46
Cornish coal mines, 22
corporate laboratories, 12
Corporate R&D Lab, 12
corporate research and development, 12
cost of market entry, 137
creative destruction, 1–3, 5, 8–9, 15, 17, 19, 24, 29–30, 38, 71–72, 90, 106, 110, 125, 134, 141, 157
creativity, 20, 54–55, 57–58, 61, 66, 69, 75, 105, 129, 192
crisis, 146, 156–157, 159, 161–165, 170, 179, 183
crop yields, 26
crowdsourcing, 198, 201, 203

DARPA, 153
Darwinism, 79
data center cooling, 23
data extraction and analysis, 166
DeepMind, 21, 207
deliberate perturbations, 74
democratic socialism, 157
deployment period, 161, 163
diabetes, 194
diapers, 29
Diffusion of Innovation, 111
digital cameras, 29
Digital Revolution, 199
digital transformation, 179, 183
digital watches, 34
disruption, 45
Disruption Dilemma, 44
disruptive innovation, 29, 40–41, 43–45, 57, 62, 95, 119, 169, 194
diving suit, 132
divisionalized corporation, 180
DNA, 209
doctors, 171, 184
Dolby, 32
dominant design, 16, 18, 25, 30–34, 47–48, 60, 112, 176
dot-com crash, 162, 166
double helix structure, 209
drug discovery, 206
DVD, 32
dye industry, 12
dynamic random access memory, 153
dynamo, 40, 50, 179

early adopters, 111–115, 117
early majority, 111–114
ecological validity, 60
economic growth, 6, 9, 14, 22, 52, 69, 141, 144–145, 151–152, 156, 205–206, 208
  Marxian growth, 6
  Schumpeterian growth, 6, 148
  Smithian growth, 6
  Solovian growth, 6
ecosystem, of technology complements, 37
Edison, Thomas, 22, 51
efficiency, 15–17, 20, 25, 30–31, 48–49, 72–75, 88, 132, 148, 152, 158–159, 171–172, 175, 183, 187, 215
elasticity, 172
electric cars, 37
electric lamp, 51
electricity, 22, 29, 50–51, 161, 163, 180, 182
emergence challenges, 38–39
Engel's Pause, 175, 177
Engels, Friedrich, 174, 177
entrepreneurial imagination, 136
entrepreneurial state, 146, 151–155

Index

entrepreneurial strategy, 28, 136
entrepreneurs, 9, 13, 21–22, 28, 41, 44–45, 57, 63, 105, 111, 125, 127–130, 132–136, 139, 141, 146, 151–152, 155, 160–162, 168, 210
   heroic, 13
environmental control, 174
environmental scanning, 88
era of ferment, 31, 33–34, 37–38, 49, 106, 108, 175–176
Era of Incremental Change, 31
eras of ferment, 32, 34–35, 81, 88, 164
Erie Railroad, 181
established firms, 5, 9, 29, 40–43, 135
European Middle Ages, 130
everywhere but in the productivity statistics, 50–51
evolutionary economics, 78
experimental innovations, 57–58
exploitation, 2, 5–6, 14, 17–20, 24–25, 30–31, 44, 49, 71–80, 85, 115, 160, 168, 174
exploration, 5, 17–20, 24–25, 28, 30–33, 44, 51, 71–80, 84–85, 89, 94, 100–101, 108, 152, 199, 214
extension opportunities, 38–39
extractive institutions, 147

Facebook, 116, 166–167, 169
factories, 2, 10, 50–52, 139, 169, 173–174, 176
failure framework, 41, 43
failure of imagination, 22
failure trap, 19, 99
fallacy of obviousness, 23
fashion, 13, 50, 92, 94, 104, 107
feudal society, 131
fiber optics, 23
financial innovation, 164
first-mover advantage, 116, 118–119, 123, 139
first-mover disadvantages, 116
first-scaler advantage, 117
fluidity, 14–17, 25, 30, 36, 49, 76, 105, 109
forecasts, 27
free lunch, 6
frenzy, 161–164
Friedman, Milton, 6, 142
Frontloading, 93

gazelles, 125, 141
General Electric, 12
general purpose technologies, 50–52, 63–64, 161, 163, 165, 169, 179–180, 206
generalized Darwinism, 79
genius, 128–129

German Romanticism, 128
GitHub, 104
glass, 31
Go, 21
Go/Kill/Hold/Recycle decision, 93
Google, 43, 45, 104, 116, 144, 165–166, 168–169, 201
GoPro camera, 46
government loans, 154
GPS, 153
gramophone, 22
Great British Leap, 163
Great Depression, 162
Green Industrial Revolution, 155

health care measurement systems, 97
hearing aids, 105–106
Hegel, 129
hiding, 102–103
High Technology Marketing Illusion, 112
hip hop, 23
hockey stick, 5–7, 204
Holacracy, 104
HTTP, 153
Hugo, Victor, 174
Hundred Years War, 132
hunter-gatherer economy, 204–205
hydraulics, 23
hype, 7–8, 27, 41–43, 52, 144, 162, 216

IBM, 32
ideas, ix–xi, 4–7, 11–12, 15, 18, 20, 26, 29, 41, 45, 47, 51, 54–62, 66, 69, 72, 74–75, 78, 83, 90, 92, 94–95, 100–103, 108, 116, 126, 128–129, 136, 138–140, 148, 152, 166, 168, 180–181, 183, 188–189, 191, 199, 205, 212–216
ideology, 1, 7–9, 30, 39, 53, 77, 152, 177, 216
Ikea, 202
IkeaHackers, 202
imagination, 22, 41, 54, 58–62, 66, 68, 127, 129, 136, 140, 186
IMAX, 32
Impossible Foods, 122
inclusive institutions, 147
incumbents, 5, 29, 33, 37, 39–41, 43–46, 88, 116, 135, 139–141, 143, 145, 208
industrial change, 5, 31, 41, 46
Industrial Revolution, 5, 7–8, 132, 161, 170, 174–175, 182, 204–205
inertia, 29, 49, 73, 116
ingenuity, 28, 103, 186
InnoCentive, 201
innovation, definition of, 3

234   Index

insight, 12, 20–21, 28, 45, 56–58, 64, 69, 72, 94, 126, 142, 202–203, 211, 214
installation period, 161, 163
institutional contexts, 132–133
institutions, 85, 133–135, 141, 146–152, 159
intellectual property rights, 138
interface function, 87
internal combustion engines, 23, 180
internal hybrid, 105–106
International Space Station, 198
internet, 50, 52, 129, 152–153, 155, 162, 166, 183, 197, 200, 208
investments, 6, 25–29, 33, 37–38, 42, 52, 63, 83, 89, 93, 96, 114–117, 132, 137, 142, 152–153, 155, 176, 179, 193–194, 208–209, 215
iPhone, 152–153, 155
IPO, 142

Jobs, Steve, 129, 151, 153
JVC, 32

Kasper, 48
knowledge, x, 6, 13, 18, 25, 29, 33, 46–49, 54–58, 60–61, 63–66, 68–70, 72, 82, 85–90, 105–106, 153–154, 158, 166, 168, 173–174, 185, 188, 201, 203, 209, 212–213
knowledge search, 88
Kodak, 12, 43

labor market polarization, 173
labor-saving technologies, 170
laggards, 111
laptops, 16
Large Language Models, 188, 207
laser, 22–23
late majority, 111–113
Latin America, 149
leading-edge industries, 162–164, 179–180
lean production, 72, 180
Lee Sodol, 23
Legitimate peripheral participation, 82
Lego, 195, 202
Library of Alexandria, 131
lifecycle
    of creatives, 55
    of industries, 31
lighting, 22, 51
limits, 26, 28
line-and-staff model, 180–181
liquid crystal displays, 153
lithium-ion batteries, 153
logic of accumulation, 168–169
Lowell, Massachusetts, 175–176
LP, 29

machine gun, 132
mainstream customers, 42
major technology bubble, 162–163, 179, 183
management consulting, 120, 188
management models, 179–180
managerial capitalism, 10–12
managerial techniques, 12, 78
Mandarin, 131
Marconil, Guglielmo, 22
marginal improvement, 31
market category, 119–121, 124
market creation, 4, 47
market for ideas, 139
market intermediaries, 139–140
Marx, Karl, 2, 6, 174–175, 177
mass media, 22
mass production, 50, 196
mathematics, 57
mechanical watches, 34
Medieval China, 130–131
Medium, 104
meta-routines, 74
metrics, 96, 99, 115, 143
Mexico, 148–149
micro hard drives, 153
middle management, 11
middle managers, 11
minicomputers, 31
miracles of production, 128
modular innovation, 47
monks, 132
monopoly, 2–3, 45
Moore, Gordon, 26
Moore's Law, 26–27, 199
multi-touch screens, 153
Muppets, 125, 141, 144
Musk, Elon, 129

NASA, 198, 201, 203
National Institutes of Health, 153
National Science Foundation, 153, 165
Naval artillery, 110
neoclassical equilibrium theories, 63
Neolithic revolution, 205
neo-Schumpeterian theory, 161, 165, 178, 203, 206
Netflix, 32
net-zero, 156
new entrants, 5, 29, 33, 39–40, 49, 65, 143, 215
Newton, Isaac, 68
niche markets, 29, 45
    low-end, 42, 46
Nietzsche, 129
Nobel Prize, 21, 67
Nogales, 149

Index

normal science, 67, 69
North Korea, 148–149

obsolescence, 32, 34
old masters, 54, 56–57
open source software, 193, 195
organization chart, 180, 181
organizational innovation, 4, 12, 17, 47, 94, 180, 182, 204
organizational learning, 14, 18, 49, 99, 114
O-ring, 23, 36–37
Orr, Julian, 81
Oticon, 91, 104, 106–108

package-delivery robot, 28
Packard, David, 151
Page, Larry, 165
PageRank algorithm, 165
patents, 22, 64, 117, 134, 138
patent trolls, 134
Pepsi, 31
performativity, 45
persistence, 150
pharmaceutical industry, 88, 139, 153
photographic film, 29, 87
physics, 26, 57, 67–68
Picasso, Pablo, 56–57
plastics, 179
poetry, 57
Polymerase Chain Reaction (PCR), 21
post-World War II boom, 163
preemption of scarce assets, 117–118
pressures toward bigness, 11
primitive condition, 22
prior knowledge, 54, 64–65, 86–88
Private Government, 158
process innovation, 16, 25, 31, 47, 81, 85
product innovation, 15–16, 25, 47, 77, 93, 193
Productivity Dilemma, 14–15, 17, 50, 66, 71–72, 75–76, 78–79, 81, 90
productivity paradox, 50–51
Progressive Era, 163
psychological theories of entrepreneurship, 63
psychological uncertainty, 21–22
punctuated equilibrium, 31, 164
Pythagorean moonshine, 165

quantum computing, 20
quantum physics, 68
QWERTY, 16, 32

R&D, 9, 12–13, 78, 81, 84, 88–90, 95–98, 103, 106, 114, 152, 158, 193, 198–201, 207

radios, 22–23, 46, 110, 120–121, 123, 179, 183, 201
  transistor radio, 46
radiologists, 183
railroads, 12, 161, 179–180
reactivity, 100
Rebrickable, 202
records, 29
Reddit, 202
referencing, 112
reformation, 7
Remington Rand, 32
Renaissance, 8, 10–11, 132
Renaissance Man, 69
repertoire, of theoretical distinctions, 32, 47
research productivity, 26
resilience illusion, 39
retractable airplane landing gear, 24, 36
reverse salient, 35
rivers, 52
Roaring Twenties, 162
robotic mailman, 28
robots, 160, 170, 184
robust coexistence, 38
robustly resilience, 38
Rosenbergian uncertainty, 22, 62
routines, 47, 49, 73–74, 78–79, 184
the rules of the game, 133

salaried managers, 11, 181
satellite radio, 120–121
Schopenhauer, 129
Schumpeter, J. A., 1–5, 8–9, 13–18, 21–22, 29–30, 41, 61, 71, 79, 125–126, 128–129, 133–134, 141, 155, 157, 161, 165, 175, 193, 198
Schumpeterian firms, 30
scientific instruments, 97
Scientific Management, 77, 83, 180
S-curve, 24, 26–29, 33, 36–37, 46, 51–52, 89
  riding the, 52
self-driving cars, 28
semiconductor lithography, 37, 39
semiconductors, 29
serendipity, 20
shadow learning, 184
ships, 25
signal compression, 153
Silicon Valley, 136, 151–152, 154, 175
singularity, 205–206
Siri, 153
Sirius, 120, 123
Situated Learning, 82
small-E exploration, 80

236 Index

Smith, Adam, 2, 6
socialized economy, 157–158
sociological imagination, 136
solid state battery, 38
Solow, Robert, 6, 50
Sony, 32
Sony PlayStation, 199
South Korea, 148
Spaghetti Organization, 91, 104–109
Sparta, 170
specificity, 14–19, 23, 25, 30, 41, 48, 67, 74–76, 78–79, 83–84, 92, 97–99, 108–109, 111, 114, 116–117, 121–122, 133, 136, 139, 141, 151, 176, 178, 180, 182, 192, 196, 200, 206, 211–212, 214, 216
spillovers, 27
stage-gate systems, 91–94, 101
startups, 135–137, 139–142, 144, 166, 169, 193
static-hedonic disposition, 127
steam engine, 22, 52, 131
   Corliss Steam Engine, 52
steam engines, 50, 161, 179–180
streetcar, 23
structural ambidexterity, 80
sub-component, 24
substitution, 170
   technological, 32, 37
sub-systems, 35–37, 39, 46–48
surgical skills, 184–185
surveillance assets, 167
surveillance capitalism, 166
sustaining innovation, 41

tapes, 29
taxi drivers, 171
teaching-learning ecology, 184
techno-economic paradigm, 163, 179, 181
technological almanacs, 67
technological discontinuity, 27–29, 31–34, 37–38, 45, 66, 80, 106, 109
   competence-destroying, 33–34, 42
   competence-enhancing, 33, 42
technological environment, 88
technological leadership, 116, 118
technological paradigm, 25, 28, 31, 33
technological systems, 24
technological trajectories, 28
technological uncertainty, 13, 20–22, 30
technological unemployment, 170

telegraphs, 161, 179
telegraphy, 22
telephone, 22, 162, 170
Tesla, 117, 154
textile industry, 175, 177, 179
The Theory of Economic Development, 10, 125–126
Thiel, Peter, 65, 140
TikTok, 167
TopCoder, 201
total quality management, 180
Toyota, 72, 76–78, 84
transcendence, 78, 81
transparency, 103
truckers, 171
typewriter, 32, 51

Ulysses, 19
unattractive markets, 40, 42–44, 49
uncertainty, 13–15, 18, 20–23, 27, 31, 33, 35, 40, 51, 56, 62–63, 74, 86, 89, 92, 112, 114, 116–118, 155, 210
   psychological, 20
Unites States, 148
unserved markets, 42
urbanization, 53

vacuum tubes, 29
Varian, Hal, 165
vertical integration, 10–13
VHS, 32
Victorian Boom, 163
video and audio transmission, 97
voice control, 153

wages, 101, 155, 160, 172–177
Water mills, 132
Weber, Max, 7
wheel, 50, 189
whole product, 114, 117
wind tunnels, 206
windmill-powered war wagon, 132
windshield wiper, 137–138

Xerox, 81
XM, 120, 123

young geniuses, 56–57, 68
Young Men's Christian Association, 181

Zappo's, 104

For EU product safety concerns, contact us at Calle de José Abascal, 56–1º,
28003 Madrid, Spain or eugpsr@cambridge.org.